HOW TO BUILD MAX-PERFORMANCE BUICK Engines

Jefferson Bryant

CarTech®

Copyright © 2008 by Jefferson Bryant

All rights reserved. All text and photographs in this publication are the property of the author, unless otherwise noted or credited. It is unlawful to reproduce – or copy in any way – resell, or redistribute this information without the express written permission of the publisher.

All text, photographs, drawings, and other artwork (hereafter referred to as information) contained in this publication is sold without any warranty as to its usability or performance. In all cases, original manufacturer's recommendations, procedures, and instructions supersede and take precedence over descriptions herein. Specific component design and mechanical procedures – and the qualifications of individual readers – are beyond the control of the publisher, therefore the publisher disclaims all liability, either expressed or implied, for use of the information in this publication. All risk for its use is entirely assumed by the purchaser/user. In no event will CarTech®, Inc., or the author, be liable for any indirect, special, or consequential damages, including but not limited to personal injury or any other damages, arising out of the use or misuse of any information in this publication.

This book is an independent publication, and the author(s) and/or publisher thereof are not in any way associated with, and are not authorized to act on behalf of, any of the manufacturers included in this book. All registered trademarks are the property of their owners. The publisher reserves the right to revise this publication or change its content from time to time without obligation to notify any persons of such revisions or changes.

Edited by: Paul Johnson

CarTech®

39966 Grand Avenue
North Branch, MN 55056
Telephone (651) 277-1200 • (800) 551-4754 • Fax: (651) 277-1203
www.cartechbooks.com

OVERSEAS DISTRIBUTION BY:

Brooklands Books Ltd.
P.O. Box 146, Cobham, Surrey, KT11 1LG, England
Telephone 01932 865051 • Fax 01932 868803
www.brooklands-books.com

Brooklands Books Aus.
3/37-39 Green Street, Banksmeadow, NSW 2019, Australia
Telephone 2 9695 7055 • Fax 2 9695 7355

ACKNOWLEDGMENTS

Writing this book required many days, nights, and weekends assembling the information found in these pages. To bring you the best content, many experts were consulted in the process. I would personally like to extend a grateful "thank you" to the following helpful professional builders and manufacturers of high-performance Buick parts:

Mike Tomaszewski, TA Performance
Russell Martin, Nailheadbuick.com
Tom Telesco
Jim Burek

CONTENTS

Introduction 4

Chapter 1: Blocks 6
   Nailhead 6
   Small-Block 350 7
   Big Blocks 8
   V-6 Turbo 11
   Main Bearing Cap Studs 11

Chapter 2: Pistons, Rods and Cranks 15
   Crankshafts 15
   Main Seals 17
   Connecting Rods 18
   Rod Bolts 20
   Pistons 21
   Piston Pins 24
   Rings 26

Chapter 3: Oiling System Upgrades 30
   Disassembly and Modification 30
   Crankshaft Mods 34
   Close Bearing Tolerances .35
   Oil Pumps 36
   Rear Oil Pressure Gauge Installation 40
   Oil Pans 40
   Motor Oil Considerations .41

Chapter 4: Cams and Timing Covers 42
   Cam Bearing Options 42
   Oiling System Upgrades .44
   Timing Cover Options 44
   Oil Pump Booster Plate 45
   Cam Thrust Control 45
   Distributor Gear Oiling 46
   Front Main Seal 47
   Lifter Bore Reinforcement 47

Chapter 5: Cylinder Heads 50
   Gasket Port Matching 51
   Blending the Bowls 52
   Exhaust Porting 54
   Valve Sizing 54
   Valve Jobs 55
   Combustion Chamber Polishing 56
   Heat Crossover Vent Modification 56
   Flow Testing 57
   High-Performance Head Parts 58
   Big-Block Heads 59

   Big-Block Head Porting 60
   Nailhead Cylinder Heads .60
   Aftermarket Head Options 62

Chapter 6: Valvetrain 67
   Rocker Arms 67
   Pushrods and Lifters 71
   Camshaft 71
   Lifters 74
   Timing Chain 75
   Retainers, Keepers and Springs 76

Chapter 7: Ignition and Fuel Systems 82
   Distributors 82
   V-6 Turbo 85
   Electronic Timing Boxes 85
   Fuel Systems 86
   Engine Cooling 87

Chapter 8: Intake, Carbs and Exhaust 89
   Carburetors 89
   Intake Manifolds 92
   Sheet Metal Intake Fabrication 94
   Headers, Manifolds and Exhaust Systems 101

Chapter 9: Race Engines 105
   Block Preparation 105
   Rotating Assembly 109
   Camshafts 110
   Heads 110
   Induction 111
   Oiling System 112
   Factory Racer Kits 118

Chapter 10: V-6 Turbo .119
   Turbo System Porting 120
   Turbo Replacement 121
   Intercoolers 123
   Downpipes and Wastegates 124
   Intakes 126
   Fuel Pump 128
   Electronics 128

Appendix A: Source Guide 133
Appendix B: 1953-1955 Nailhead Engine Specifications .135
Appendix C: 1953-1971 Engine Specifications 142
Appendix D: 1987 3.8L V-6 Turbo Engine Specifications . .144

INTRODUCTION

David Dunbar Buick founded the Buick Manufacturing Company in 1902. By 1906, David was no longer a part of the company that bears his name. While many consider Buick a stepchild to Chevrolet, the General Motors Corporation held Buick as its cornerstone brand, and many of GM's innovations came from the Buick division.

Since the very beginning, Buick has brought important new technology to the automotive market. The first Buick engine was the only engine of its time and kind to feature overhead valves. Eventually, Buick moved forward with the legendary Buick Eight. This inline 8-cylinder powerhouse led Buick into the 1950s. In 1953, Buick introduced the Nailhead V-8 engine series to replace the Eight.

The Nailhead derives its name from the positioning and size of its valves. The engine's small valves are mounted straight up and resemble nails. The first Nailhead was not without its drawbacks. The 1953 models had a poorly designed combustion chamber and lacked a balancer, leaving this engine at the bottom of the performance pile. This engine in stock form is best for restoration.

In order to compensate for the smaller-sized valves, the Nailhead engines utilize a high-lift, long-duration camshaft, which certainly adds to its mystique. In 1954, Buick introduced a smaller engine, the 264, which replaced the last of the straight-8s. The 1954 and 1955 versions produced 143 and 150 hp, while the 322 cranked out 255 hp and remained in production until 1956.

In 1957, Buick brought out its new Nailhead. The 364-ci engine generated 300 hp, certainly pushing the Nailhead-powered cars to the front of the pack in terms of horsepower. The 364 continued production until 1961. In 1959, the 401 became available in the Invicta and Electra models. From 1959–1961, the 364 was only used in the LeSabre model, mostly in a 2-barrel version. The 325-hp, 401-ci engine found a home in Buick's first muscle cars: the Gran Sport and Wildcat. Buick added the 340-hp, 425-ci Nailhead to its stable in 1963. It was also available in a 360 hp dual-quad version with two 4-barrel carbs.

Many big-name drag racers built their reputations with the Nailhead. TV Tommy Ivo built several Nailhead-powered dragsters, included his infamous 4-engined *Showboat* dragster.

The final Nailhead rolled off the assembly line in 1966. Buick had fallen behind in the engine-design department, having hung its hat on the Nailhead design for 14 years. It needed a fresh face to propel it into the raging horsepower wars; the new big-blocks did just that.

When the 340-hp 400 and potent 360-hp 430 arrived in 1967, Buick owners had plenty of power to rival the best of the boulevard. Buicks, by design, have always been torque monsters, making these muscle cars stoplight-to-stoplight kings.

In 1970, Buick's 455-ci engine upped the ante at the pinnacle of the muscle car era. Based on the 400/430 platform, the conservatively rated 350-hp 455 packed quite a punch. Most builders consider 410 hp to be the real baseline figure for the non-Stage 1 engines. According to the Buick figures, the Stage 1 package added 10 hp, but anyone who has driven one knows that the number is considerably

INTRODUCTION

higher. Torque numbers make a Buick a Buick. Stage 1 and non-Stage 1 455 engines crank out 510 ft-lbs of tire-shredding torque. This number is more than any other muscle car.

The real beauty of the 455 family is that most of its parts easily interchange. Bolting a set of 400 or 430 heads on a 455 adds a significant bump in compression. This simple change easily upgrades the later low-compression engines without getting into the block. In 1971, reduced compression ratios delivered decreased horsepower output, and the 455 lost 15 horses. Gross power ratings were taken at the flywheel on 1971 and earlier models, leaving the engine unencumbered by the transmission and rear end. By 1972, the 455 was rated at 270 hp, but horsepower was now measured at the rear wheels rather than the flywheel. While the changes look drastic on paper, in reality, the drop in power was not that substantial.

Amid the horsepower wars of the muscle-car era, Buick had a potent small-block in the stable. The Buick 350 4-barrel engine was pumping out 280 hp and 375 ft-lbs of torque in 1968. By 1970, this lightweight small-block was churning 315 hp, with 410 ft-lbs. It put the 350-powered Gran Sport in serious contention for Friday-night bragging rights.

Horsepower ratings dropped in 1971 and continued to fall throughout the 1970s, as the EPA and insurance companies pushed their agendas. The popular Buick 350 was available in every mid- to large-size vehicle in the Buick line-up.

Contrary to popular opinion, the Buick 350 shares absolutely nothing with the small-block Chevy. The small-block Buick has a lot of design features that the Chevy does not. For instance, the Buick's cylinder head has tall skinny ports for generating high-flow velocity. This port design allows the engine to build higher torque numbers at lower RPM. Several late-model GM engines, such as the 231-ci V-6 and the 3800 V-6, share the same basic design as the little Buick.

Buick introduced another groundbreaking engine — the first in American automotive history — when it brought out the 198-ci V-6 in 1962. Based on the aluminum 215 V-8, this V-6 shared the same bore and many other parts with the V-8; however, the odd firing order made it idle roughly. The 198 V-6 proved unpopular, and the design was sold to Jeep in 1967. Flash forward 18 years: Buick no longer had a V-8 in the stables. So, in 1980, the 231-ci V-6 was called into action, and a turbocharger was added to increase HP to 235. While the first turbo appeared in the 1976 Indianapolis 500 Pace Car, the first regular-production turbo engines were released in 1978.

By the mid-1980s, turbo technology began to improve. Sequential fuel injection was added in 1984, followed by an intercooler in 1986. Shoehorned into the Grand National, the 3.8-liter V-6 turbo was capable of delivering 13-second ETs in the quarter-mile in bone-stock trim. This wasn't bad, considering that the same-year Corvettes couldn't turn those times with a V-8. With minor tweaking, the 3.8-liter V-6 turbo could push a G-body to the low-12s.

As Buick engines have evolved, one thing has remained clear: They are full of potential. From the potent 455 Stage 1 to the early-era Nailhead, Buick delivers high performance. This book will get into the details of how to produce Buick power like never before. We will take apart an engine in each family, break down each system, and explain the advantages and shortcomings. Buick engines are not perfect, and all share some common problems — such as the oiling system. We will show how to alleviate the issues and what it takes to build max-performance Buick engines.

Built from 1970-1972, the Gran Sport GSX represented the ultimate in Buick high-performance. With the Stage 1 package, the 455-ci V-8 cranked out a conservative 360 horsepower and a whopping 510 ft-lbs of torque. This 1972 GSX clone carries a 455 that has been stroked to 464. It has been clocked at an impressive 11.74 seconds in the quarter-mile.

CHAPTER 1

BLOCKS

There are many things to consider when building a Buick V-8. Depending on the desired use and function, there are several options. The undervalued Buick 350-ci engine rarely gets any attention by the aftermarket, even though it is superior in several ways to the small-block Chevy. The lightweight and slightly undersquare 350 features a 3.8-inch bore and short 3.85-inch stroke for making lots of torque. Other than the 350, the 400/430/455 family has most of the aftermarket support for Buick V-8s. A new cast-iron or aluminum 455 block is available, which can be custom bored to over 4.5 inches. There is more material around the main webs for added strength, and the cam journals have more material to facilitate running custom diameter camshafts. In all, there is a world of opportunity to build whatever your heart desires. For older restos and custom rods, the Nailhead is a unique option with a lot of history, making it perfect for a traditional rod or custom.

Nailhead

Built from 1953 to 1966, Buick Nailhead engines were offered in the following sizes: 264, 322, 364, 401, and 425. All have rear-mounted distributors and starters mounted on the driver's side. The Buick 215 and 300 engines have Nailhead-type valve covers, but instead are related to the V-6 turbo and 350-455 engines.

When choosing which Nailhead block to build, you need to ask several questions. Are you building a vintage racer, cruiser, or restoring a classic? Each engine has its own unique requirements. How much displacement is required? While the big-displacement engines (364, 401, and 425) are the most popular, the 322 and 264 engines should not be ruled out. Are you performing a basic rebuild or building a high-performance engine? Installing rings and bearings for a simple rebuild is easy, but we want to make some real power.

The early 1953–1956 264 through 322 engines have few parts interchangable with the later 1957–1966 364, 401, and 425 engines. As the deck height increased, the distance between the heads increased and the engines became wider, so the intakes, rods, pistons and crankshafts won't swap.

The 1953 322-ci block has a hole to time the engine at the flywheel, and it was offered for only one year. Later model engines were timed at the damper. The 264 was used only on Buick Specials in 1954–1955, and it was cast for a 3-5/8-inch bore. The 1953–1956 322 blocks were cast for a 4-inch bore. The 264 and 322 blocks have a larger bellhousing diameter than the 364, 401, and 425 blocks. There were three different 364s for the 1957–1958 and 1959–1960 model years. The 1961 carried the same basic casting as the 1957–1960, but it was machined for the 1961–1966 oil filter adapter and starter bolt pattern. The 1957–1958 models used the same canister oil filter mounting as all the 1953–1956s. All 1959–1960 engines used a spin-on filter adapter that bolts to 1953–1958 blocks. The 401 came in three blocks, the 1959–1960, the 1961, and the 1962–1966. It contained the same characteristics as the 364 block from 1959–1960 and 1961. However, the 1962–1966 block used a different oil pump designed for the center sump oil pan. Prior to 1961, all Buicks used the rear sump oil pan. The 425 had one block style.

All 1961–1966 oil filter adapters are the same. All 1966 401s and 425s have a loop cast on the rear of the block for lifting the engines. The 1961 and older Nailheads do not fit the 1962–1966 Buick frames because the older engines cannot use the center sump pan. However, 1961 and earlier Buicks accept 1962–1966 engines if a 1965–1966 Gran Sport oil pump pickup and a 1957–1961 or 1965–1966 GS pan is used.

There are two different oil-pan flange patterns: 1953–1956 and 1957–1966. These oil pans cannot be swapped. The 1953 is a one-year-only design, but it looks like a 1957–1961 pan. The 1954–1956 pan is the same as the 1953 pan, but it has an extra hump. The early 322 pans have double the number of mounting holes. All 1953–1956 blocks for 264 and 322 engines have three-bolt engine mounting, and all 1957–1966 blocks for 364, 401, and 425 engines have four bolts on each side.

The upright, horizontal position of the valve covers easily identifies the Nailhead. Beyond that, casting numbers determine the engine displacement. Buick used a system similar to most manufacturers for identifying an engine. From 1953 to 1956, the engine code was stamped into the head-gasket flange. It used a sequential number code followed by a single digit for specifying the engine series. Beginning in 1957, Buick stamped the engines with a portion of the VIN (vehicle identification number) which matched a particular engine to a particular vehicle. This ID number is located on the block behind the water manifold. In 1957, Buick also placed the ID code on the right side of the block. In 1957, Buick also added a two- or three-digit code that identified the engine and production sequence.

This bone-stock Buick 350 has a lot of life left in it. These undervalued blocks are capable of supporting well over 1,000 hp without any major block enhancements. This particular block is a 1971 four-barrel unit, but that really only matters in restorations because the 1968–1980 350s remained the same throughout their production run.

Small-Block 350

The 350-ci block remained unchanged from 1968 to 1980, so sourcing the correct parts is very easy. However, Buick made many changes to the 350's internal engine components over the years. Before performing the build-up, there are certain engine systems and components that need to be checked and possibly corrected. The crank alignment should be checked and squared. The deck height from the crank centerline needs to be equal on each side, and it can be checked and corrected when align-honing. The block we used for our build-up was in excellent shape and did not require align honing. Core shift is not a huge problem with the 350, but sonic testing verifies the alignment of the bores and how much support material is available.

Most builders recommend using a torque plate when boring the cylinders because it adds support for most engines. Other builders hold the opposite opinion. Jim Burek of Performance Automotive Engines says, "Torque plates on Buick engines are a waste of time and money. They simply are not needed." The choice is yours. We bored our 350 without torque plates and had no issues.

This is the main area for casting numbers on 1968 and later 350 or big-blocks. If this was a 455, you would see "455" where the two 5s are located on this 350.

The Buick 350 is a little different from many engines. The head bolts on most engines end in water jackets, which allow the block to twist when the head nuts are torqued. The Buick blocks have blind head-bolt holes that do not go through water jackets, so the block doesn't distort when the heads are bolted down.

Aftermarket support for the 350 is very limited; internal components are limited to pistons and cams. In turn, the engine work required for a 350 is

CHAPTER 1

pretty basic. Unlike the small-block Chevy 350, the Buick 350 cannot be stroked because there is not enough camshaft clearance. Buick 350s have very tight internal tolerances.

Big Blocks

There are quite a few options when it comes to building a big-block Buick. The 400 and 430 engines certainly benefit from the aftermarket support for the 455. Choosing a 455 block requires careful consideration of several aspects. Intended use is the main question. A basic street engine requires much less attention than a serious performance engine, and race engines require even more. If serious high performance is the goal, there are a few things to weigh when picking a block.

Core shift is a major problem in Buick 455s, and this problem originates in the actual casting process. If the patterns moved during the mold casting, the centerline of the block ended up off-center. Some blocks have a very high amount of core shift; so much, in fact, that it is visibly obvious. These blocks are not suitable for a high-performance build-up and should not be used. The Buick-designed 455 has a lightweight casting — 100 lbs lighter than the 454 Chevy — that certainly contributed to the core shift problem. A minor amount of core shift is acceptable, and it can be corrected with align-boring.

Look at the lifter bores to quickly check for core shift. If the bores are not centered horizontally in the casting, the cylinders will be off, as well. A sonic test is the best way to detect core shift. Similar to radar, sonic testing sends a sound wave through the metal and counts how long it takes for the signal to return. This precisely measures the thickness of the cylinder walls for determining core shift. A block with heavy core shift has cylinder walls that are thinner than others. This leads to overheating and boring limitations. The 1976 and service replacement 455 blocks have 10 percent more material and minimal occurrences of core shift, making them ideal candidates for building.

The 1970–1972 455 blocks have the unfortunate distinction of having

Using a dial bore gauge, the block is checked for clearance. It is important to check your block for square, as well. Align-honing your Buick ensures a proper fit and adds a good deal of longevity to the engine.

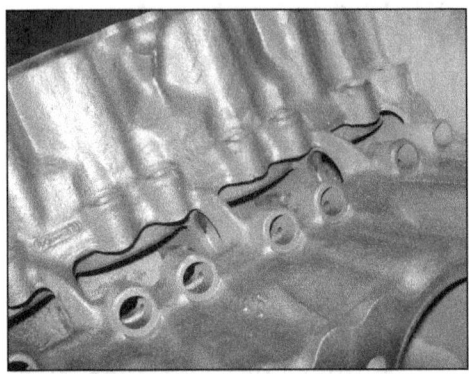

Core shift is a major problem for pre-1973 Buick big blocks. Check the lifter bores for core shift. If they are off center in the casting, then you have issues. The best solution is a different block. Thin lifter bores are another issue here. If any type of roller lifter is used, the bores are going to break.

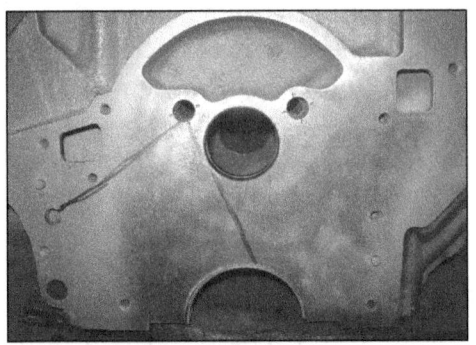

These marks on this stock 455 block show the oil path from the main oil-feed hole. The oil first travels to the passenger-side oil galley, next to the main cam bearing, and finally to the crank mains. This engine suffers from serious lubrication problems that need to be fixed in the stock block.

Whether or not to use torque plates is a matter of fierce debate in the Buick world. TA Performance uses this torque plate on every 455 it builds. Some builders say that the Buick engines do not need torque plates because the head-bolt holes are blind. This keeps the block from tweaking when the heads are bolted down. However, most builders recommend using torque plates, figuring it can't hurt.

BLOCKS

the worst production tolerances. Although these are the highest-performing blocks from the factory, they have the highest core shift, and the oiling issues are numerous. That is certainly not to say that these are unworthy of a high-performance build. Once a suitable block has been selected, the oiling system troubles are easily remedied. The stock block is certainly capable of supporting 500, even 600, hp, and it was designed to produce massive amounts of torque. High RPM is a problem because these engines were never designed to spin over 5,000 rpm. If you rev a 455 to more than 6,000 rpm, it will eventually come apart—maybe not the first time, but soon and in a big way. The stock block does not have enough material in the bottom end for high RPM. The 455 crank was designed first, leaving the engineers to lighten the bearings and reduce the main webbing. The lighter bearings burn up in high-RPM situations, leading to failure. While this is not a huge problem for engines under 600 hp, engines turning out 600-plus hp need a stud girdle. These girdles bolt onto the oil pan rails and allow pre-load to be added to the main caps. If you are building a serious high-performance Buick, this is a good idea.

Cylinder boring is another aspect of big Buick performance. Never bore a 455 beyond 0.040 inch; the cylinder walls will be far too thin and catastrophic failure will occur. The 430 may be bored up to 0.060-inch and the 400 to 430 specs (4.187 inch). Anytime you bore an engine this much, it needs to be sonically tested to ensure adequate wall thickness.

Beyond using a stock casting, Bulldog Performance has created a brand new 455 casting in cast iron or aluminum. The Bulldog 455 resolves all of the previous shortcomings of the stock block. As seen in the accompanying images, the Bulldog block is far better than the stock casting. The cast-iron Bulldog weighs about 20 lbs more than the stock block without any strengthening devices, such as block girdles. The new aluminum block weighs 120 lbs with main caps for a savings of more than 100 lbs over the stock cast-iron block.

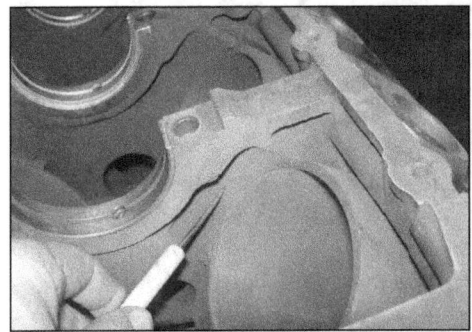

The factory created a major drawback by carving out sections of the already-thin main webs and leaving very little strength in this area. The spot shown here is only about 0.100 inch thick. This is why the main webs break on a Buick engine under heavy output without additional strengthening devices, such as block girdles.

The cylinder walls extend out of the main casting in the block. The problem here is that the material is so thin, and boring these blocks 0.060 inch over stock leaves very thin walls, typically 0.120 to 0.140 inch.

The stock iron big-block was designed to be a lightweight, large-ci engine that made a lot of torque to drag around land yachts. To accomplish this, Buick engineers shaved off a lot of material in the main webs to save weight, and utilized a crank with large main journals. Essentially, the crank was used to strengthen a weak block.

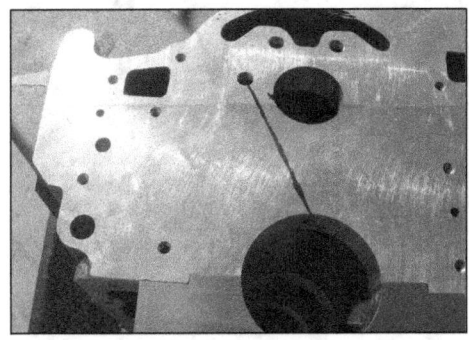

The Bulldog block reroutes the oil, creating a priority oiling system that oils the crank first and eliminates these oiling issues.

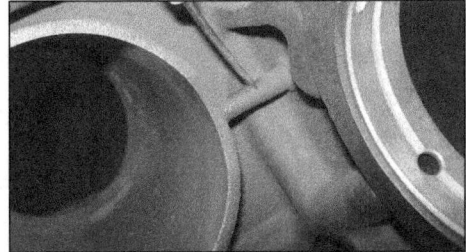

The stock block also uses these tiny cylinder wall supports, and this is supporting the exposed cylinder wall to the block.

CHAPTER 1

The Bulldog block uses 1-inch thick main webs in its castings. A set of four-bolt main caps (included) adds significant strength to the block.

The bottom end of the Bulldog block is available in three different bearing sizes: 2.75 inches, 3.0 inches, and the stock 3.35 inches. The smaller journal sizes experience less friction and require less oil pressure to survive, which means more power to the ground.

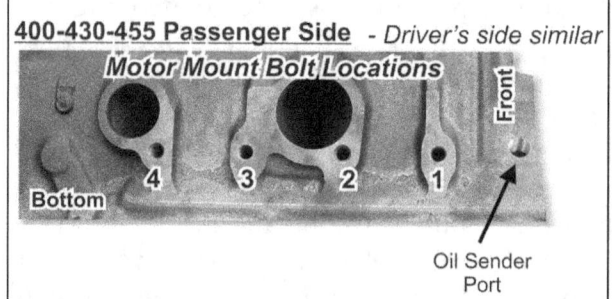

The motor mount positioning is important for engine swaps in GM cars. Use the number two and four positions for engine swaps in GM A- and G-body cars. For most full-size GM cars, numbers one and three are best.

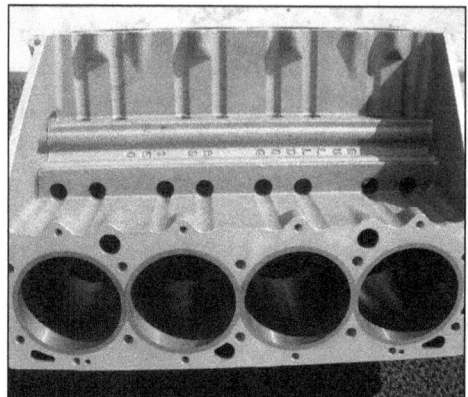

The Bulldog block features cast-iron sleeves that can be bored out to 4.5 inches. This bore combined with a max stroke of 4.5 inches yields a 573-ci Buick behemoth.

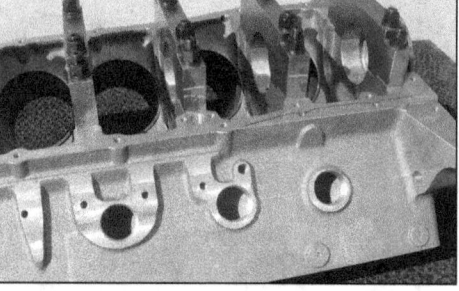

The Bulldog block uses screw-in freeze plugs instead of press-in units. Notice the pan rail. This marker line indicates where the stock pan would sit. These blocks were cast to accept more stroke. In the event the motor is stroked to the max of 4.5 inches, the inner section can be machined off for clearance for the rods. A stock pan cannot be used on these blocks because front mains are too large.

The Bulldog aluminum big block resolves every stock block issue. Notice the solid lifter bore area — no roller lifter is going to break this. There's still some machining to do on this block; the oil drain holes have not been drilled yet.

The Bulldog blocks also have a lot more material in the main webs for added strength and custom machining options. The new blocks can be ordered with custom machining, fitted with Chrysler rods, and bored out to over 4.5 inches for yielding over 600 ci. In addition, these high-performance blocks have much more material in the cam journals, allowing easy installation of custom-diameter camshafts.

The Bulldog block is certainly capable of supporting HP figures well beyond 1,000, while the stock block is suited for 600–800 hp. The Bulldog cast-iron blocks list for $3,200, and the aluminum unit is priced at $5,250. Certainly not inexpensive, but your engine is as strong as your weakest link. While the stock block can be band-aided with girdles and other pieces, the new block is a better choice for race engines. Spending $5,000 for a high-performance block on top of a $10,000 engine build is a wise

V-6 Turbo

The 1978–1987 3.8-liter V-6 turbo is basically a Buick 350 without two cylinders. These engines have matching 3.8-inch bore sizes, but the V-6 turbo has slightly less stroke at 3.4 inches. Over its lifespan, the 3.8-liter block received a few changes, some of which might make a difference in choosing which block to use. Though the 3800 engine is produced today as a 3.8-liter, it is a redesign from the previous engine for front-wheel-drive vehicles, and parts will not interchange.

The 1980 and later 3.8-liter V-6 turbo blocks use larger oil sump and feed passages enlarged from 0.500 to 0.625 inches for increased oil supply. In 1982, Buick added a boss for a knock sensor to the back of the engine, an important feature for a turbo engine. The 1984 blocks use a 0.030-inch larger cam base circle, and a groove was added behind the number-1 cam bearing for better oiling. In 1985, Buick brought out a new block with 20-bolt oil pan and new timing cover. Consequently, the 1978–1984 units will not fit the newer block. In 1986, the deck height was reduced by 0.035 inch to accommodate thicker head gaskets. The 1985–1987 engine is capable of handling over 750 hp and is considered the best. Although the 1985–1987 engines are the most desirable, any of the 1978–1987 blocks are certainly suitable for building into a serious street-performance/strip engine. The same basic steps for machining the V-8s apply to the V-6 turbo blocks. The V-6 turbo engines do not have drastic issues with core shift. The V-6 bore should be kept to 0.060 inch at the maximum.

When the machine work has been completed, it's highly recommended to replace at least the number-2 and number-3 main bearing caps with billet main caps. Pro Gram Engineering aftermarket caps are much stronger than stock main caps, and these fit tighter in the block, eliminating cap walk under heavy load. Whenever the main caps are changed, they need to be align-bored. It is very important to torque the cylinder heads in place when align-boring this block. The 3.8-liter block has a tendency to twist slightly with the heads installed, which can tweak the number-2 and number-3 main bearing caps. Without the heads installed, the align-bore will not be accurate, and the number-2 and number-3 main bearings will be in danger of failing.

An extreme-performance aftermarket aluminum engine is on the way. Champion GN1 plans to build a new aluminum 3.8-liter block that's enhanced in all the right places for maximum strength at high boost levels. This new block adds thicker main webs and more meat in the lifter bores, which adds a significant level of strength.

The TA Performance aluminum V-6 turbo block is capable of supporting 2,000 hp. All of the inherent oiling issues have been fixed on this block.

Main Bearing Cap Studs

The main bearing caps are obviously an important piece of the puzzle when building any engine. Why skimp on the bolts that hold them in place? Every engine builder we spoke to said the same thing: Use main bearing cap studs. By adding studs, the possibility of main bearing cap walk is virtually eliminated. Every engine — street, street/strip, or race — should have main studs installed. It is simply good insurance against failure.

Installing a set of ARP main studs is simple. The stud threads into the block using the supplied thread dressing. If you lose this compound or run out, then you can use moly lube. The studs are only torqued to about 8–10 ft-lbs. The upper threads should also be coated with the supplied thread compound; use the supplied thread lubricant because it can affect the torque setting, and follow the instructions. Next, the caps are installed and the nuts are torqued to the supplied specification, which is typically 80 ft-lbs. Anytime you use new caps or studs, the caps should be align-bored. This is an important step. Tell your machine shop what parts you will be using. Give them the parts so the block can be properly prepped for assembly.

CHAPTER 1

Compression Ratios *by Len Emanuelson*

Several factors determine the compression ratio. Piston height and dome (or dish), deck height, cylinder head combustion-chamber size, and even the head gasket affect the final compression ratio. Most standard V-8 and V-6 Buick pistons come in a 10.2:1 compression ratio. There are other options in production pistons, such as 8.5, 11.0, and 12.0:1 ratios. Depending on your application, any one of these pistons would be suitable. The trick is determining exactly what you want and what you need. A compression ratio higher than 10.5:1 is excessive for any reliable street engine. You will not only pay much more for premium or race fuel, but it will also lead to detonation and other problems. As compression ratios increase, so does heat. As the engine revs higher, the cylinder pressure increases, and so does the heat. This excessive heat can pre-ignite the air/fuel mixture and produce a damaging explosion before the piston is in position to take the charge. This is commonly referred to as knock. An engine with high-compression needs high-octane fuel because it runs hotter and resists heat better: the higher the octane rating, the higher the fuel's resistance to heat. Therefore, higher resistance to pre-ignition helps prevent knock. For street use, select pistons with a 10.5:1 or less compression ratio or less if you want to run pump gas. A 10.2:1 Buick 350 piston with the block decked at 0.030 inch and stock combustion chamber provides 10.1:1 compression – just right for pump gas.

Of course, proper cylinder head prep is important, too. Polishing the combustion chamber increases the engine's resistance to pre-ignition. In addition, if you are adding forced-air induction, such as a turbo or supercharger, keep the compression ratio down. The cylinder pressures created by a forced-air induction system are much greater than in a naturally aspirated engine. For anything other

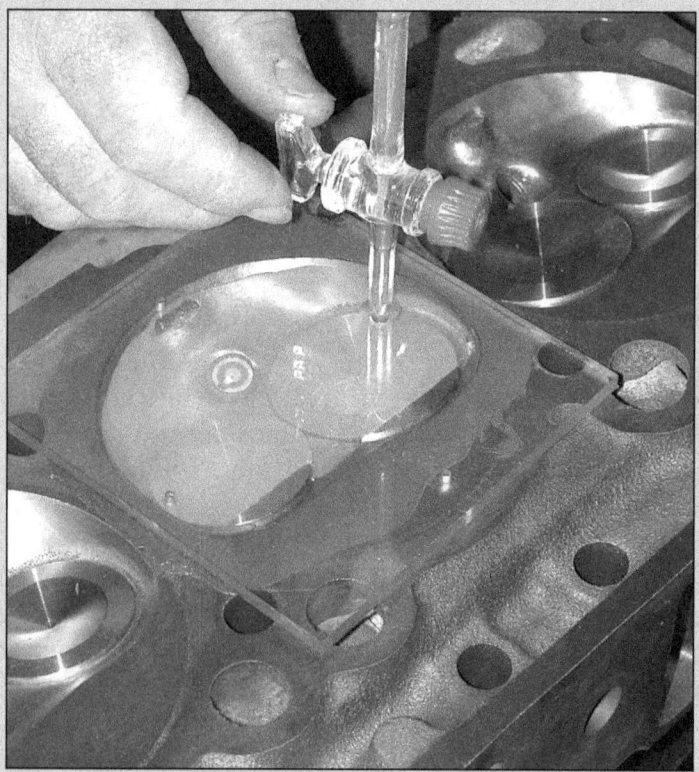

A piece of Plexiglas, or other clear acrylic plate, seals to the head with a little dab of oil. Use a burette to accurately measure how much fluid the combustion chamber can hold in cubic centimeters (CCs).

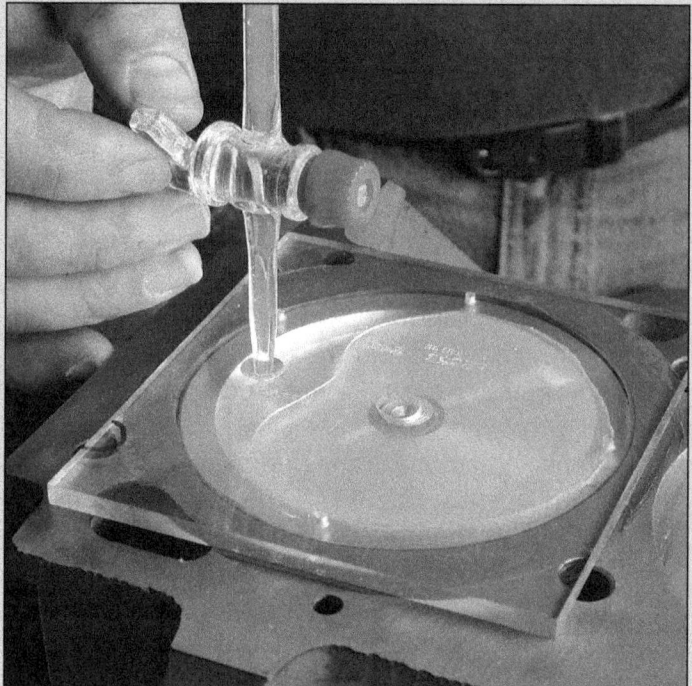

The same process works with measuring cylinder volume. This is a little harder to do with pop-up or high-dome pistons. You must roll the piston down in the cylinder, take your measurements, and remove the empty volume of the cylinder to obtain the complete measurement.

than a full-race engine, including turbos and supercharged, an 8.5 or 9.0:1 compression ratio is sufficient and retains longevity. It would not be a good idea to build a 13.0:1 supercharged engine for your daily driver.

Calculating Compression Ratio

To accurately calculate compression ratio, you must determine:

1. The cylinder bore.
2. The stroke of the piston.
3. The volume of the combustion chamber. (Chapter 5 explains how to obtain this figure.)
4. The compression height of the piston, which is available from the piston manufacturer.
5. The dome/dish volume of the piston. (This figure is available from the piston manufacturer.)
6. The piston-to-deck clearance.
7. The thickness of the head gasket.
8. The bore of the head gasket.
9. Engine displacement.

Obtaining this information requires some measuring, and some of the figures should be readily available. The thickness and bore of the head gasket should come with the gasket set. If it is not included, contact the manufacturer. The exact cylinder bore is measured at the time of machining, but the standard bore plus the amount of overbore is sufficient for our purposes. The standard bore and stroke for each engine is listed in the appendix at the back of this book. Measuring the heads is somewhat more involved and will be demonstrated in Chapter 5 on cylinder heads.

The calculation is relatively simple. First, we need to calculate the exact engine displacement:

**Engine displacement =
(bore x bore x stroke x 0.7854) x number of cylinders.
The 0.7854 is the magic number that converts everything to ci.**

The equation for a Buick 350 is:

(3.8 x 3.8 x 3.85 x 0.7854) x 8 = 349.3082208 ci

For our equation here, we need the displacement of one cylinder, which would be 43.6635276 ci.

That is the easy part. The next step involves calculating different volumes and converting the volumes to ci. The following equation calculates the compression ratio and the definition of each figure.

$$CR = (D + PV + DC + G + CC) / (PV + DC + G + CC)$$

**CR = Compression ratio
D = Displacement of a single cylinder
PV = Piston volume
DC = Deck clearance volume
G = Gasket volume
CC = Combustion chamber volume**

We already know the displacement, and there are several ways to get the remaining figures we need. Calculating the gasket volume is similar to calculating the displacement:

Gasket volume = bore x bore x 0.7854 x thickness of compressed gasket. The compressed thickness spec should be available from the manufacturer; they may even have the volume already calculated.

The next two steps can be a little tricky. First, measure the distance from the top of the piston to the top of the deck at top dead center (TDC) to calculate DC volume. While this can be calculated from the numbers and a simple measurement with the piston in the bore at TDC, this does not take into account the piston-to-cylinder wall clearance. We also need to know the actual piston volume. Usually, the manufacturer has this spec, but we can determine it and the DC at the same time.

Compression Ratios continued

To calculate these figures, use this formula:

Deck clearance volume = bore x bore x 0.7854 x distance between piston and deck at TDC

As long as the top of the piston is even or below the deck, you can also measure cylinder volume directly using the same method for determining a head's volume. If the piston sits above the deck, lower the piston in the bore by exactly 1 inch. When doing it this way, subtract that inch (bore x bore x .7854 x 1) from the converted cubic inch measurement.

To measure volume manually, start off by wiping the top ring of a piston with a little Vaseline to seal it, and rotate the crank until that piston is at TDC. Next, place a plexiglass block with two small holes in it over the entire cylinder bore. One hole is used for filling while one is used for letting air escape. These can be purchased in a kit complete with a graduated burette for measuring the fluid. You can measure fluid into the bore to come up with the actual piston volume at TDC. This figure would take the place of both the deck clearance volume and piston volume in the compression formula. Of course, this measurement typically is in cc, which needs to be converted to ci:

Volume in cc x 0.061037 = volume in ci

The head volume is the last measurement we need. To arrive at the correct figure, use the same method mentioned above. (Details on how to determine this measurement are provided in Chapter 5.) Again, the measurement needs to be converted from cc to ci before it can be used in the CR equation.

After we have this information, we can calculate our compression ratio. We use the following figures:

D = 43.6635276
PV + DC = 1.23648272 as measured or 0.22682352 calculated + 15cc piston dish volume converted to CI equaling 1.0096592

G = A single 0.040-inch compressed gasket for Buick 350 calculates to 0.457909512
CC = 48cc converted to ci = 2.929776

Punch those numbers into the formula:

CR = (43.6635276 + 1.23648272 + 0.457909512 + 2.929776) / (1.23648272 + 0.457909512 + 2.929776)

Therefore:

CR = 48.287695832 / 4.624168232

Therefore:

Compression Ratio = 10.44

This compression ratio is 10.44:1. These calculations were made on an engine with a standard bore. Boring the cylinders will increase the compression ratio. In addition, machining the block, milling the heads, or altering the gasket thickness changes compression ratio. Complete these calculations before you make any modifications to establish reliable baseline figures. In turn, you will be armed with the information to make the best build-up decisions. These calculations were done using standard bore. Once again, do your homework before you by any parts.

CHAPTER 2

PISTONS, RODS AND CRANKS

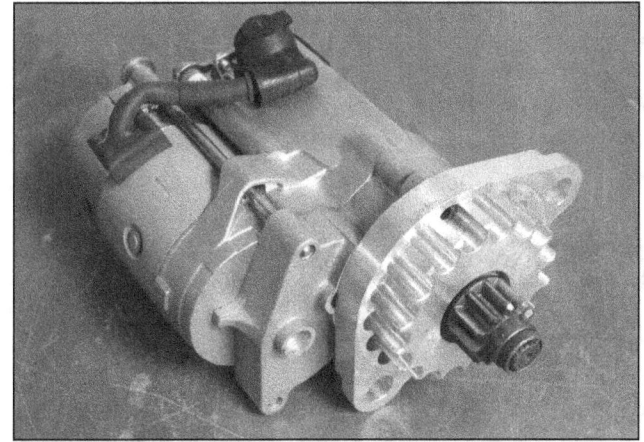

This is the Thomas Telesco gear-reduction starter for the 1964–1966 Nailheads.

A strong engine starts with a strong crankshaft, and all Buick engines use quality cranks. This is good because there are not many aftermarket cranks for Buicks. The small- and big-block engines, as well as the 3.8-liter V-6 turbo, use nodular-iron cranks, while the Nailheads run forged-steel cranks. Some people will tell you that the only way to tell if a Buick crank is made of nodular iron is if it has an "N" cast into it. While this is true for some Buick cranks, it is not a steadfast rule. In 1970 and earlier Buick engines, many of the cranks were marked with the telltale N and manufactured in the Flint, Michigan, plant that produced nodular cranks as well as plain steel units. In 1971 and later, Buick used a foundry that only manufactured nodular cranks, which eliminated the need for the N.

Crankshafts

Nailheads

The Nailhead uses four different forged-steel cranks. These forged-steel cranks are used in the 1953–1956 264/322 and 364, 1959–1963 401 and 425, and 1964–1966 401 and 425. The two different 401- and 425-ci cranks were a result of the transmission converter hole on the back. The Dynaflow transmission, used until 1963, had a larger pilot hole in the end of the crank than the 1964–1966 crankshaft that used the ST300 and ST400 transmission. Nailhead specialist Russell Martin, sells an adapter bushing that fits in the rear of a 1957–1963 crank. He also offers a dual-pattern Nailhead starter. With this adapter and a 1964–1966 flexplate, the ST300 and ST400 transmissions can be installed on all 1957–1963 engines. However, the 1953–1956 engines use the same crankshafts except the factory stick shift, which had a smaller hole for a pilot bushing. Small, lightweight mini gear reduction starters are available from nailheadbuick.com and Tom Telesco. The Dynaflow starter has about a 1/2-inch longer snout so the shorter 1964–1966 starter or special mini starter must be used. The 1961–1966 block accepts the 1964–1966 starter as is, but the 1957–1960 block has a different starter bolt pattern.

Small-Block 350

The smaller of the Buick powerhouses, the 350, does benefit from the same aftermarket support as its

CHAPTER 2

big brothers. The 350 had but one crankshaft, a cast nodular-iron unit. Fortunately, the stock crank is strong enough to support well over 500 hp. The 3.85-inch stroke crank will handle this magnitude of power, but the oiling system must be modified and the bearings need to be nice and tight. For power-added motors, such as turbos and superchargers, the stock crank is fine for engines up to 600 hp. If you plan on developing more than 500 hp, a custom crankshaft is required. Although expensive, the typical $2,000 price is cheap when you look at the overall price of building an extreme performance engine. Supercharged Buick 350 engines with stock blocks have been dyno'd at over 1,000 hp, so it certainly is capable of producing mega-power as long as the right components are used.

One drawback of the 350 is that the engine is built so tight, and there is literally no extra space between the rods and camshaft for any additional stroke. As a result, the cam must be installed before the crank; otherwise the crank and rods have to be rotated during the cam installation. By installing a custom-ground crank and custom pistons, you can increase displacement by a few ci, but the expense does not justify the performance benefits.

Big Blocks

The 400/430/455 crankshaft is also made from cast nodular iron, but these cranks easily support up to about 800 hp. For engines spooling more than 800 hp, there are aftermarket alternatives. All of the big blocks use the same 3.9-inch-stroke crank. The late-1970 and later cranks were cast without the telltale N, so don't let this confuse you; it is assuredly a nodular-iron unit.

The stock crankshaft has very large 3.25-inch main journals because these large main journals added critical strength to the thin block. In most applications, the stock crank is more than enough to provide a solid, dependable base for the rotating assembly, as long as it is properly prepped and oiled. When using large amounts of nitrous (200-hp shot or more) or building extreme-output

This 455 steel stroker crank has the full treatment with chamfered oiling holes, which increases oiling to the rods and main bearings.

There are aftermarket options available. This ATI Super Damper bolts onto any Buick 350, but it comes with a caveat. The externally balanced version requires the factory pulleys to be moved out from the engine about 1 inch because the crank snout was built long to clear the timing cover. This can be altered with some machining.

A micrometer, like this one, is the best bet when measuring clearances. This 350 crank was turned 0.010 inch to get perfectly concentric journals.

PISTONS, RODS AND CRANKS

Buick engines were externally balanced from the factory. This SFI-approved harmonic balancer from TA Performance should fit the bill for your Buick. If the stock balancer's rubber insert is cracked, missing pieces, or squished out of the groove, it needs to be replaced. A defective balancer's poor harmonics can rattle an engine apart. If the two pieces separate, there will be a lot of damage.

precision indexed, and magnafluxed. In addition, each crank has chamfered oil holes and is micropolished for superior oiling.

V-6 Turbo

There are two types of 3.8-liter V-6 turbo crankshafts: the nodular iron crankshaft used in the turbo engines, and the standard 3.8-liter crankshaft. The nodular turbo crankshaft features a rolled radius on the main and rod bearings that adds concentricity and uniformity, which increases load distribution through the journals. This also adds a good deal of strength to the crankshaft and reduces stress risers, which can cause catastrophic failure. All 1978–1987 turbo 3.8-liter crankshafts are nodular iron with rolled radii. The standard 3.8-liter cranks have rolled

For the V-6 turbo, this lightweight GM balancer is the ticket.

fillets on the main bearings only, and this crank will not survive in a turbo engine.

Main Seals

The Nailheads, the 350, and the big blocks used a factory rope seal, which originally sealed the crankshafts. But these seals were difficult to install and should be replaced

race engines, a custom forged-steel or steel-billet crankshaft is necessary. The stock crank cannot handle the hit of a 200-hp nitrous shot for long. It might work a few times, but it will eventually break, and then every single part on that engine will be unusable. You can build a custom billet crank for about $2,500, but this process often takes 6 to 10 months.

For those who subscribe to the gearhead adage, "there's no replacement for displacement," TA Performance's 455 stroker kits are a good option. The 494-ci and 523-ci stroker kits offer more displacement for extreme performance. The TA cranks feature 4.150-inch stroke and a 2.0-inch crank-pin diameter. Each stroker crank is custom ground,

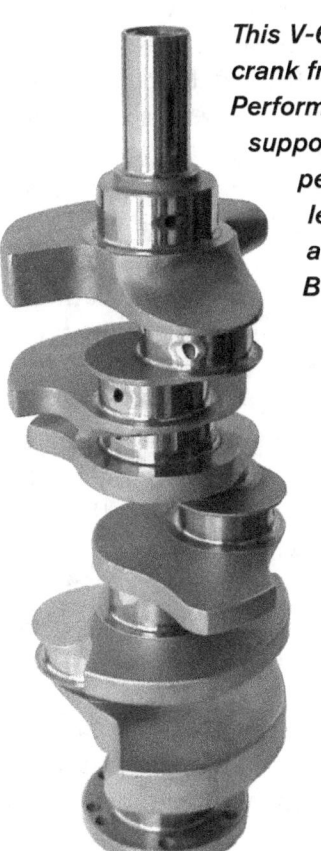

This V-6 turbo crank from TA Performance supports the performance level of about any Buick engine.

The rear main seal was originally a rope seal. These types of seals leak constantly and are a nightmare to install. Replacing it with a neoprene seal is a simple conversion but does require a little preparation.

with neoprene seals. There are, of course, a couple of techniques to make it easier.

The groove for the seal should be modified with three divots in the block and in the main cap. This keeps the seal from rotating in place. The grooves should also get a little squirt of silicone. The silicone seals the perimeter of the seal and keeps oil in the crankcase where it belongs. The neoprene seal comes in two halves. Each half should be installed with about 1/8 inch rotated out of one side of the groove (make sure they are opposite each other, top and bottom). This ensures there will be no leaking at the joint.

Before installing the rear seal, add a few divots in the block with an awl or small punch. This gives the seal something to grab, so it won't rotate.

Place a little dab of silicone in the seat and push the seal in place. Rotate the seal so that there is about 1/8 inch above the lip on one side and the same amount below on the other. This prevents the seal from leaking at the joint.

Connecting Rods

Nailheads

All of the Nailhead engines had forged rods. The 1953–1956 rods were 6 inches long and featured a wider bearing than the 1957–1966. There are two different rods: 1953 to mid-1955 264 ci and 322 ci; a pinch bolt held the wrist pin. On the mid-1955 to 1956 models, a more contemporary press-fit unit held the wrist pin, which was suitable for performance rebuilds. The 364 rods are 6-1/8 inches, and the 401 and 425 rods are 6-1/4 inches. The Buick rods are long for the stroke, so they have excellent rod/stroke ratios. This is even more evident with the 264, 322, and 364 engines. There are two different 364 rods, one used in 1957–1958 and one for the 1959–1961. The latter rod uses the 1959–1966 401 rod bolts and ARP bolts are available for these rods, but not the rods prior to 1959.

Forged Pontiac rods can be used in the 401 and 425 engines. These rods are longer and increase the rod/stroke ratio for better breathing. However, it takes a lot of work to make the 389 poncho rods for the Nailhead. These rods need to be lightened up and narrowed at the big end so the stock 401 bearing can be installed. The rod bolts hit the bottoms of the cylinders, so these must be clearanced on the block. The rod nuts contact the oil pan so a 1/4-inch spacer must be installed to drop the pan slightly. The Pontiac rod is 6-5/8-inch, and the 401-425 rod is 6-1/4-inch; therefore custom pistons with the wrist pin moved up are required.

Stock rods require very little work because they are forged and very strong. When rebuilding a Nailhead, a machine shop needs to magnaflux, shot-peen, and resize the rods and install ARP bolts. Always check the small ends of your rods, too. Buick had problems with wrist-pin knocking, and dealers installed oversize pins to fix it. If a standard pin is installed in these rods, it will slide out and ruin your cylinder wall.

Small-Block 350

The connecting rods for the 350 are quite durable and handle 500–550 hp, even though they are cast iron. When properly prepped, the stock rods are even suitable for all but the most extreme 350 builds. For prep guidelines, follow the steps in the next section for the big-block rods. While there are not many aftermarket Buick options, there are some. TA Performance offers reconditioned 350 rods that have been magnafluxed and shot-peened. In addition, the wrist pin end is

These 350 rods and pistons have been assembled and are ready for installation. Notice the discoloration on the little end (piston pin). This is from the heating process for press-fitting the piston pins to the rods. These rods have also been fitted with ARP rod bolts for security, and the pistons are Sealed Power Hypereutectic 10.5:1 units.

PISTONS, RODS AND CRANKS

checked for size, the crank end is resized, and ARP rod bolts are installed. TA Performance's high-performance forged-aluminum connecting rod is an extreme-performance alternative. This rod is the strongest aftermarket Buick 350 rod available. Of course, it is the only aftermarket Buick 350 rod produced. This rod is ideal for racing or adding nitrous to your small-block Buick.

Machining other makes' rods, such as Chrysler or Chevy, for the Buick 350 is another option. However, this is a very costly option and it yields a miniscule benefit. With the availability of the TA forged rod, the custom option just isn't worth it.

Big Blocks

Buick installed forged-steel rods on the big blocks, which provides adequate strength for many high-

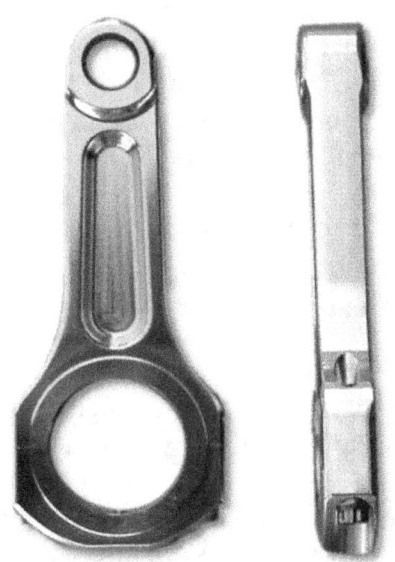

For the 455, these billet-aluminum rods are recommended for engines revving over 7,000 rpm or putting out more than 800 hp. They use 4304 chrome-moly rod bolts, which offer ultimate strength for 350 and big-block engines.

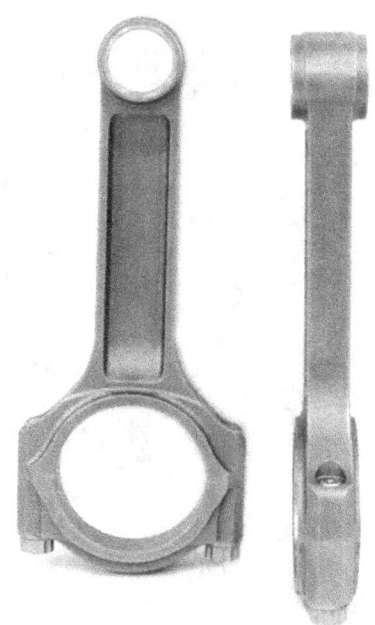

The TA Performance billet-steel rods are the very best connecting rods. These rods are the strongest available for Buicks and will clear the block with stroker cranks.

performance applications. If the stock rods are properly prepared, they are even strong enough for racing, a nitrous oxide system, or revving up to 6,500 rpm. If you are going to spin the engine more than 6,500 rpm, the stock rods will not be strong enough. In addition, a set of aftermarket rods is required for a 125-hp, or more, shot of nitrous.

Numerous aftermarket connecting rod offerings provide a significant increase in strength over the stock rods. Some even provide a better rod/stroke ratio, but these rods require custom pistons. Chevrolet big block, Chrysler, and Pontiac rods require modification but can be adapted for use in a Buick, which opens up an entire selection of aftermarket options. Use of any non-Buick rod will require a custom piston. A big-block Chevy rod requires rod journal machining to

When fitting a Nailhead or big block with ARP rod bolts, you must check for clearance around the cap inset. The larger head can ride the inner edge, giving a false torque reading. Refacing the cap with a 21/32-inch counter bore eliminates the problem.

accommodate the smaller Chevy bearing. Anytime you choose to run a non-Buick rod, the corresponding bearings and pins reference the rod type, not the Buick engine.

While there are lots of non-Buick rod options, there are quite a few aftermarket offerings, as well. TA Performance offers both forged-steel and billet-steel connecting rods. The 4340 billet-steel rods offer the most strength and lightest weight comparable to billet rods.

The length of the connecting rod is good for a little cheap HP. Some builders, such as Jack Merkel of Merkel Performance Engines, suggest that a 6.800-inch rod in the 455 engine will deliver a little extra power, but there is no more power to be found by using a longer rod. TA Performance, however, sells 455 rods up to 7.350 inches.

Properly prepping rods takes a little patience and time. When it's done correctly, it yields a quality piece that will serve any vehicle well. When disassembling the motor, correctly label the rods for convenient assembly. The rods have matching caps that must be used with the same rod; otherwise, the bolts will not line up in the rods. Simply stamp each cap and rod on one side by using a mallet and set of number stamps.

CHAPTER 2

This ensures the rods are also installed in the right order and in the right direction. There is a small dimple on each rod, and each pair of rods must have the dimples facing each other for correct installation. Ask your machine shop to perform this process if it disassembles the engine. In addition, the shop should Magnaflux the rods and make sure they are not bent or cracked. Once the rods' straightness and integrity have been verified, it's time to get out the sander.

Use a belt sander with a small-diameter roller; or, a small-diameter sanding drum with medium-to-fine grit is ideal for removing the forging seam along the length of the rod. This reduces the stress risers, which accumulate heat and lead to cracking. Run the sander along the length of the rod, as you want the cuts to run the lengthwise instead of across the beam. An air-powered mini-belt sander works perfectly for this task. Once the rods are polished, a set of ARP rod bolts should be installed. At this stage, the rods are ready to be resized. A properly prepped set of rods should be good to 6,500 rpm without any issues.

V-6 Turbo

The 3.8-liter connecting rods used in all Buick V-6 turbo engines utilize a strong cap-screw design. This is the same design of connecting rod used in racing, including NASCAR. Introduced in 1975, this design proved to be twice as strong as the previous style. For most high-performance builds, the stock connecting rods provide more than enough strength for a turbo engine. In fact, rods are very seldom the cause of a turbo engine breakdown. The stock rods can take a tremendous amount of abuse.

These ARP rod bolts for the V-6 turbo are the best you can buy. The stock units are acceptable for street motors, but when an engine is apart, install new rod bolts. The new bolts will not have any prestretch, so the initial torque setting will be accurate.

There are several aftermarket rods available for those who are building extreme-performance and race-only turbo engines. K1 Technologies, a division of Carrillo, produces an H-beam 4340 forged-steel connecting rod fitted with ARP2000 rod bolts. These rods are suitable for just about any performance level turbo engine.

One note on the factory turbo rods: the bolt hole in the cap is not chamfered from the factory. This needs to be corrected when using aftermarket rod bolts, such as ARP. If not, the bolt head will not sit flush on the cap, and the bolt cannot be torqued correctly.

Rod Bolts

Always use ARP or similar high-performance rod bolts. They offer superior holding power and accurately measure bolt stretch. Reusing

ARP has quite a selection of bolts for Buick engines. Whenever possible, use top-quality ARP bolts. This crank balancer bolt features a 1/2-inch square-drive head, which allows the builder to rotate the engine using just a breaker bar.

the stock bolts is never a good idea because these used stock bolts have been stretched, and they cannot be accurately measured and torqued. Save yourself a headache and pay the nominal amount for a set of good-quality rod bolts.

The rod bolts need to be torqued to the proper specs, or there will be problems with your engine. Too much torque can cause excessive friction in the engine, leading to bearing failure. Not enough torque and the oil pressure will lead to failure, as well. While the factory specs call for 35 to 45 ft-lbs for the connecting rods, most builders recommend 50 ft-lbs for high-performance applications. Once the rods are torqued down, the side clearance for the rods is an important clearance to be checked. There should be between 0.007- and 0.016-inch total clearance on the rod journals for performance rebuilds.

A forged piston yields the best strength, but at a slightly heavier weight. For low-revving engines, this is certainly a reasonable tradeoff for the improved performance. This Nailhead piston is a lightweight forged unit, which saves a lot more weight than traditional forging. The pent shape of the Nailhead combustion chamber requires a large pop-up in the center of the piston.

These Sealed Power forged pistons are exactly as stock but are forged instead of cast. They easily handle stock compression and deliver the strength of a forged piston.

A stock-style low-compression V-6 piston is perfect for applications in which massive amounts of boost will be added.

Pistons

Nailheads

The original Nailhead pistons on the 264 are 3-5/8-inch diameter and 4-5/16 inches on the 425. The 1953 has a very large dome — almost like a Hemi — while all others have the same basic dome shape. It is common for people to confuse a 10:1 Nailhead piston for a 12:1 piston because the dome profile makes it look like a higher compression unit. The large pent-roof chamber of the Nailhead cylinder head requires large piston domes, unlike the later Buick engines and most other makes. Buick used the size of the dome to change compression ratio of the piston. All factory pistons were cast, except a limited number of the 11:1 forged pistons for 401s offered in 1966. Cast pistons are perfectly acceptable for a Nailhead build. They are quiet when cold, and lighter than most forged pistons.

Some racers have claimed they lost horsepower by switching from cast to forged pistons. Max Balchowsky, who built the cars in the movie *Bullitt* and a Buick Nailhead authority, said he ran cast pistons in Nailhead engines up to 7,000 rpm. The 1954–1955 Buick 264 and 322 pistons did not provide sufficient durability. These pistons often cracked and should be replaced with aftermarket cast or forged. There are a couple of ways to finish off cast and forged pistons, including CNC machining and cam grinding. "I have had some problem with CNC'd pistons," said Russell Martin, a Nailhead engine expert. "They don't seem to have a nice wear pattern when I have inspected used ones, so I prefer old-school cam-ground pistons." Computer numerical control (CNC) machining uses a computer aided design (CAD) program to operate the machine. Cam-ground pistons feature an elliptical-shaped cross-section. This elliptical shape allows the piston to fit in the cylinder regardless of being hot or cold and allows for more expansion.

Small-Block 350

The stock pistons, while decent, are not really suitable for high-performance use. The stock castings have a large, dished-out center with a little nipple sticking up. An easy way to identify the compression ratio of the piston is to look at the height of the nipple. A deep dish with a tall nipple is a low-compression engine. The stock compression ratios for the 1968–1980 350 are: 10.25:1 (1968–1969), 10.5:1 (1970), 8.5:1 (1971–1975), and 8.0:1 (1975–1980).

The 10.2:1 compression pistons are the only stock cast pistons currently available for the Buick 350. There are two types of aftermarket pistons: hypereutectic cast, and forged. To make an informed decision on piston selection, here is a brief description of each type.

The term "hypereutectic" means over eutectic, and eutectic is a metallurgical term that refers to the percentages of one element to another in a specific alloy for maintaining a common bond. Once the alloy reaches a certain percentage, any material that's added remains a separate entity.

Typically, in aluminum alloys, the silicon content is eutectic at 12 percent. In the 1970s, it was discovered that adding more silicon to a cast piston produced less expansion when heated. This was very important for emissions, and it created a process of forcing additional silicon into the alloy, which remains in its granular form up to the 16 to 19-percent range. At 25 percent silicon, the pistons become hard and brittle and are subject to cracking.

Hypereutectic pistons can be machined for a tighter fit, and can run much closer tolerances in the cylinders because these pistons do not expand very much when heated. The rings form a tight seal on the cylinder wall, and this translates into less oil blow-by at start up. However, these pistons are not as strong as forged pistons and should not be used in any engine that uses more than a 125-hp shot of nitrous.

Forged pistons are formed from a heated slug of aluminum alloy. The alloy is forced into several increasingly detailed dies until it comes out as a very close representation of a finished piston. The forging is machined to precise specs and ready for installation. Forged pistons are very strong, and they can take a lot of abuse without breaking apart. Most importantly, these pistons are the only choice for any serious high-performance engine, but there are drawbacks.

Forged pistons are more expensive and fit more loosely in a cold cylinder than hypereutectic pistons because the forged pistons require loose tolerances to accommodate for a large expansion range. The expense of a forged piston depends on the engine. For a small-block Chevy, these pistons cost a little more than a cast piston. For a small-block Buick, however, they cost a bit more. As a matter of fact, TRW recently ceased production of the only production forged piston for the Buick 350. The other drawback is loose cylinder tolerances, which only affects the engines when they are cold. For basic mid-level daily driver engines, the strength of forged pistons would not justify the expense. For serious high-performance and race engines, forged pistons are a must.

Currently, a forged piston is not available; custom pistons are the only option besides stock cast or hypereutectic. Several manufacturers produce on-demand, custom pistons for Buick 350 engines. Diamond Racing is one of those companies. TA Performance and Poston Enterprises also offer forged Buick 350 pistons in a variety of compression ratios. Hypereutectic pistons for the Buick 350 typically have a 10.5:1 compression ratio. The price difference in a custom forged Buick 350 piston and a hypereutectic piston is typically $300 – $400. The Sealed Power hypereutectic piston is probably the most commonly used Buick 350 piston, and we used this piston on our 400-hp 350 build-up.

Big Blocks

The big blocks, predominately the 455, have quite a few brands of pistons available. As stated earlier, stock cast replacement pistons are not suitable for any application other than stock rebuilds. For high-HP engines, forged pistons are the best choice. In fact, forged pistons

This 11:1 flat-top 455 piston from JE Pistons is a complete custom unit, which features 7-cc valve reliefs and is capable of producing 13:1 compression.

are required for any big-block engine that will turn more than 5,500 rpm or use more than a 125-hp shot of nitrous. The premium material for forged pistons is 2618 aluminum alloy because it's both strong and light. In most cases, a thinner 1/16-inch file fit ring is used. For most street or light strip-duty engines, the TRW forged pistons fit the bill. Beyond running a custom piston, there are several specialized forged pistons available for the 455. TA Performance offers a 2618 alloy lightweight race piston in 12.0:1 and custom compression ratios. This is the piston of choice for building a stroker engine. These stroker pistons also have the top ring placed higher on the piston, reducing the compression distance. In addition, this accommodates a longer rod for better rod ratios. TA also carries forged stock replacement pistons available in 8.5 and 10.1:1 compressions.

The camshaft used in any particular build may require notched pistons, so it is wise to speak with your cam supplier before ordering pistons. If your block has been decked or the heads have been milled, valve notches may be necessary. It is very important to dry-assemble your engine before final assembly to check valve clearance. A minimum piston-to-valve clearance of 0.100 inch should be maintained. A piston hitting a valve would not be a good way to break-in an engine.

Piston-to-wall clearance is also an important issue to consider. Inadequate piston-to-wall clearance can cause an engine to run hot. This is why most builders recommend honing every engine with torque plates. If you hone a block without a torque plate, you may have tight spots in your piston travel because the cylinders can potentially tweak when the head is torqued in place. Still, quite a few Buick builders dispute the value of torque plates for Buicks and will not use them. The choice is yours. For cast pistons (including hypereutectics), a clearance of 0.0015–0.002 inch is sufficient. The TRW forged pistons should run 0.003 to 0.004 inch of piston-to-wall clearance. Always follow the manufacturer's instructions when using custom pistons. For most 2618 alloy pistons, at least 0.005- to 0.006-inch piston-to-wall clearance is required.

According to Mike Tomaszewski, owner and founder of TA Performance, "We do not sell, nor do we recommend, hypereutectic pistons. We have noticed an increase in failures due to the use of these types of pistons." There are a few manufacturers that offer a hypereutectic piston for the 455, but these pistons are certainly stronger than the OEM cast piston and feature valve notches for use with larger camshafts. In addition, they are available in higher compression ratios than the stock cast pistons with their smaller dish and 0.010-inch less deck clearance. These hypereutectic pistons cost considerably less than forged pistons. TA Performance does not recommend these pistons because several customers have experienced piston breakage. In their opinion, hypereutectic pistons are too hard and brittle, allowing detonation to break a hypereutectic piston. This is an area of great debate. TA Performance is not alone in this argument, and they are certainly not opposed either. Many builders use hypereutectic pistons for high-performance street build-ups. It is this author's opinion that there is a place for both.

The stock cast piston is not suitable for anything other than a stock rebuild. If you are building a mid-performance engine that's below 600 hp for big blocks and less than 450 hp for the 350, the hypereutectic pistons will be more than adequate and should prove to be excellent in a properly built engine. With that said, *do not use* large amounts of nitrous on a hypereutectic piston. These pistons cannot take the shock and will break. A stock engine with stock cast pistons can typically take a 125-hp shot of nitrous. Use any more and you will start breaking pistons. If you plan on using nitrous, it would be a wise choice to use forged pistons. The same goes for any engine that is going to be revved over 6,000 rpm. If you are going to rev your engine this high, it is probably not a daily driver. If it will be raced, forged pistons are a must.

Turbo-V6

The pistons for the 3.8-liter V-6 turbo engines require special consideration. The forced-air induction engines place incredible demands on these pistons and make selection critical. The compression ratio for a turbo engine should not exceed 8:1 because a higher compression ratio can cause detonation, which can lead to engine failure. While high-octane or race fuels can remedy detonation, most owners don't want to deal with hassle and/or expense of finding and running race-type fuel in a street car. Forged pistons are the best option for performance turbo engines because cast and hypereutectic piston are generally not strong enough to handle high-boost pressures. In fact, cast and hypereutectic pistons, if subjected to high enough intake pressures, can break apart in the cylinder and wreck the engine. Non-turbo pistons are not engineered or manufactured to withstand heat and stress of a turbo engine, so never use these pistons. The ring lands on a turbo piston are strengthened to support the boost pressure. Jack Merkel of Jack Merkel Performance engines recommends using TRW forged pistons with a

 **Spiral**  **True Arc**

There are two styles of locks for floating piston pins. The traditional lock ring on the right will work, but for more security — especially for street-driven engines — a spiral lock works better. However, it is more difficult to install.

piston to cylinder wall clearance of 0.0045-inch. Otherwise, you should follow the recommendations of the particular piston manufacturer. Piston weight is also a factor. Heavy pistons create more rotating mass and lose a fair amount of HP. Lightweight turbo pistons, made of 2618 aluminum, are recommended and provide superior performance.

Piston Pins

There are two types of wrist pins: press-fit and free-floating. Press-fit means the pins are pressed into the piston and rod. This wrist pin style has slightly more friction, so the pin remains stationary and the piston rotates on the pin. Controlled heating of the wrist pin side of the rod allows the pin to slide through the rod. As the rod cools, the pin is grabbed by the rod and held tight, leaving no possibility of the pin sliding out, ruining the cylinder walls. This is the most common method for Buick pistons. Jim Burek of Performance Automotive Enterprises recommends this style for all but race-only engines.

Free-floating wrist pins require honing the small end of the connecting rod so the pin can slide though easily. The wrist pin is held in place with two locking rings on both sides of the pistons. Some builders say these clips are prone to breakage. If one breaks, the pin can slide out and destroy the cylinder wall. Free-floating pins reduce friction and may free up a little HP on high-revving race engines, and they are certainly easier to assemble and disassemble. It's a big plus for a race engine that gets torn down frequently. For street applications, they just are not necessary.

The key is to file fit your rings or use gapless rings, such as these rings from Total Seal.

Once the rings are installed, the pistons can be installed into the block. Use a spring compressor to help hold the springs in place before tapping the piston in the block with a soft mallet. This can be done without a compressor, but the $30–$40 to buy the compressor is well worth the added ease. This also reduces the risk of breaking rings.

A set of ARP main bolts securely holds down the crank. The crank should spin easily in the bearings with pre-lube. If it does not, there are several likely culprits: the tolerances are too tight, machining is incorrect, or a set of caps has switched positions.

PISTONS, RODS AND CRANKS

This fully installed 455 rotating assembly is ready for some heads.

ARP main studs were installed on this 350. Using studs instead of bolts greatly improves strength. The bolts stretch evenly since the threads are fully threaded in the block, and they do not twist while being torqued.

Measuring crankshaft end play is an important step. End play of 0.006 inch is acceptable.

The flexplate rounds out the rotating assembly. Since the Buick engines are externally balanced, using the correct flexplate is important. This stock unit is safe for engines up to about 500 hp.

This SFI-approved unit from TA Performance is good for everything above 500 hp. Replace your flexplate on every rebuild. There's no reason to risk a failure over a $50 part.

HOW TO BUILD MAX-PERFORMANCE BUICK ENGINES

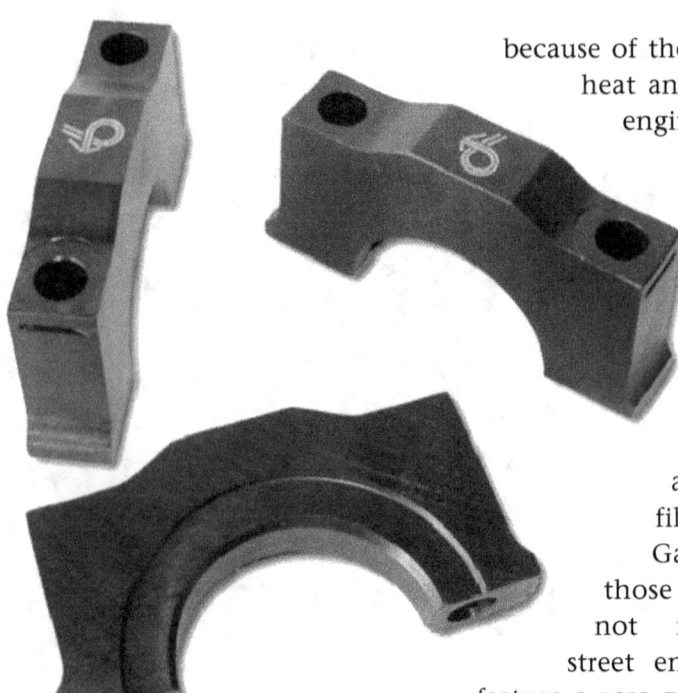

For the V-6 turbo, the billet main caps are a good idea for anything more powerful than stock. The block requires align-honing with main caps in place before assembly.

Rings

There are quite a few choices when it comes to piston rings. For stock and street-performance engines, a chrome-moly ring set provides good sealing and oil control. For high-horsepower and high-revving engines, the Federal Mogul or Speed-Pro plasma moly rings with a 1/16-inch-wide top ring is the best choice. These rings have superior resistance to moly flaking. The plasma coating increases lubrication, and the high melting point of the moly ensures a higher resistance to scuffing. When in doubt, use the plasma moly rings. If you are running nitrous, the plasma moly rings are the best choice because of the high resistance to heat and detonation. Most engine builders recommend a file-fit ring set. This allows the builder to set the gaps rather than use a by-the-chart gap in a standard set. Any high-performance application requires file-fit rings.

Gapless rings, such as those from Total Seal, are not recommended for street engines. These rings feature a zero-gap second ring that interlocks, virtually eliminating combustion gas escaping through the rings. Removing the end gap can improve sealing, cooling, and HP. Some claim as much as a 5 percent hp increase by using a gapless top compression ring. Using a gapless top ring can eliminate the second compression ring on drag-race only engines. Deleting the second ring reduces friction and adds HP. But this is not something you would want to run on street engines. It's for drag-race-only engines that get torn down after every race.

There is a lot of debate on this subject. In fact, many top builders recommend running a larger gap in the second ring because it reduces the pressure buildup between the rings. When the pressure drops, the top ring loses its seal at high rpm, resulting in better compression, better piston cooling, and reduced oil consumption. Pressure build-up between the rings will eventually force oil out of the rings, reduce lubrication, score the cylinders, and inevitably ruin the engine. By opening the gap on the second ring, the top ring is allowed to float, increasing sealing and allowing the gases to escape. This eliminates the possibility of the top ring lifting off the ring land.

After the type of rings has been selected, the file-fit process begins. Each ring is inserted into the cylinder bore, and a piston is used to push the ring inside, keeping the ring square. A set of feeler gauges is used to measure the gaps. Then each ring is filed using a ring grinder (available from Powerhouse tools, Snap-On, Matco, K-D, etc.) to keep the edges clean and burr-free. You could use a hand file, but why waste all that energy and time when a $40 tool does a better job? The ideal gap for the top ring is 0.016 to 0.018 inch, and the second ring is commonly set at 0.012 to 0.014 inch. The oil rings typically do not need sizing.

When the rings are sized, they need to be installed on the pistons. Opinions vary, but many contend that keeping the gaps apart is important for good sealing. Jim Burek, of Performance Automotive Enterprises, recommends setting the oil-ring spacer with the gap over one of the wrist pins. One oil ring is placed about in the middle of the piston between the wrist pins on one side. The other oil ring is placed 180 degrees opposed on the other side of the piston. The compression rings are typically installed with one gap over each wrist pin. It's important to keep the gap opposed for the initial installation. The rings will move once the engine is running, so starting off with them opposed is the best bet.

PISTONS, RODS AND CRANKS

Max-Performance 1970 Buick Gran Sport 455

Mike Garrison, owner of mrbuick.com, a Buick-specialty restoration shop, drag races this 1970 Buick GS as often as he can. TA Performance and Ruge Automotive built the bored and stroked 455 that runs as fast 10.18 seconds at 135.30 mph in the quarter mile. His business offers parts, such as core support rebuild kits, flywheel covers, and transmission brackets.

Engine Package:

- 535-ci V-8, 830 hp at 6,300 rpm; 802 ft-lb at 4,600 rpm
- 4.30-inch bore x 4.50-inch stroke
- 13.96:1 compression
- Steel billet 7-inch connecting rods
- TA 1610 inverted dome pistons with 1/16th rings, pin size: 0.927 inch x 2.950 inch, double spiral locks, piston weight: 546 grams
- Intake valve 2.19, 0.372 stem; Exhaust valve 1.75, 0.372 stem; Dual springs TA1190; seat pressure 230 lbs, open 540 lbs
- Comp Cams roller cam, 0.636 lift, 1.6 rockers 107-degree centerline
- 296-degree duration
- Cam degreed to 105 degrees
- Push rod size is 9.50 inch x 0.312 inch
- TA Street Eliminator heads: 58 cc
  Intake side flows: 334.9 cfm at 0.600 inch
  Exhaust side flows: 243.8 cfm at 0.600 inch
- Block supported with a block girdle
- Block is filled 50 percent with block hard
- Lifter gallery has been filled to the top of the bores with epoxy

TA Performance and Ruge Automotive bored and stroked Mike Garrison's 830-hp, 535-ci Buick behemoth. Garrison owns and operates mrbuick.com, which sells parts for Buick restoration.

Garrison's 1970 Buick GS hangs the wheels at Thunder Valley Raceway in Noble, Okalahoma, and is certainly a force to be reckoned with. Garrison is running low 10s and only a few tenths away from 9-second quarter-mile times.

HOW TO BUILD MAX-PERFORMANCE BUICK ENGINES 27

CHAPTER 2

Measuring Piston-to-Value Clearance *by Len Emanuelson*

Building a high-performance engine with various speed parts is complex business. To help avoid problems, you need to follow the basic engine-building rules, measuring every part to ensure they meet specs and trial-assembling the engine to check clearances. Valve-to-piston clearance is one of the most critical clearances and should be physically checked. Many first-time engine builders try to calculate the amount of valve clearance by the piston at top dead center (TDC) and the total lift at the valve. It just doesn't work that way. You won't know if the valve notches in the pistons are in the right place and exactly how everything meshes unless you go through the process. The most accurate test is to put clay on the top of the pistons, install the cylinder heads and valvetrain, and rotate the engine through a complete cycle – two complete revolutions.

Clay-Mation

Most professional engine builders recommend 0.100 inch for manual transmissions and as close as 0.070 inch for automatic transmission vehicles. Use 0.100 inch to be safe – and even more if you can get it – unless you're building a world-championship race engine and need every bit of compression you can get. One missed shift at 7,000 rpm and valve float could instantly turn an expensive engine into a pile of junk. First, rinse the piston top with lacquer thinner for a clean, oil-free surface that clay can stick to. Then cut a couple of strips of clay about 3/16-inch thick and place them where you think the valves could hit the piston.

Engine Rotation

Spray the valves with a light coat of oil to prevent them from sticking to the clay and put the cylinder head back on the engine with a head gasket; torque to spec. Next, install the valvetrain and adjust the valve lash. Here's the tricky part. Swap the hydraulic lifters for a mechanical lifter, a piece of wood dowel, or an aluminum slug that matches the pushrod seat height in the lifter. Why? A hydraulic lifter in a non-running engine will

Clay is placed on the piston in the area where it comes in contact with the valves. Give the valves a light coat of lubricant to ensure the clay does not stick.

The cylinder head is placed back on the engine. The pushrods and rockers are installed for a particular cylinder and set to spec.

deflect the plunger and not give you true valve lift. In addition, you can take an old hydraulic lifter apart and fill it with something solid so the pushrod seat remains up against the retaining clip. Once you figure out this little issue, the rest is easy. Finally, rotate the crankshaft through two complete rotations. Slowly turn over the crank and feel for any resistance. If the engine doesn't want to rotate completely, don't force it. Remove the cylinder head and see what's hitting.

Squish Check

Once you've successfully run the crankshaft through two complete revolutions, remove the cylinder head and inspect the clay. Hopefully, the clay was placed in the right location and stayed put for the valve opening and closings. (By cleaning the piston, the clay has plenty of stick, and by spraying the valves with light oil they won't stick to the clay.) If you used thick-enough clay, the valves should leave fairly large impressions that are easy to identify.

Measurements

To determine valve-to-piston clearance, measure the deepest part of the groove made by the valve in the clay. Also, you must measure the deepest groove at the highest portion of the piston dome. Our Buick pistons had a big dish in the center, so the clearance was more than adequate. However, out on the raised edge of the piston, we measured the clay thickness with the wire-rod depth gauge of our dial caliper and measured only 0.075-inch clearance – just enough to squeak by. This big Buick redlines at 6,000 rpm, and the automatic transmission should provide the safety factor.

Perform this valve-to-piston inspection when you trial-assemble your engine – you'll be doing yourself a favor. Inadequate clearance means disassembling the engine, having the pistons notched at a machine shop, and starting the assembly process all over – a real pain!

Slowly rotate the engine by hand. If any hard resistance is encountered, stop and determine the source of the resistance. Resistance means something is wrong, and you need to resolve the issue to avoid serious damage. If all goes well, remove the head, and you will discover the valves have left marks like these.

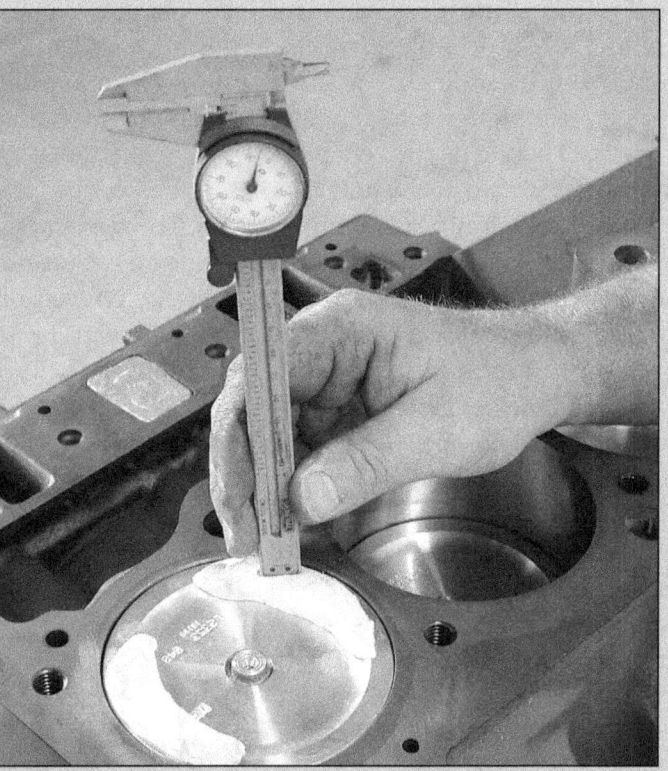

Use the backside of the caliper to measure the depth of the clay. Do not press the base of the caliper into the clay; this alters the measurement.

CHAPTER 3

OILING SYSTEM UPGRADES

The single biggest weakness of any Buick engine is the oiling system. The original design of the oiling system has more than a few issues, including small oil feed holes, misaligned bearings, and poor cam and lifter oiling. All of these issues are easily fixed if you take the time to learn the proper techniques and buy the right parts. The next two chapters focus on the 350 and 455 family and 3.8-liter-engines; Nailhead engines do not have the oiling issues the others have. To understand how to fix the oiling issues, knowing the path the oil takes is important.

On every Buick engine except the Nailhead, the oil pump is located in the timing cover and powered by the distributor. It's driven from an integral drive gear on the camshaft. The pump draws oil from a 1/2-inch oil pick-up tube (5/8-inch on 1971 and later 455s) on the passenger side of the oil pan. The pump gears are pressurized and the oil is forced through the oil filter. Then, oil is sent to the crankshaft through holes in the main bearing journals. Next, oil is pumped to the connecting rods through passages in the crankshaft. At the same time, oil is pumped up to the passenger-side lifter galley, across the front cam bearing to the driver's side lifter galley. For 455, 1970 and later 350, and 400 Stage 1 engines, pressurized oil from the lifters is pushed up through hollow pushrods and enters the rocker at the pushrod tip and oils the rockers. The 1968–1969 non-Stage 1 400, 430, and 350 engines use specific rocker arm shafts to oil the rockers and pushrod tips. These engines use solid pushrods. While these pushrods are still available, the conversion to the later (and more efficient) hollow-pushrod design is simple and will be discussed in the next chapter.

Disassembly and Modification

The block should be fully disassembled and cleaned before any modifications are made. Each engine build is different, so how deep you go into the engine determines how much you will modify. If you are boring the engine, oil system modifications should be done before the machine work, so you have a perfectly clean and prepped block that's ready to be built. These mods are not an absolute must, but since the engine is apart, it's a good idea to do them. Each of these modifications

Cleaning up the 3.8-liter V-6 turbo bores is a quick way to increase the speed at which the oil returns to the pan. A basic clean-up gets the job done.

OILING SYSTEM UPGRADES

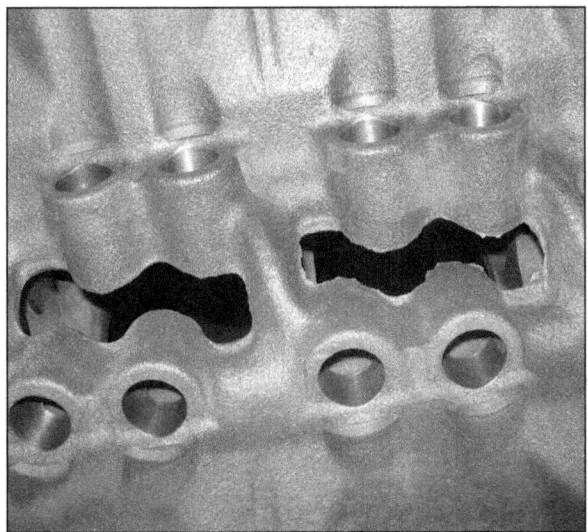

Here is the difference in the stock casting and the cleaned-up section.

The weak lifter bores need to be reinforced for a high-lift cam profile or roller lifters. The bores will break out under the outward stress from the lifters. This TA Performance bolt-in lifter girdle is a simple way to eliminate the problem.

can be performed on all of the later Buick blocks. However, some of the hole sizes may be different.

Cleaning up the flashing on the casting should be done on every engine build. It is quick, easy, and results in faster oil flow from the rockers back to the pan. Mount the engine on a rotating stand. A die-grinder with a fine carbide cone bit is the best tool to use for this job. Smoothing out the flashing in the lifter galley is most important. The idea is to eliminate the rough edges that will catch the oil and inhibit its downward flow. Perform a basic cleanup and don't go crazy. The Buick engines don't have a lot of material around the lifter bores, so you don't want to remove too much material and create a problem. Use the same process for cleaning up the casting flash around the main webs. This job isn't mandatory, but it will certainly reduce the chances of them becoming a stress riser and cracking. If you are building a severe-duty engine, this is a really good idea.

In addition to cleaning up the flashing around the lifter bores, adding a lifter bore girdle is required when a roller cam is used. There are bolt-in lifter girdles and custom-built epoxied-in units. These are only necessary when using a roller cam, and will be discussed further in Chapter 9: Race Engines.

Now that everything is trimmed up, the real work can begin. On the main bearing journals, the number-2, -3, and -4 oil-feed holes should be opened up. Do this by drilling the original 1/4-inch hole with a 5/16-inch drill bit. It is extremely important to start the drilling straight on the hole, or you run the risk of running off the edge of the corresponding cam bearing. These holes must be drilled all the way past the cam bearing, to a depth of 3-3/4 inches; a standard-length drill bit should be able to accomplish this task; just make sure it is sharp. The stock main bearings (on a 350) have a 3/16-inch hole in them. If you are leaving the stock oil holes alone, the main bearing holes should be opened up to 1/4 inch; if you are making the previously mentioned modification, the bearing holes should be opened up to the corresponding 5-1/16-inch size.

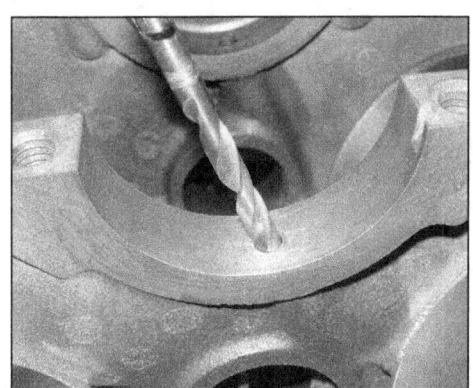

The number-2, -3, and -4 main bearing saddle oiling holes on this 350 were opened up from 1/4 inch to 5/16 inch, while being careful not to hit the cam bearing. These holes must go to a depth of 3-3/4 inches.

Main bearing oil hole alignment is one of the biggest problems with Buick engines. To check this, you will need either the original bearings, or even better, the bearings used in the rebuild. On our 350, we found the number-2, -3, -4, and -5 main journals had to be corrected. This is a very important step — if you skip it, you could end up covering more than half of the hole, which could result in a catastrophic failure. Once the problems have been identified, the fix is pretty simple. With the bearing in place, mark the journal inside the hole where the misalignment occurs. Using the die-grinder with the cone carbide, chamfer the oiling holes where the journal was marked. This allows the oil to easily enter the bearings and not get hung up on the edges. It is all right if the hole ends up slightly larger than the bearing hole, just as long as they line up afterwards. This step should be done on every single Buick engine build: stock, high performance, or race.

The next step is to open up the main oil suction feed on the front of the block. This step is paramount to increasing the oil flow to the rest of the engine. Use a 12-inch long 1/2-inch drill bit, and drill the suction side oil galley from the front of the block to the oil pick-up tube. Patiently drill and add cutting oil as you go. Don't try to do this all at once. Drill about an inch, pull the bit out, remove the chaff from the drill bit, and proceed another inch or so. Be sure to keep the bit level and do not go off at an angle. This passage is 10-1/2 inches deep, so take your time and be patient. You can do all the drilling with a cordless drill, but it's much better to use a corded drill

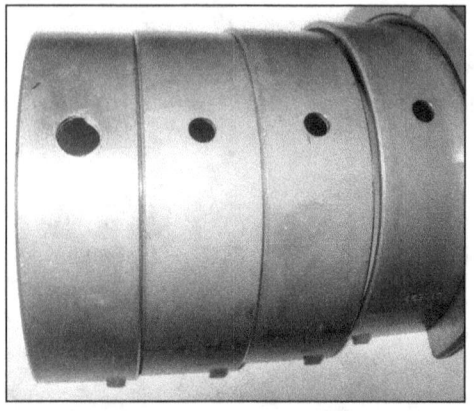
The bearing oil feed holes must be enlarged. Otherwise, the block mod does no good.

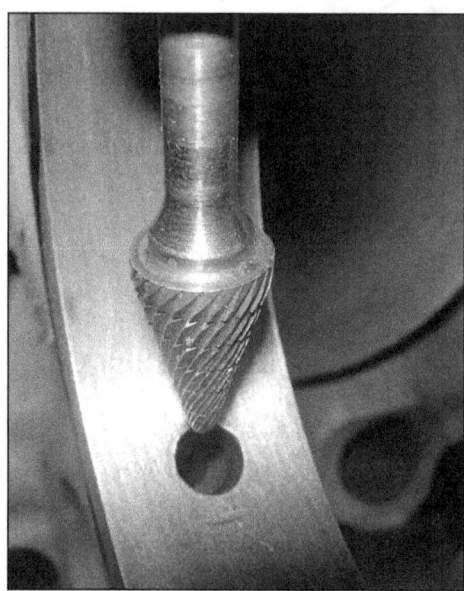
Using a carbide tip, chamfer the edge of the hole in the bearing saddle. This had to be done to the number-2, -3, -4, and -5 saddles.

On the 350, the oil suction passage from the block to oil pump hole needs to be enlarged to 1/2 inch.
The passage is 10-1/2 inches deep.

Checking the bearings for alignment is important. This must be correct in order to get adequate oiling.

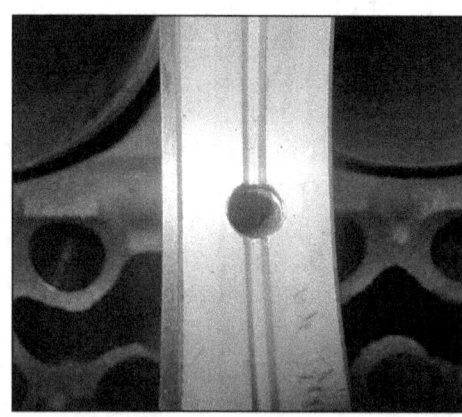
Rechecking the bearing shows a proper fit.

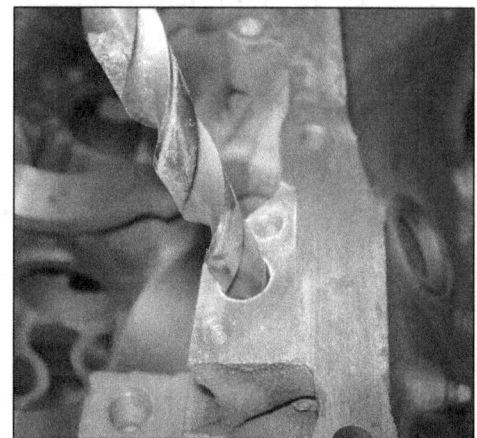
Enlarge the oil pick-up tube passage to 1/2 inch. This will intersect the previous passage at 3 inches.

OILING SYSTEM UPGRADES

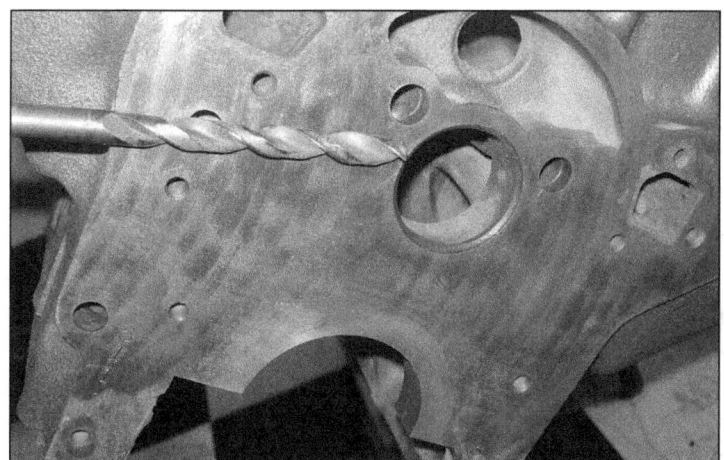

The main oil-feed passage needs to be opened from the oil-pressure sending unit to just short of the main cam bearing. The depth is 4 inches, and it's drilled out to 7/16 inch. The passage can be opened up to 1/2 inch, but it requires tapping the oil sensor to a 3/8-inch pipe thread.

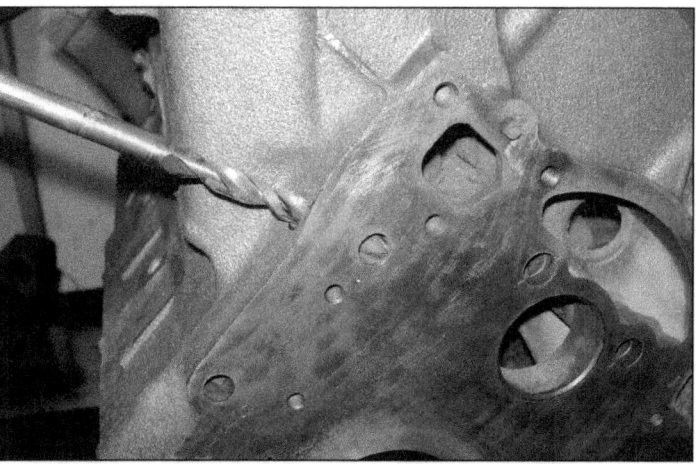

Again, drill slowly and keep the drill depth to 4 inches. Using cutting oil makes the work a little easier and keeps the chaff from binding up the bit. Pull the bit out of the hole after drilling each inch, and clean off the chaff.

because the lighter weight will reduce the strain on your arms and allow you to drill level. Another plus of a corded drill is more torque and no recharge time.

The 350 requires the following procedure: Drill the oil pick-up tube passage to 1/2 inch. This will intersect with the previous passage from the front of the block. The depth on this passage is 3 inches. Again, take your time and use cutting oil — it will help.

The previous step can also (and should) be performed on the early big blocks (1968–1970 400, 430, and 455 engines). In 1971, Buick realized the 1/2-inch suction feed line was not adequate and bumped the oil pick-up tube size to 5/8 inch. Opening the 1/2-inch passage in the 400 and 430 blocks to 9/16 inch is sufficient; the 455 blocks can be drilled to 5/8 inch. Whether you choose to drill the passage or leave it as is, the 5/8-inch pick-up tube should used in all big-block builds.

Buick engines tend to lose oil pressure to the lifters over time. The problem is the way Buick engines feed the lifters. The oil must travel across the front cam journal before it feeds to the driver-side lifters. After the engine has some miles on it (typically after 10,000 miles), the cam bearing begins to fill the oiling hole with bearing material, cutting off the oil supply to the driver-side lifters. Part of the fix for this is to open the main feed line from the pump to passenger side lifter galley. By using a 12-inch-long 7/16-inch drill bit, the passage will be opened up enough to add significant flow to the lifter galley and more pressure to the cam bearing. This passage runs from the oil-pressure sending unit to just shy of the front cam bearing, a depth of 4 inches. Using the 7/16-inch bit, the threads for the sending unit will remain untouched (if you are careful). You can open this to 1/2 inch, but that will require retapping the oil-pressure sending-unit hole to 3/8-inch pipe thread from the factory 1/4-inch thread.

For the 3.8-liter turbo engines, there are a couple of extra steps that should be taken, because the oil pump not only feeds the engine but the turbo, as well. In high-performance street and street/strip engines, deburring and smoothing out the oil-pump walls provides a serious increase in oil flow. Extreme-performance engines, such as full-race applications, should have an external oil line running from the turbo oil supply fitting to the passenger-side lifter oil galley in the rear of the block. This external line will increase volume and pressure to the rear mains and rod bearings because oil is being supplied from both the front and the rear ends of the oil galley, rather than just from the front. To accomplish this, the turbo-feed fitting at the block (front, passenger side) is drilled to 9/16 inch to just before the cam bearing as in the 350 and big-block engines. Then, using a 19/32-inch standard drill bit, the passage is drilled 1 inch deep. The threads must be retapped to 3/8-inch pipe thread to accommodate the new fitting and 3/8-inch external line.

Crankshaft Mods

There are two camps when it comes to increasing the oiling capability of the crankshaft. One side advocates cross-drilling the crank, while the other group argues that cross-drilling weakens the crank, and therefore the best bet is to use fully grooved main bearings. Here are the advantages and drawbacks for both:

Cross-drilling the crankshaft supplies more oil to the crank, and therefore the rods. By adding a second oil feed hole, oil is supplied to the crank during its entire rotation. Otherwise, with a half-groove main bearing, oil is supplied to the rod bearings only when the oil feed passage aligns with the oil groove, which is about half the rotation of the crankshaft. This leaves the rods waiting for fresh oil for the second half of the crank rotation. Under high RPM, extreme heat is generated on the surface of the rod journal and rod bearing, requiring an abundant supply of oil to maintain reasonable temperatures. This is reason for continuous oil feed. Therefore, cross-drilling provides this constant supply of oil as one feed hole rotates past the oil feed groove, and the other feed hole enters into the groove.

In the early 1970s Buick released a service bulletin instructing dealers to cross-drill the crankshaft for heavy-duty applications. This solution worked well for Buick and quite a few manufacturers. There are, however, a few drawbacks. With increasing RPM, centrifugal force pushed oil away from the center of the crankshaft. The oil pump must then overcome this force with higher pressure to continue to feed adequate oil volume to the rod bearings. The original oil feed hole is drilled at an angle, so the oil passes through the center of the main journal. The centrifugal force acting on that passage is not as high as the cross-drilled passage, so the oil pressure does not have to be as high. Cross-drilling a crank can actually force oil out of the hole and reduce oil flow to the rods. Some builders feel cross-drilling a nodular iron crankshaft will weaken the crank and lead to failure.

Engine builders on the other side of the fence recommend using fully grooved main bearings. These bearings feature 360-degree grooves, which accomplish the same thing as cross-drilling without the drawbacks of weakening the crankshaft and centrifugal force pushing the oil out. However, the proponents of cross-drilling believe that grooved bearings reduce the bearing surface too much, resulting in a shorter life. Since the big Buick crankshafts have such large main journals, this is a good point. If you are building a mild-performance engine and it won't rev beyond 5,500 rpm, then the stock bearings and crank will be sufficient. If you are building anything more potent, then either method will increase oiling over stock. The simplest and most inexpensive method is to use fully-grooved bearings. As a side note, the 401- and 425-ci Nailhead engines came with grooved crankshafts, which do the same thing as grooved bearings.

TA Performance is one of several Buick specialists that offer fully grooved main bearings for the small- and big-block Buicks. Yet there are some other options. Federal-Mogul offers 3/4-grooved main bearings, leaving a little more bearing surface and saving the builder from cross-drilling the crank. The other option is to buy a standard set of main bearings and have them grooved at the machine shop. The number-5 main journal bearing should *not* be grooved, as this could lead to a leak at the back of the block.

Use high-quality bearings in the 3.8-liter turbo engines because a 6-cylinder engine puts more load on its main bearings. Federal-Mogul manufactures an aluminum alloy main bearing set for the turbo engine. These bearings offer a more accurate finish because they are bored to size, not stamped like other brands. The Federal-Mogul units have a smaller oiling hole than the feed holes in the block, so the bearings need to be drilled out to 5/16 inch in all 3.8-liter builds to increase oil volume. Once the bearings are drilled, they should be cleaned and deburred with a deburring tool and hit with an ultra-fine Scotch-Brite pad and motor oil. These bearings are of the 3/4-groove variety, which can be machined to fully grooved by your machine shop if you choose to have it done.

While on the subject of crankshafts, there is another inexpensive

The cheaper alternative is running a set of 3/4-inch groove bearings. This option slightly reduces the bearing surface but not enough to be an issue with a properly modified oiling system.

modification that adds extra insurance. Chamfering the oiling holes in the crankshaft allows the oil to flow inside the crank with less restriction and increase the area for the oil to move into the crank. Also, it is always a good idea to have the crank degreed and indexed. Most of the time, the stock crank is not accurately indexed, and the machine shop will perform this job to ensure the rod journals are 90 degrees apart. Indexing the crank takes the stroke and swing degrees and grinds the crank to match. This ensures proper crank timing, which is important for proper camshaft timing.

Close Bearing Tolerances

One of the most important steps in building any Buick engine is measuring bearing tolerances. Be careful when taking your Buick engine to a builder that specializes in Chevy engines. Chevy engines are built to run loose, running bearing tolerances .0035-inch and more. This is perfectly acceptable for a Chevy. If you run a Buick engine that loose, it will likely blow up before you can even shut the hood. Most Buick builders recommend a tolerance of .0020 inch for the number-1, -2, -3, and -4 main bearings for high-performance street or street/strip applications. For serious drag cars, a tolerance of 0.0025 inch is sufficient. For the number-5 rear main bearing, a 0.002 inch to 0.0025 inch tolerance is recommended for all engines. For the connecting rods, the same 0.002 inch to 0.0025 inch tolerances are recommended. The reason for the tight tolerances is due to fact that the Buick's large 3.25-inch main bearing journal diameter requires more pressure to supply oil to the rod bearings.

Checking the crank for clearances can be done with a micrometer or plastigauge. Most top-end builders only use precision tools, such as micrometers and calipers, but these tools can be expensive.

If you run the bearings loose, the oil will be allowed to squeeze out of the bearings, limiting supply to the rods. The stock specs on a 455 are 0.007 0.0011 inch, which is a little too tight for a high-performance Buick.

It is highly recommended that all 350 and big-block Buick cranks be turned down 0.010 inch. The reasoning being: most of these engines will not have maintained the factory tolerances and will have flat spots and be seriously out of specification. You can build a Buick without turning the crank this much, but to achieve the tight tolerances, it is a good idea to start with a smooth, concentric journal that will yield the best fit in the block. When checking your tolerances, there are two methods: Plastigauge and micrometers. Using micrometers is the most accurate, and therefore it is the method of choice. They are however, fairly expensive and can be confusing for the novice builder to use. Plastigauge is fairly simple to use and typically yields fairly accurate results. If you are building a mild street engine, plasti-

We checked the main bearing clearances with a micrometer and dial bore gauge, and verified the measurements with plastigauge. Both readings were accurate. If you have the means, use the precision tools because they will always yield accurate results.

gauge will probably get the job done, but for serious performance engines, a micrometer is the best way to ensure proper measurements. If you do not have access to a set of micrometers, most machine shops will measure the tolerances for a nominal charge. You should have this done when the machine work is performed to save some time and money.

As for the 3.8-liter V-6 turbo, only turn the crank the minimum amount, and do not exceed 0.010 inch for any performance application. Be sure to tell your machine shop to cut the crank on the high side (tighter, less cut). The turbo engines need even tighter tolerances than the V-8s. A main bearing clearance should be 0.0015 to 0.002 inch (closer to the 0.0015-inch side is better), while the rod bearing clearance should run 0.0018 to 0.0025 inch. When using the 3/4-grooved main bearings, clearances run slightly larger but do not exceed the top end of the range.

CHAPTER 3

Oil Pumps

There is one thing that cannot be said enough about high-volume oil pumps in a Buick engine: be very careful if you choose to run one. High-volume pump kits can damage your cam bearings if you use the wrong relief spring. Do not use the 60-lb spring (typically the red spring), because it is wound too tight. The coils tend to stick and bind before the relief valve can fully open, causing your pump to build oil pressures well over 100 psi. This high-pressure oil will cause your cam to float in the bearings, knocking on and destroying the bearings.

Most builders recommend a rebuilt oil pump with a minimum of 60 lbs. of pressure. An adjustable oil pressure regulator can supply this amount of pressure. If your tolerances are a little loose or if the engine will be spinning over 6,000 rpm, a high-volume pump is a good idea, but a stock pump will do the job. That said, the 350 does not have the same issues with high-volume oil pumps. In fact, the 350 high-volume pump gear is the same size as the stock 455 pump gear. For our 350 build, we chose to run the stock pump with a booster plate in

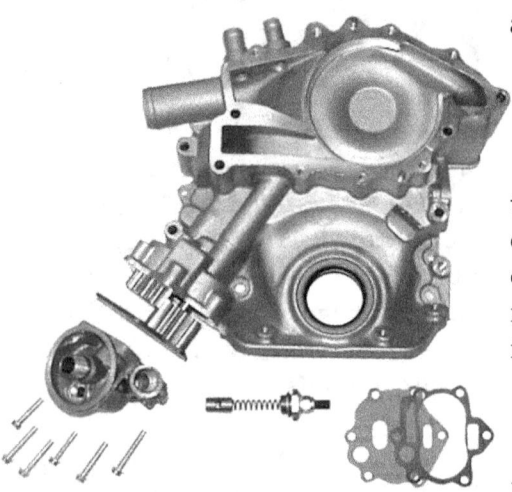

This TA Performance oil pump kit makes rebuilding the oil pump much simpler.

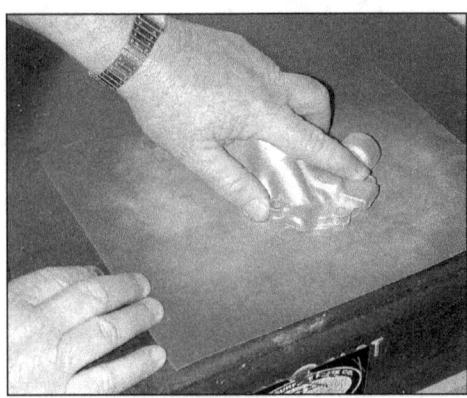

The pump build begins by refinishing the oil filter cover with a surfacing job. Lightly sand the cover with a piece of 220-grit sandpaper to even up the surface.

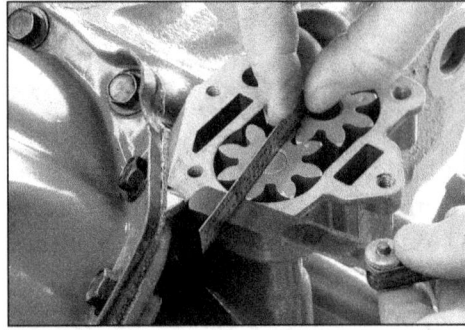

Check the end clearance once the pump gears are in place. There should be no more than 0.002-to 0.003-inch clearance. If the clearance is more than that, install high-volume pump gears.

Here the stock oil pump gears are compared to the high-volume pump gears. The 350 high-volume pump gear is the same size as the 455 stock gear (shown to the left). While most builders shy away from the high-volume pumps in big-block engines, the 350 readily accepts the high-volume pump with no issues. The gears on the right are stock 350 gears.

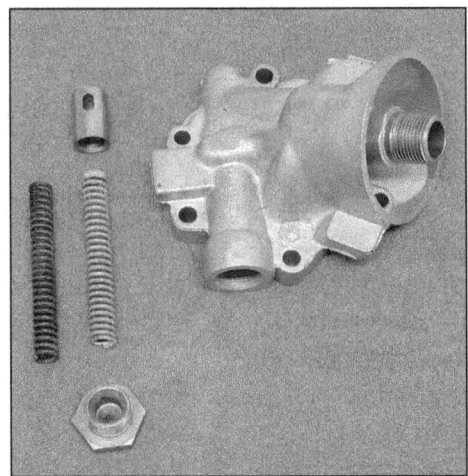

The red spring on the left is the 60-psi high-volume spring. If you use this spring in a street-driven engine with the correct tolerances, the cam bearings will be destroyed from too much pressure. This spring can develop over 100 psi, which is just too much.

The inner clearance must be checked, too. The gears require a clearance of 0.004 to 0.005 inch. If the clearance is 0.007 inch or more, then the timing cover is beyond specification and needs to be replaced.

OILING SYSTEM UPGRADES

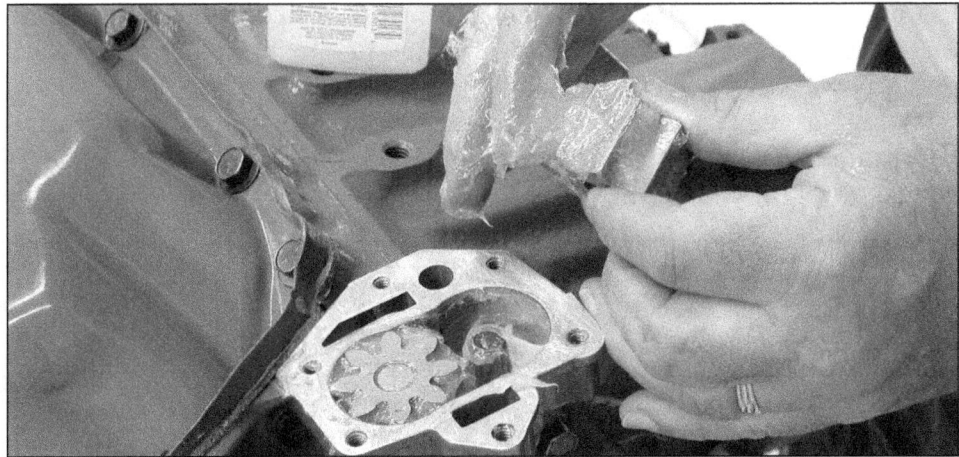

With everything in check, the pump needs to be packed with either Vaseline or pre-lube.

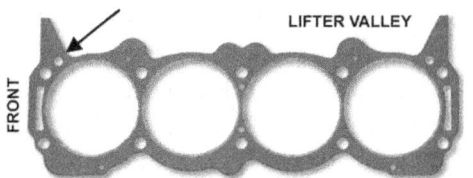

If you are swapping a set of 400 or 430 heads to a 455 or converting a 400 or 430 block to pushrod-style rocker arm oiling, the oiling hole shown needs to be blocked. If you are running an early block, this can be accomplished with a 3/8-inch x 16 set screw. If you are running a 455, block the driver side only; block both sides for a 400 or 430 block.

If the pump is not packed with lube, it will never prime, leaving the engine completely without oil for the initial start up.

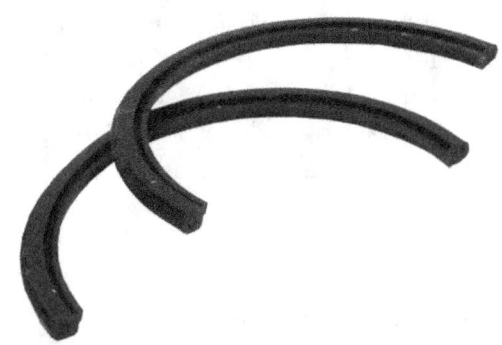

The neoprene rear main seal is an important upgrade to the block oiling system. The stock-style rope seals simply do not work as well.

The oil filter housing was reinstalled and tightened down. An externally adjustable oil pressure regulator can be installed at the large hex-head bolt on the front of the filter housing.

Do not leave out the factory windage tray. This tray prevents the crank from whipping the oil into a foam, and it keeps the oil from splashing on the crank and robbing power.

HOW TO BUILD MAX-PERFORMANCE BUICK ENGINES

the timing cover (this will be discussed in the next chapter). When assembling the oil pump, the end clearances should be kept to 0.002 to 0.003 inch. Once the oil pump is assembled, it should be packed with Vaseline or assembly lube. If this step is skipped, the pump will never prime.

When using a high-volume oil pump in a 455, Jim Burek, Performance Automotive Enterprises, recommends breaking in a new engine using the stock oil–pump pressure relief spring. This 40-psi spring should be good for 60–70 psi (with a high-volume pump) at the 2,000–3,000 rpm break-in speed you will

Euro Muscle – A Unique 1972 GSX

Dutchman Robert Noeken has a particular fancy for American classics. Purchased by Noeken in 2004, this 1972 GSX clone currently resides in the Netherlands. Jim Burek, of Performance Automotive Engines, El Paso, Texas, built the engine. It is a 455 stroked to 464, backed by an SP400 transmission. Noeken enjoys drag racing the car at Explosion race events, the car has been featured in a Dutch car magazine, and it has appeared in a Dutch TV show. This street-driven Buick runs as good as it looks. Time slips show 11.74 best quarter-mile ET. This

The 455 was stroked to 464 ci and built by Jim Burek of Performance Automotive Engines. The engine features ported Stage 1 heads, 11.5:1 pistons, and a Poston intake.

Robert Noeken's 1972 GSX clone has a storied history. The car was shuffled between various owners while Robert was trying to get his hands on it. He finally managed to purchase the car and had it shipped to the Netherlands, where it has been shown, cruised, and drag raced. The GSX even landed a part as the "meanest street racer" on a Dutch TV show.

OILING SYSTEM UPGRADES

run the engine. This allows the engine to be safely lubricated and not go overboard on the oil pressure. One hundred psi would put too much strain on the fresh bearings and can destroy the distributor gear, cam gear, and front cam bearing. If you see the oil pressure falling off, you can always swap in a bigger spring. A 30–40 psi oil pressure level is plenty at the low break-in speeds. If you don't have a stock spring and are planning on running the big pressure spring (typically red), you can trim down the lower-pressure spring by 1-1/2 coils, which will yield excellent pressure when the engine is warm. Also, if

GSX has won numerous Dutch OSL (Operation Street Legal) street racing trophies. The GSX trim package includes hood tach, front/rear spoilers, and correct decals. By the end of the 2005 season, the GSX won 4th place in the OSL championships and an 11th place in the Explosion championship.

Equipment Package:

- Jim Burek-built 464-ci V-8
- Stage-1 ported heads,
- Ross true 11.5:1 coated pistons and bearings
- Block O-ringed
- Deep sump oil pan
- MSD ignition
- S-divider lightweight aluminum intake
- Lunati cam; duration 251/273 at 0.050 inch
- Holley 850 DP carburetor
- Aluminum two-core radiator
- High-torque starter
- 2-inch Jet-Hot coated T/A headers; 3-inch full aluminized exhaust
- 3:73 12-bolt strong rear-end with C-clip eliminators
- Strange yoke
- 33-spline Moser axels
- LPW axel tube brace and LPW girdle
- Jim Burek-built T400 Switch-Pitch transmission and converter
- B&M shifter
- 6-point roll cage
- Factory bucket seats, console, and tilt column
- Front disc brakes
- Fiberglass hood
- Front and rear Koni drag shocks

The street-driven GSX runs 11.74 seconds in the quarter-mile, and this mighty Buick beats tuners and Euro-sport cars on a regular basis.

CHAPTER 3

you find that you need the big spring to make enough oil pressure, you have a serious problem. Too much bearing clearance or a heavily worn timing cover is the likely culprit, and the engine needs to be torn down. The same approach effectively remedies low pressure problems in the 350 and V-6 turbo engines. The oil-pump pressure relief springs are shorter, but use the same principles.

Nailhead engines used several oil pumps. The early 264 and 322 had beveled gears and different pickups. Top Nailhead builder Russell Martin recommends using the 1955–1956 pump in the 264 and 322. "I don't think the beveled gears in the early oil pumps were better, just more expensive to manufacture," Russell tells us. The 1957–1958 364 used an oil pump with a vacuum pump on it for wipers; a 1959–1961 oil pump eliminates the extraneous function. The 1962–1966 engines use one pump but have two different pickups, one for center sump and one for rear sump pans.

Rear Oil Pressure Gauge Installation

It is common for a Buick to show 4 to 5 less psi at the rear of the block than at the front. The trouble is, the stock oil-sending unit is located at the front of the block. There is a quick and easy way to add a rear pressure sensor so you can monitor the oil pressure at the rear of the block, or run two gauges and monitor both.

There are two ways of performing this task; one is a little more involved than the other. I prefer the following easier version. There are two pipe plugs at the back of the block, just above the freeze plug behind the cam. Remove the passenger-side plug. Install a 90-degree elbow that has 1/4-inch pipe threads on one side and compression fitting on the other. Be sure to wrap the threads with Teflon tape or other thread sealant. While you could use a copper capillary tube, the best feed line is a 1/4-inch braided line. This ensures the line will flex with the engine and not kink or break over time. Attach this line to the fitting. Drill a small hole in the rear of the engine, either up through the top, at the flat pad behind the intake, or to the driver's side. Run the line through the hole and secure the line with a little silicone sealant to hold it in place. If done correctly, there will be plenty of clearance for the flywheel/flexplate. If you choose to run dual gauges, you will be able to monitor the pressure difference. If there is a substantial difference (10 psi or more) you can shut it down before any serious damage occurs.

Oil Pans

The 455's stock oil pan is suitable for any street-driven engine, provided it does not rev past 5,500 rpm. When the engine starts spinning faster than 5,500 rpm, the oil pump often drains the pan, resulting in oil starvation. Some builders suggest that any Buick-powered car running 13s or less in the quarter-mile

A really trick mod is to add a rear oil pressure gauge to the engine. By removing one of the rear freeze plugs (shown here), the oil pressure sending unit can be added with 90-degree elbow.

Next, drill out the rear webbing (marked by the pointer) on the block to pass the line through. You should use a rubber or plastic grommet on this hole to protect the capillary tube or wire coming from the sending unit.

OILING SYSTEM UPGRADES

needs a 7-quart oil pan. Depending on your engine and how you plan on using it, there are a couple of choices. TA Performance and Poston Enterprises offer several oil pans that accommodate the 7- and 8-quart capacity and add some extra features (we will discuss these in the race engine section). Stef's Fabrication Specialties offers a 6-quart aluminum oil pan designed to fit the Buick A-body (Skylark/GS) and maintain proper oil control. TA Performance also sells a larger capacity deep sump sheet metal oil pan for the big blocks.

Welding the two pans together to create a larger pan is the last option. This is a good choice if you need the extra capacity for an engine up to 600 hp but don't need the girdled aftermarket oil pans that can cost well over $500. Just be sure you use a good welder who is capable of stitching together thin sheet metal without burning it. This is also the only option for a 350; even Buick specialists do not make a bigger pan for the 350.

Motor Oil Considerations

Standard motor oils are not efficient enough to adequately cool and lubricate a high-performance engine, especially a Buick. That's not to say that Buicks require ultra-expensive oil, but with their inherent oiling issues, truly high-performance oils are the best way to go.

MotorHead Classic heavy-duty oil is one of the best oils for a Buick. It has high concentrations of the anti-wear chemicals needed in older engines. Choosing the right viscosity is also very important. The thinner 5W-30 oils used in late-model engines will not have sufficient viscosity to shield your older, high-compression, larger-tolerance engine. Buick engines need heavier weight oil, such as 20W-40 or 20W-50, with the colder climates using 10W-40, for adequate lubrication. In addition, if you are running a mechanical non-roller cam, you will need oil with significantly better anti-wear characteristics to keep your engine properly lubricated. Mechanical camshaft engines require racing oil with high levels of anti-wear additives, such as phosphorous and zinc. Some builders even suggest using four-stroke 20W-50 motorcycle oil. These oils have the correct chemistry and are safe for use in high-performance applications. Here is a trick: If you smell the oil and it smells a little like gear oil, then it probably has enough anti-wear chemistry and stabilizers to be sufficient to run in your big Buick.

For the blow-dried engines (we're talking turbos here), the same types of oils are recommended. As an added bonus, you might try a little extra oil additive, like Lucas or Pro Blend. These add a little more stabilization that is needed for the high heat transferred to the oil by the turbo.

The 3.8-liter V-6 turbo engines use oil coolers to help remove the extra heat induced in the oil from cooling the turbo. Keeping the stock oil cooler clean and operating at its maximum capacity is paramount to keeping these high-powered engines cool. Better yet, upgrading the factory oil cooler to a high-performance four-core unit is a wise choice. The excessive heat generated in these engines has to go somewhere, and you certainly do not want it in the crankcase.

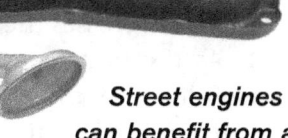

Street engines can benefit from a 7-quart oil pan. This stock steel pan has been modified to accept an extra quart of oil. The pick-up tube is constantly immersed in oil, even under heavy acceleration and cornering.

Choosing the right oil is a very important decision. This Royal Purple oil is specially formulated for high-performance and race engines. It has the right levels of zinc and other high-wear additives that are crucial to high-performance engines.

HOW TO BUILD MAX-PERFORMANCE BUICK ENGINES 41

CHAPTER 4

Cams and Timing Covers

With the bottom end and oil pump issues resolved, it's time to address the top of the block. The 1968 and later engines have a lot of issues in the top end of the engine, particularly in the cam bearing area. The problem arises from the fact that the driver-side lifter galley gets oil only from what crosses the front cam bearing. As the front bearing wears, it starts filling up the oiling holes that feed the lifters. This eventually plugs the entire feed hole, which then stops sending oil to the driver-side lifters. This is very common and typically starts happening at around 15,000 to 20,000 miles. This is also a big problem when running high-lift camshafts; the extra force exerted on the cam bearings tends to melt the babbitt materials. The solutions to alleviate this problem are varied and involve both proper parts and block modifications.

Cam Bearing Options

In the past, using bronze cam bearings was the preferred choice, as the bronze materials held up without overheating and melting. This solution worked great until most manufacturers stopped making bronze bearings. Finding these types of bearings can prove difficult.

One of the other options is to relocate the oiling hole. There are several ways to do this. The first involves modifying the front cam journal. By adding a groove into the block, the oil feed hole would be moved to the four o'clock position from the eight o'clock position. Using a die grinder and a small cutting wheel, the groove should be made 1/8-inch wide to as deep as 1/8 inch. This groove does not have to cover the entire journal, although it can. You should run the groove from

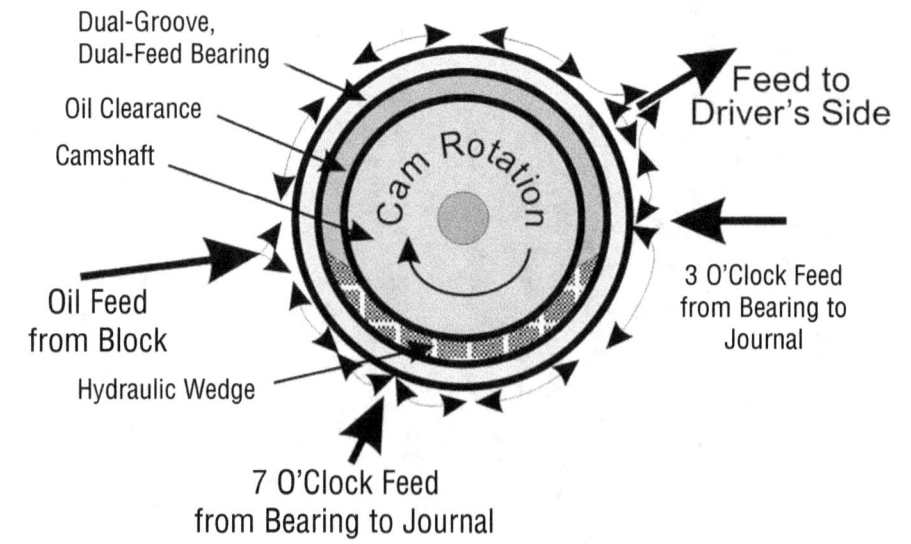

This illustration represents the camshaft oiling properties. As you can see, the driver side lifters and rockers are only fed through this front main cam bearing.

CAMS AND TIMING COVERS

The stock cam bearings (on the right) are smooth, so the camshaft transfers all the oil itself — not a good thing. The grooved bearing (on the left) allows oil to move around the outside of the bearing, reaching the driver-side oiling hole much faster, which increases the volume considerably. This eliminates the possibility of oil starvation on the driver-side lifters as the cam bearing wears.

The front cam bearing was installed at the three o'clock position, which helps the oil flow easier.

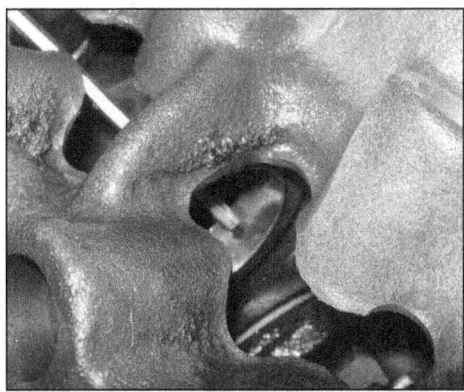

The number-2, -3, -4, -5, and -7 cam bearings were installed at four o'clock on this 350. The four o'clock position provides better oiling.

This TA Performance double-grooved cam bearing adds a second groove. This not only further increases oiling, but it reduces the strain on the bearing by supporting the center section.

the oil feed hole to about the one o'clock position. If the groove follows the entire journal circumference, then you can place the oiling holes from eight o'clock to three o'clock. This will minimize any bearing material clogging up the oiling holes and supply more oil flow to the driver-side lifters.

Another option for increasing the driver-side lifters is to bypass the cam bearing oiling altogether. By using a lifter galley to bypass the oil line (available from Poston Buick), both of the lifter galleys are fed through the back of the block. This option does not pose any threat to the oil pressure at the back of the block (you can monitor it yourself if you install the previously mentioned secondary rear oil pressure gauge). This part costs only $15 and adds peace of mind.

Using grooved cam bearings is the last option. These specialized bearings available from TA Performance and Poston Buick are designed to help increase oiling to the driver-side lifters and the rest of the cam journals. These bearings should be used on any high-revving or high-lift-camshaft engine. They cost a few dollars more than non-grooved bearings, but are ideal for any performance engine. We recommend two or three options listed here for serious, high-output engines. If you do not groove the block, run grooved bearings and the oil bypass line. You can groove the block, and that will fix the problem, but there will definitely be more cleanup involved. For our 350 build, we used the grooved cam bearings, since the cam lift was under 0.550, and we used the high-volume oil pump.

With the front cam bearing taken care of, the rest of the cam bearings should be installed. There is some debate about the best oiling hole location when using grooved bearings. Performance Automotive Engines recommends installing the bearings at the four o'clock position. This positioning increases oil flow due to the optimum oil hole placement. Placing the oil feed holes at four o'clock also increases cooling and the bearing's ability to handle loads — particularly important for high-lift cam profiles. TA Performance, however, recommends using the three and seven o'clock positions for its dual-grooved cam bearings. TA claims that these bearings, with their pair of grooves around the backside, provide more load-bearing capacity than a single-groove bearing and improve oil control. Since the Buick engines oil the cam and lifters before

CHAPTER 4

oiling the crank and rods, oil control here is important.

All of the above steps are recommended for 350, big-block, and V-6 turbo builds.

Oiling System Upgrades

Since the 1968 and later Buick blocks have an external oil pump, the oil is fed from the pump through a passage in the timing chain cover into the block. At this spot, the oil must make a sharp 90-degree turn. Any time you can radius a turn, the flow will increase. This is the area where all of the fresh oil enters the engine, and this opening needs to be as free and clear as possible for maximum flow and lubrication. Using a ball-shaped fine-tooth carbide tip and a die-grinder, radius the sharp turn on the backside of the feed hole. Add as much radius as you can, keeping it smooth. A shallower, smooth radius is better than a large, rough radius.

Timing Cover Options

The timing cover on a Buick engine is unique. Not only does this cast-aluminum part cover the timing chain and seal the crankshaft, it also mounts the water pump, the distributor, the oil pump, and oil filter housing. If there is a single critically important piece of a Buick engine, this is it. There are several modifications to be made to the timing cover that should be made to every single 1968 and later Buick engine.

The timing cover oil passage should be opened up on every build. The main oil feed, which delivers pressurized oil from the oil pump, is on the small side and can certainly be enlarged. This passage should be opened up to 1/2 inch on the 350 and V-6 turbo, while the big blocks should be drilled to 9/16 inch. Be sure you enlarge the corresponding oil feed hole in the oil pump spacer plate, booster plate, and gaskets.

While you could take the time to modify your existing timing cover,

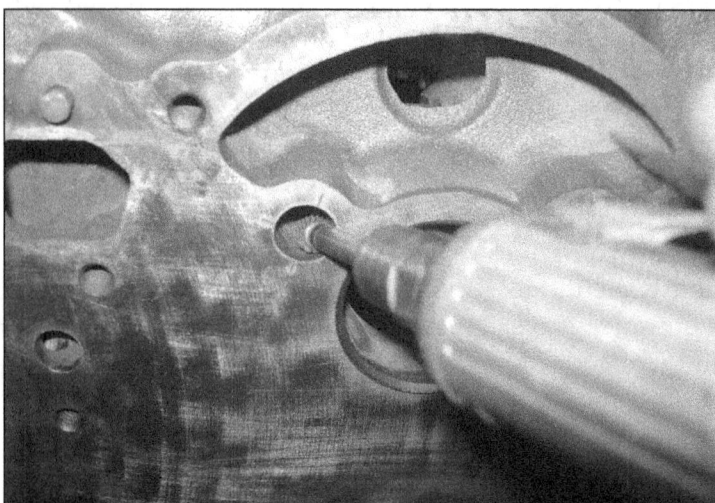

Any time you can radius a 90-degree turn, you will increase flow and remove restriction. This oiling hole is the main oil feed to the passenger side lifter galley. Using a ball-end carbide, the turn is smoothed and radiused.

The finished job should look like this. Take care and work as much as you can.

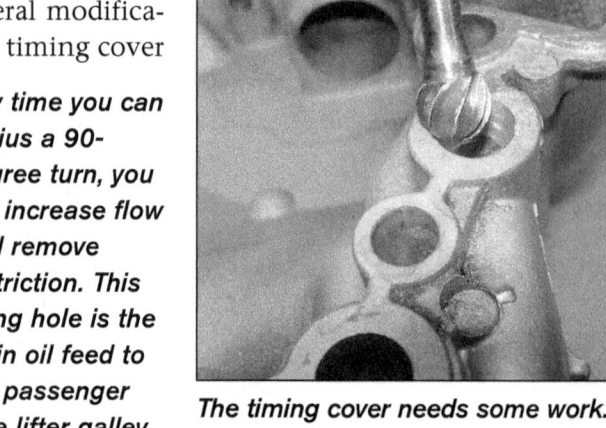

The timing cover needs some work. A ball-end carbide bit was used to radius the oil feed passage to the block.

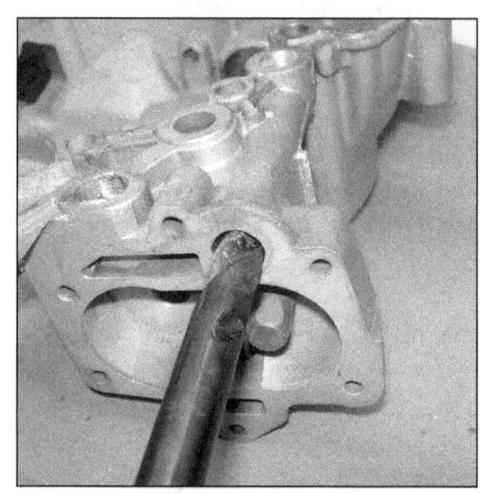

The oil feed from the pump to the block needs to be opened up to 1/2 inch.

CAMS AND TIMING COVERS

Buying a completely new timing cover is one option. This unit has all of the previous mods cast right in and is ready to go, complete with an adjustable oil pressure regulator.

Installing the timing cover and water pump requires a little bit of anti-seize compound on the bolt threads, so the bolts do not rust as they pass though the water jackets.

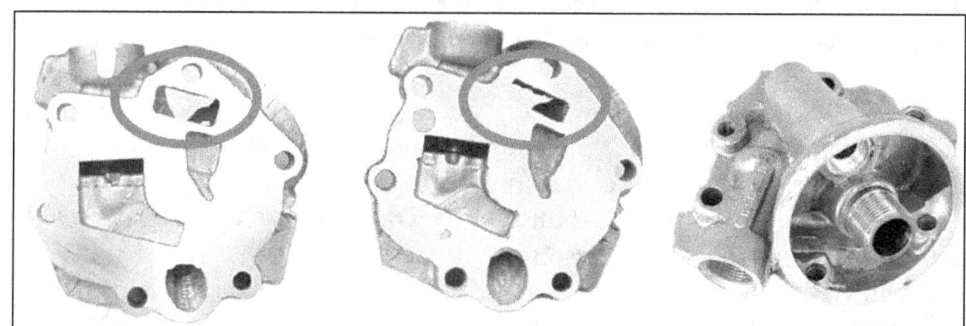

This oil filter/pump cover for the 455 features a modified oil feed (on the left) for increased flow.

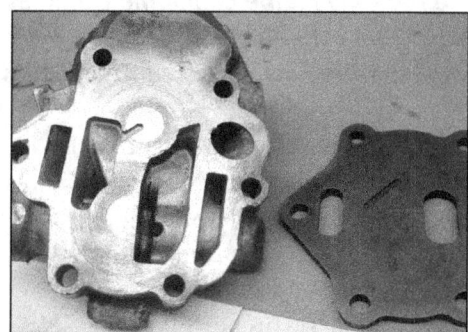

The stock oil filter cover has some scoring, but this is not bad. The oil pump booster plate (on the right) will be used to help increase flow and gives the new oil pump gears a new surface to ride on.

there is another option. TA Performance and Poston Buick both sell brand-new timing covers; TA Performance even offers a high-performance version with all of the above modifications built in to the new casting. This allows the builder to simply bolt on the timing cover right out of the box. It certainly saves time, but they do cost a little extra.

Oil Pump Booster Plate

The oil filter housing installs over the oil pump gears, completing the oil pump assembly. The problem with this design is that the oil pump gears ride against inside of the oil filter housing, which leads to scoring and, eventually, a lot of oil bypassing the gears and reducing oil pressure. These housings are now available new from TA Performance for the 350, big-block, and V-6 turbo engines. There is also a less-costly option, which has other benefits, as well. Installing an oil pump booster plate gives the oil pump gears a new surface to run on, thereby fixing the original oil filter housing. In addition to repairing the scored housing, the booster plate also increases oil flow with its modified oil passages. This booster plate is a must for any engine that is not getting a high-volume oil pump; it will work great with a high-volume oil pump, as well.

Cam Thrust Control

The cam in a 1968 and later block has the tendency to walk forward. This cam walk can cause erratic timing and prematurely wear out the distributor gear. While this fix is not an absolute necessity, it helps on engines with excessive camshaft endplay. Jim Burek, Performance Automotive Engines, came up with a

CHAPTER 4

After the block mods are complete and the machine work is done, the cam and the timing chain should be installed. There is very little room inside the Buick 350. If you do not tie the cam to the crank with the timing chain, the rods will hit the cam if the crank is rotated. If you install the cam after the rods, you will have to rotate the engine as you install the cam. Doing it this way is easier.

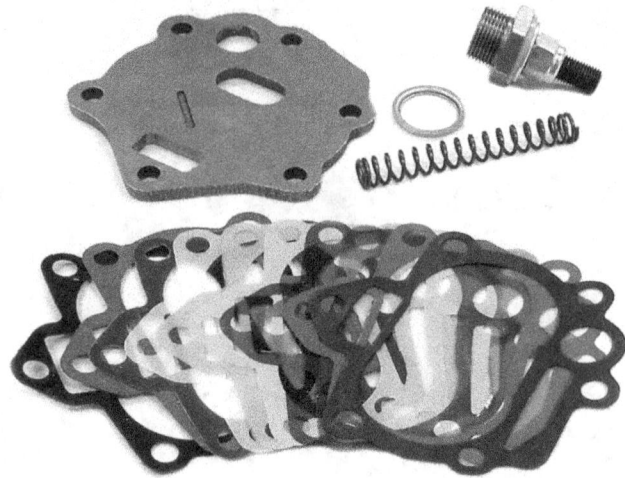

This TA Performance shim kit includes these shims – amber (0.001 inch), purple (0.0015 inch), red (0.002 inch), green (0.003 inch), blue (0.005 inch), transmatte (0.0075 inch), brown (0.010 inch), black (0.005 inch), and dark gray (0.008 inch). First install the black or dark gray gasket and add Mylar shims as needed to obtain proper end clearance of 0.002- to 0.003-inch.

custom fix to eliminate cam walk on these engines. The fix is fairly simple, but takes a little work.

To create a cam bumper, you will need a brass 1/4-inch coarse thread bolt, a 1/4-20 thread tap and a 7/16-inch drill bit. Locate the small raised pad on the timing cover just below the distributor shaft (positioned directly above the notched ledge in the top half of the cover). Using the 7/16-inch bit, drill the center of the pad through the cover. Clean off any chaff from the drilling and tap the hole with the 1/4-inch-20 tap. Run the tap through the hole several times to make sure it is good and clean. Install the bolt in the hole, then mark the end where it comes out of the cover. Remove the bolt and trim it back so it is recessed slightly in the hole when installed. Using a die grinder or hacksaw, cut a slot in the threaded end of the bolt, this will allow the bumper to be adjusted from outside the cover. Clean up the head of the bolt so that it is smooth and burr-free. The head of the bolt will run against the cam gear, so it is important to use a clean bolt. (This is also the reasoning behind using brass, as brass is softer and will wear down before the cam gear does.) Install the timing cover.

At this point, you need to check the clearance. The recommended clearance for this bumper is 0.005 to 0.010 inch. You may need to grind the head or the pad to get this clearance, depending on your bolt and your engine. Once the correct clearance has been obtained, remove the cover and remove the bolt. Mix up some JB Weld or other epoxy and place some under the head of the bolt. Reinstall the bolt and adjust the bumper to the correct position. Put a little epoxy in the front side of the hole, where it is adjusted. This ensures a tight seal and no leaks. Jim Burek also recommends adding a little Permatex Cold Weld compound to make doubly sure it is watertight. In the event the bumper needs to be removed, heating the bolt will soften the epoxy, allowing bolt removal.

Distributor Gear Oiling

For the big blocks, the cam gear that drives the distributor is not replaceable. As such, the distributor/cam gears could use a little lubrication. By adding a distributor oiling kit (available from Poston Buick), the gears will enjoy an increased lifespan. As mentioned earlier, the cam has a tendency to walk forward, which can ruin the distributor gears. Adding this accessory will help in reducing the heat build up caused by cam walk. Install the kit by drilling and tapping a 1/8-inch pipe-thread hole on the inside of the timing cover. This hole is placed at the top of the oil pump housing. A small fitting is then threaded into the hole and the supplied pre-shaped hole sprays the gears with oil. Oil pressure is not affected with this kit, as the volume of oil used is quite small.

In addition to the distributor gear oiler, adding a bronze distributor gear is also an option. In the event you have excessive cam walk, the distributor gear will take the brunt of the damage and not the cam. These bronze gears have a limited life, and needs to be checked occasionally for wear. A typical bronze distributor gear will last about two years before it needs replacing. It may be a little bit of trouble, but it is certainly better than ruining a cam gear, which would require total cam replacement. The composite gear from BOP Engineering is an alternative to the bronze gear. Made from Carbon Ultra-Poly material, this gear is not only strong enough to last the life of the engine, but also does not shed metal shavings into the oil, like typical bronze gear will.

Front Main Seal

The Buick engines used a rope seal to seal the crank in the timing cover. These old rope seals do the job, but they can be tricky to install.

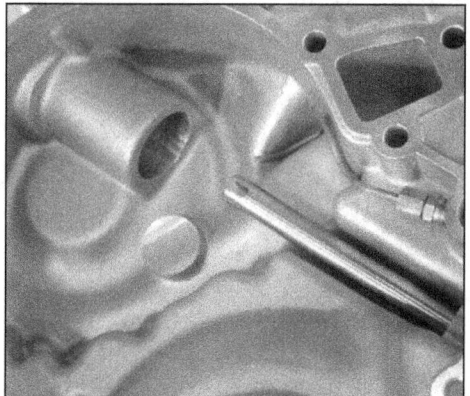

Installing a distributor oiler kit to the timing cover is a simple way to add some life to the distributor gear. Harder cam drive gears eat up these gears. Poston Buick and TA Performance offer this kit.

Modern materials are much better. Installing a neoprene front seal is a good idea, although it is not just simple to drop in.

In order for the timing cover to accept a neoprene seal, the original rope seal location must be modified. The retaining ring that holds the rope seal in the timing cover must be removed. Then the three original stake points that hold in the retainer need to be ground smooth. The new neoprene seal can now be pressed into the opening. Be sure to keep the seal positioned properly as there are several seals available, which may look different, but must be oriented front to rear.

Lifter Bore Reinforcement

While this passage may not directly pertain to oiling, it is a cam-related modification that is important to make to the block when using high-lift and roller camshafts. The original Buick casting is very lightweight; this affects every aspect of the engine, including the lifter galley. Buick only put as much material in

Upgrading the front main seal to a neoprene unit is a must for any performance engine, but it does require a little work. The original rope seal retainer must be removed first.

the block as it had to, which left the lifter bores quite thin. This is a serious problem when a roller cam is used.

Roller cams typically have much quicker ramps on the cam lobes, and this creates much more stress on the lifter. As the lifter starts rising, the top of the lifter pushes out, exerting force on the thin outer ring of the lifter bore. Eventually, the lifter bore cracks and the entire engine can be wiped out. Strengthening this area is not only important for every engine that will run a roller cam, but it is critical to any high-performance Buick engine.

There are two ways of making this modification. TA Performance sells a pre-engineered lifter bore girdle. This girdle bolts to the lifter valley and uses threaded adjustable pins to place preload on the lifter bores. This piece does not affect the oiling system and costs around $400. It is not a permanent piece, and can be installed on another engine if needed. The other option is to use epoxy. This method will affect the oiling system in a positive manner, depending on how it is done. The oil return to the pan can be directed using this method. This is the method of choice used by Mike Phillips of Automotive Machine and Performance. By redirecting the oil flow, you can free up some horsepower by keeping the oil off of the spinning crank.

In order to strengthen the lifter bores, you will need epoxy, a steel plate, and 1/2-inch PVC pipe. Devcon Titanium epoxy is preferred for its superior strength; it's available from Grainger and most hardware stores for about $60 a pound. You will need between 2 and 3 lbs. A steel plate placed in the center between the bores yields a nice flat surface

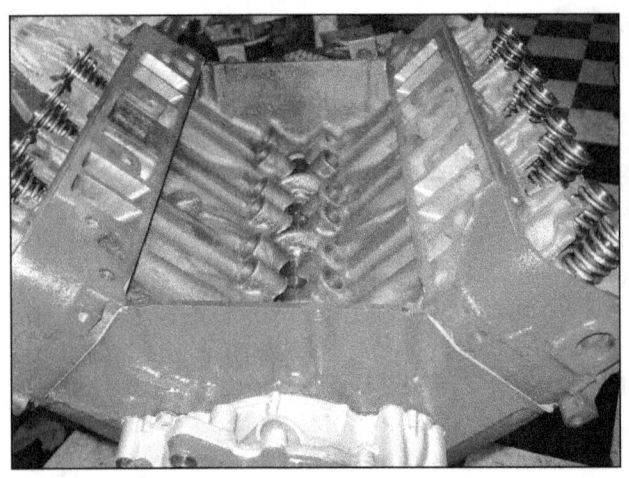

The lifter bores need reinforcement if you plan on running roller lifters or a high-lift camshaft that's over 9.600 inch.

The V-6 turbo does not have any issues with weak lifter bores.

and increases strength. A 1/2-inch PVC pipe will be cut into small sections to act as lifters.

The process is quite simple, but it will take some patience and attention to detail to do correctly. This needs to be done with a clean, completely disassembled block prior to machining. The first step is to size the steel plate. You want the plate to fit snugly at lifter bores. It should be slightly larger so it needs to be gently tapped in place. You do not want it too tight, because that would push in on the bores, creating another problem. The plate should be slightly smaller than the length of the valley; this will aid in oil return. The plate should fit snug to the front of the engine, but have about 1/8-inch gap at the back of the casting. It should be drilled to accommodate crankcase venting. This is typically done with four large holes placed roughly between the pairs of lifter bores along the centerline of the plate. These holes can also be placed to the sides of the camshaft, fore and aft of the lifters themselves. The placement of these holes is not critical, as long as they are away from the corners.

With the bore plates installed in place, the PVC pipe should be cut into sixteen 3-inch-long pieces. Each piece is coated with a little grease and gently tapped into the lifter bores, leaving at least 1 inch exposed for removal. The plugs keep the epoxy out of the lifter bores, which is very important.

Once the plugs are in place, the epoxy is mixed up. Pour the epoxy into the lifter valley, spreading it to cover all of the gaps from the plate to the engine, with the exception of the slot at the back of the block; we want that open for oil return. To make this step easier, let the block sit in the sun for a couple of hours or heat the block with a heat lamp. This will increase the adhesion of the epoxy as the pores of the metal open up, and the extra heat will help the epoxy cure faster. Don't worry about it setting up too fast; properly mixed epoxy should provide 20 minutes of work time. Use a finger and some water (wear a latex or rubber glove for easy clean up) to smooth the epoxy. You want the epoxy to be as smooth as possible, and the water will add some lubrication and make the epoxy smooth out easier while not affecting the epoxy's strength or adhesion. Mix only what you need and can use in about 10–15 minutes. Stop working the epoxy once it starts to harden; you will only create more work once it is dry. Let it cure for 24 hours; if you are in a time crunch or in a cold climate, you can use a heat lamp to speed up the curing process to about 8 hours.

Once cured, you can use Roloc buffing pads to further smooth the epoxy. Use the medium-grit pads to get rid of most of the roughness, but don't go too far or you will weaken the epoxy — you don't want any epoxy to fall into a running engine. The buffing step is not required. If you properly smooth the epoxy before curing, you can skip this step. The idea is to have as smooth a path as possible for the oil to drain; any ridges, pits, and lumps will slow the oil's path back to the pan. In order to route the oil back to the pan, the front of the valley needs to be vented to the timing cover. Two 3/8- to 1/2-inch holes need to be drilled into the front of the casting. If you angle the drill downward slightly, beveling the steel plate, the oil will flow a little easier to the pan through the timing cover. You can also add a bevel to the small slot at the back of the plate to aid in oil flow. With this modification, the block will be much stouter and will be capable of running high-lift and roller camshaft profiles.

One-of-a-Kind 1922 Buick Roadster

Russell Martin, owner of nailheadbuick.com, built this 1922 Buick Roadster in his shop using a 1922 Buick Roadster body and grille shell for the base structure. This one-of-a-kind car was created from a predominant number of Buick parts from many different eras. A 1965 401, with 0.060-inch overbore, powers a 1965 Buick ST400 transmission with shift kit. It also has a switch pitch converter from a 1964–1967 ST300 transmission. Russell did all the fabrication work and built the engine, and his brother Brian did the body and paint work. The windshield was chopped 10 inches, and the body was shortened 10 inches at the door jams. Metal replaced all the wood in the body, and a custom-made steel floor, lower firewall, and dash were installed. The steering system features a Vega steering box, 1931 Buick locking steering column, and a cut down 1937 Buick steering wheel. Body pieces include 1947–1953 Buick taillights and vintage Dietz headlamps. A set of 1947 Roadmaster front brakes and 1964 Riviera aluminum drum stop the car. Suspension and drivetrain equipment include a 6-inch dropped axle, special custom front leaf springs, a triangular four-bar with coil springs in rear, and a 1972 GS posi-traction rear end narrowed 3 inches.

Engine Package:

- 1965 401-ci V-8, bored 0.060 inches over, which equals 413 ci
- Solid lifter cam pushing Pontiac lifters
- 1959 Pontiac narrowed, lightened, and shot-peened connecting rods
- BME custom 10:1 pistons; the piston pins were moved higher on the piston to allow for the longer Pontiac rods
- Ported heads with 1.5-inch exhaust; 1.94-inch intake Chevy valves and springs
- Adjustable push rods
- 1958 iron 1.5 rockers
- B262 intake with two 600 cfm Carter carbs
- Spalding flame thrower dual-coil, dual-point ignition

The pistons were made by BME and are 10:1; the wrist pins were placed higher on the piston to allow for the longer Pontiac rods. The rods were narrowed, lightened, and shot-peened. The cylinder bottoms were cleared for rod bolts, and Russell even had to make a 1/4-inch pan spacer that dropped the pan lower for clearance so the bulkier Pontiac rods and rod bolts could be used. The cam was custom-ground at Comp Cams and the lobe profiles were from a jet boat cam for a big-block Chevy.

Nailhead expert Russell Martin built this elegant 1922 Buick roadster. The 1922 Buick body and grille shell were constructed from real steel to make it a true Buick. Unlike so many other hot rods, this roadster was built from as many Buick parts as possible. It contains a 1931 Buick steering column, modified 1937 Buick steering wheel, 1964 Riviera aluminum drum brakes, and 1972 GS rear end.

A 1965 401-ci Nailhead provides the motivation for this showstopper. Bored out to 0.060-inch, the Nailhead now measures 413 ci. It runs heavily modified Pontiac push rods and custom BME pistons.

CHAPTER 5

CYLINDER HEADS

To make big power, you must send more air and fuel into the combustion chamber. You can add a little HP to a Buick engine with a few bolt-on parts, but if you want to make any serious HP, the heads must be reworked.

Back in the late 1960s, Buick's engineers knew a thing or two about head design. The Buick 350 and 400/430/455 heads feature a tall, skinny intake runner, which yields excellent port velocity, unlike the typical first-generation Chevy, which has big and fat ports. Higher port velocity allows the engine to breathe better, letting the builder run a larger carburetor while maintaining big bottom-end torque. Buick heads have a lot of potential, and this has benefited Buick engine builders for years.

While there are a few aftermarket heads available for the 455-series and 3.8-liter engines, the Nailheads and the 350 have been left out in the cold. These heads greatly benefit from head work. The techniques shown here translate to virtually all Buick heads, but we are going to port a set of 350 factory heads. With the emergence of muscle car and factory appearing stock tire drag racing classes, using a set of aftermarket heads is forbidden; head porting, however, is perfectly legal. Quality

In order to achieve real power with bolt-on performance parts, real engine work must be performed. With such a well-designed yet under-realized head, porting offers the quickest way to awaken a sleepy Buick. Beginning with the basic gasket port-matching, a beginner can make some progress without risking too much. Next, the heads are completely ported and polished, bowls blended, and guides reshaped for opening up the heads.

CYLINDER HEADS

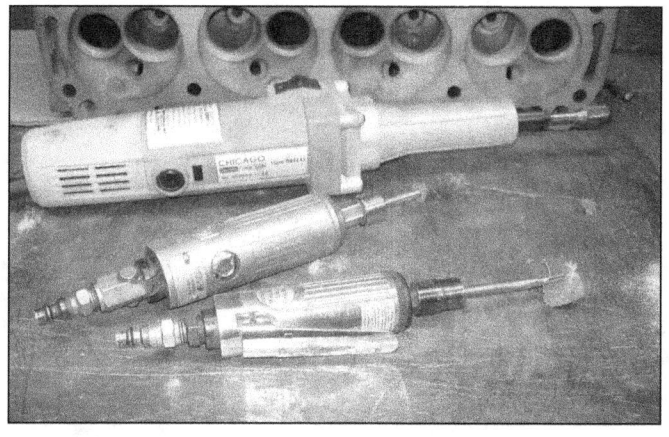

The basic tools needed to port a head are air-powered die-grinders and an electric die grinder with a foot control for precise cutting. The foot-control unit isn't absolutely necessary, but it makes things easier.

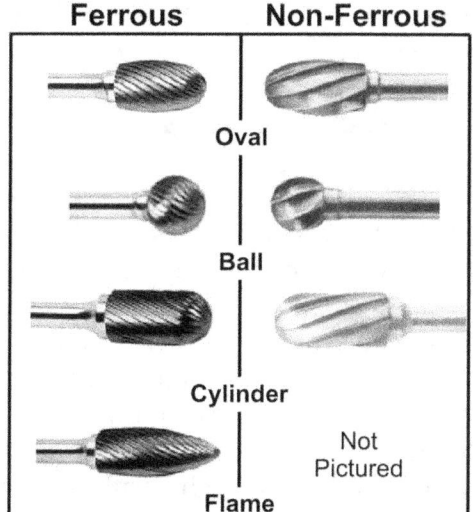

An assortment of fine carbide burrs assist in getting the most off your iron. Head porting kits can be purchased from most mail order parts warehouses and include all the tips and sanding rolls needed. Do not use coarse tips on cast iron. Coarse bits will grab the iron, making the work more difficult to accomplish.

ported heads will give your engine an advantage without compromising the factory look. For the beginner, purchasing a cylinder head porting kit is a good idea because these kits typically come with all the sanding rolls and buffing pads required for a proper port job. The carbide bits and grinders are not typically included and need to be purchased separately.

Gasket Port Matching

A basic gasket port match is the first step in porting a set of heads. This process takes a set of intake-to-head gaskets. Each intake port is opened up to the edges of the gasket in order to allow more air and fuel to enter the head. The result is less turbulence, which increases flow. To begin, the gasket is centered on the head, as it would be with the intake installed. Use a marker to trace the inner edge of the intake runner holes. This line serves as a guide to open the ports. A word of caution: It is very important to stay within the guidelines when gasket port matching. If you go beyond the guideline, you will create turbulence and possibly leaks. Once the lines are drawn, go to work on the head with a die grinder along with an assortment of metal burrs. This is where skill and finesse come in — it takes some practice learning how to work the grinder. When working with cast iron, fine carbide burrs are suitable where coarse bits will dig in and jump around; aluminum, however, should only be worked with coarse bits because they will fill up almost immediately with shavings, causing a big headache.

The ports are worked from the outside in, blending the widened outer port to the deeper recesses of the head. Using a cylindrical burr, the walls of the intake port are trimmed to the lines. The basic trim work needs to keep the lines square and straight. The grinder is worked at a high RPM, helping the tool run smooth and not grab and bounce. It is important to keep the walls flat and not introduce waves, which will disrupt flow. Next, a cone-shaped burr works well for removing the material in corners. Blending the corners to the straight sections takes

Use a marker to trace the outline of the intake gasket for use as a guide for port-matching the intake runners. Notice the large valve guides; this causes a lot of turbulence in the air flow.

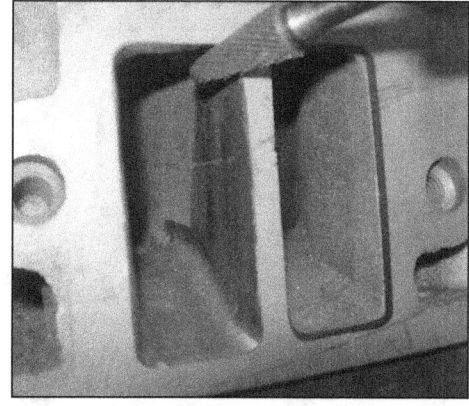

After trimming the walls of the intake port to the lines with a cylindrical burr, a cone burr works well for removing the material in corners.

CHAPTER 5

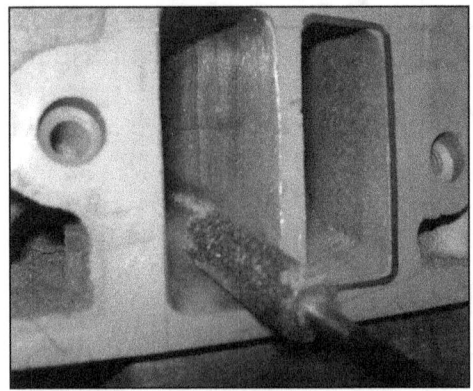

After completing the carbide work, a sanding roll finishes the job of smoothing the walls.

In comparison to a stock head, the difference is quite amazing. The last step here is to polish the surface with a modified Scotch-Brite pad.

Place the gasket on the head, again, to verify the porting. Each intake is widened by 0.100 inch.

can perform a basic gasket port-match job without risking ruining a good head.

For serious street and competition engines, the intake runner surface can be raised 0.070 inch by setting the gasket higher on the head and marking it as such. Then all the port work is done at the top of the port, as opposed to being split between the top and bottom. This allows the head to be milled to increase the static compression of the engine, and still allows the intake to fit properly.

Blending the Bowls

Blending the bowls is the next step in head work. This process involves smoothing the short turns where the port flows into the bowl and turns to exit the valve, reshaping the guides and smoothing the walls. The key here is eliminating or reducing the obstacles inhibiting flow. The process begins with laying back the short turns in both the intake and exhaust bowls. This step is crucial for improving flow. This short-turn radius creates a lot of turbulence, and reducing this obstruction lessens the turbulence. A flame-tip or egg-shaped burr allows enough room to get in the bowl and reach the back of the radius. Slow and steady wins the race, as the goal is a smooth and clean surface. Once the meat of the radius is gone, a round ball stone smoothes the surface and eliminates the bumps and pits. On the exhaust bowls, there is a large step just under the valve seat. This area requires blending into the rest of the bowl. Once the turns and radiuses are smoothed, the valve guides have their turn with the grinder.

a little practice, so it is best to work slowly and carefully.

After completing the carbide work, use a sanding roll to remove the cut marks from the carbide, smoothing the walls. Working with increasingly higher-grit rolls, sand the walls, progressing from rough to smooth, so you achieve a better-than-stock finish. To complete the job, a Roloc or surface-conditioning pad, also referred to as a Scotch-Brite pad, is used to achieve a mirror shine. There are many varieties and sizes of these pads. For port work, a cross buff fits best. A standard buffing pad can be altered to fit inside the ports by cutting several pie-shaped sections out of the pad, allowing it to easily conform to the port walls. These pads can be purchased, but making them works just as well. The smoother the walls, the better the flow characteristics will be. Polishing the ports increases flow and gets a little extra HP out of the head.

Once all the port work is done, the gasket is put on the head again to verify the porting. The work done on these heads opened up the intake ports by 0.100 inch, which is quite a big difference. The goal here is creating a smooth, blended surface, as opposed to a large, notched opening. This process is easy and a good place to start with head work. A beginner

CYLINDER HEADS

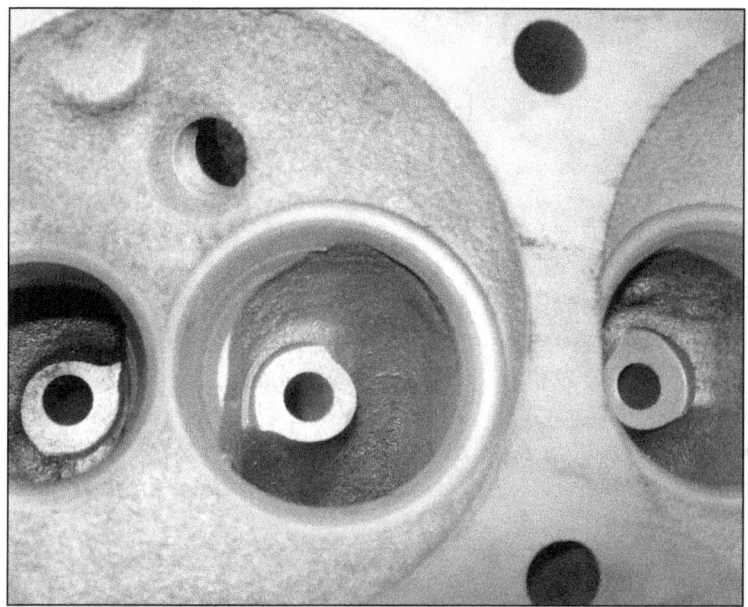

The stock valve guides (center of ports) are big and bulky, and the flat tops are much larger than needed.

The valve guides are reshaped using an electric grinder with a speed-control foot pedal. Clean up the guide until the iron is blended smooth to the opening. Use a 1/2-inch tip for the intake and a 3/8-inch tip for the exhaust bowls.

The valve guides on Buick heads are quite large and chunky. A lot of material can be removed here, which will help guide the flow around the valve and into the combustion chamber. Instead of an air-powered die-grinder, an electric grinder with a foot pedal can be used for easier speed control and hand concentration on the guides. A small round-tipped burr (1/2-inch tip for the intake and 3/8-inch tip for the exhaust) is best when working the guides in the close quarters of the bowls. The work begins with laying the edges over; blending the guide to the back of the bowl. Using the foot control to change the RPM of the bit, the guide is reshaped until it resembles a fat teardrop, with point leading away from the valve. The top of the guide will become sharp, not flat, and should be convex (rolls out like a ball), so the airflow is smooth.

With all the major work done, a flap disc and an air-powered die-grinder can be used to smooth the

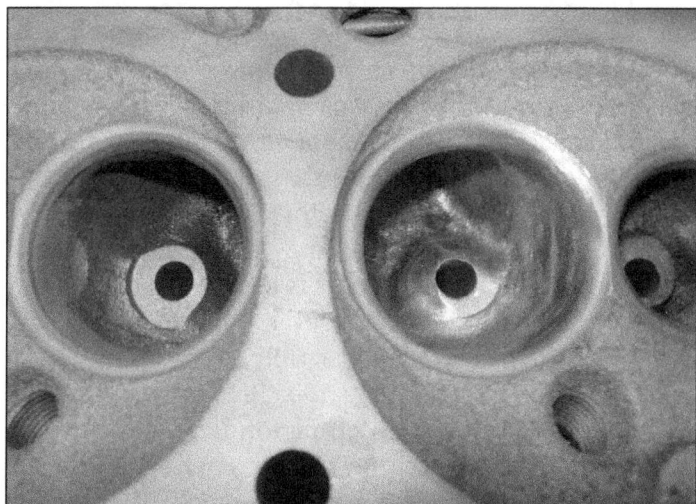

The slight teardrop shape from the top to the bottom is the difference between the stock guide and the reshaped guide. This has a vane effect, which helps guide the flow around the valve stem.

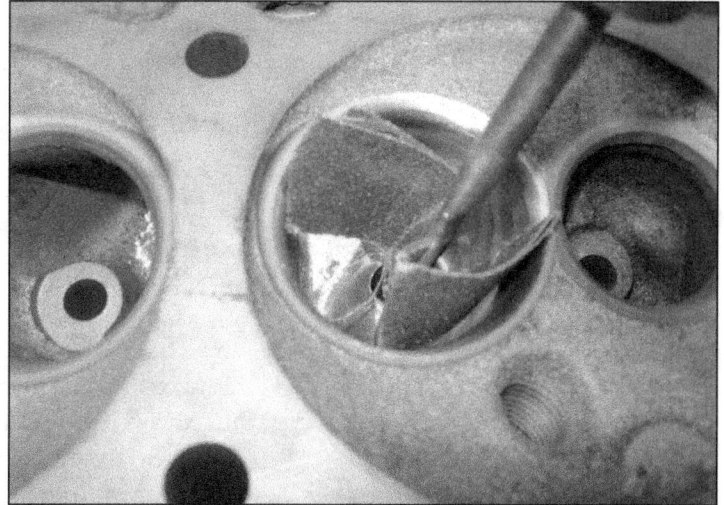

A flap disc yields a smooth, round finish inside the bowl. Use any sandpaper grit with this slotted spindle. A cross buff can also be used to polish the bowls.

bowls of all the grinding marks. The modified Roloc pads then polish the surface. The surface should be smooth and free of any pits or rough patches. On these heads, the exhaust throat was opened a total of 0.100 inch.

This is the only step that should be performed on Nailhead heads. There is very little material to work with on these heads and you can hit a water jacket quickly. Short-turn radius and bowl work is where the bulk of the power is going to be unlocked.

Exhaust Porting

The exhaust ports require a different approach. With the Buick heads, file and grind smooth the crossover holes between the two center exhaust ports with the walls. This cools the intake and eliminates some exhaust turbulence. The exhaust ports run straight out to the manifolds/headers, so they can be left stock. If they are polished, you will gain minimal flow, but I always say every little bit helps. The center exhaust ports feature a small bump on the bottom outer wall; this area can be massaged, but do not remove this hump completely.

Here is a stock exhaust runner. While not a lot of work needs to be done, polishing the runners and cleaning up the valve guides increases flow.

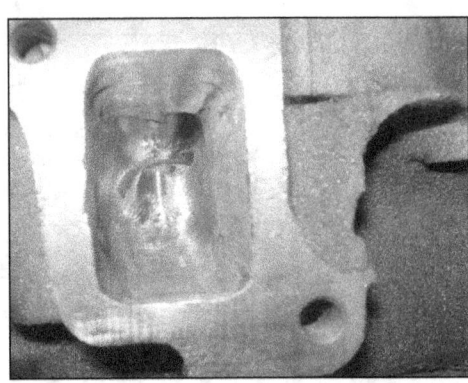

This is the completed exhaust port. The shape of the guide and the lack of flashing and pitting increase exhaust flow and reduce turbulence.

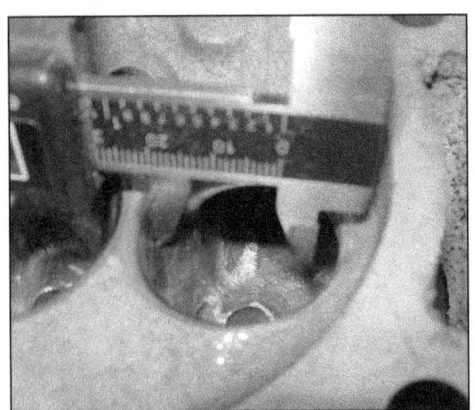

The exhaust throat was enlarged by 0.100 inch, a considerable difference compared to stock.

Compare this completed 350 head with the stock 350 head. Hardened valve seats were not required because we stayed with the stock valve sizing and the high-nickel content of Buick heads. Some builders recommend hardened valve seats for all heads.

*If you are running heavy spring pressures, hardened seats will keep the valves from recessing. Recessed valves occur when the valve seats compress and the valve sits below the surface of the combustion chamber. **Never install hardened seats in a Nailhead, as the simple installation process can ruin the head.** Most rebuilt heads with stock valve sizing do not need hardened seats because they have been work-hardened over the years.*

Valve Sizing

For the 350 heads shown here, we chose to keep the stock 1.88-inch intake and 1.55-inch exhaust valves to show the difference in flow with the port work. Adding larger valves will surely increase flow, but would not accurately represent the gains from the port work. In addition, the 350 heads can easily accept a larger 1.92-inch intake valve.

Machining a head to accept larger valves is best left to the professional. However, you need to investigate and carefully select a prospective machine shop. Is the shop qualified to do high-performance head work? Have they ever done any Buick heads for high performance? How long have they been machining heads? Any machine shop can ruin a set of heads by sinking the valves into the head, improperly setting the guides, off-setting the valve in the seat, etc. There are quite a few ways to go wrong here, so be sure your machine shop is qualified. The local parts store is usually not the best place for performance engine work.

The valve seats are the one thing to consider when increasing the valve sizing. Most other pre-unleaded gas heads require hardened valve seats to survive unleaded gas. When leaded gas burns, it forms lead oxide that deposits on the seat and valve in thin layers, limiting metal-to-metal contact and eliminating valve-seat wear. With unleaded gas, this process and protection goes away. Buick heads were cast with a high nickel content, which typically eliminates the need for hardened seats; however, things are different when using larger valves. When cutting the head for larger valves, the original seat is removed and the valve hits virgin metal, which can lead to a valve recession. There are two solutions for this potential problem: one, machining the head and installing hardened valve seats: and, two, running a lead additive for the first few thousand miles. Running lead in the gas will help seat the valves and eliminate the need for hardened seats. However, adding a hardened seat is cheap insurance against this real problem. But engines, such as the Nailhead, have very little material for milling and mounting new valve seats. Unless you must run hardened seats in a Nailhead, use the leaded gas when larger valves have been installed.

Valve Jobs

Another absolute must when reworking a set of heads is a three-angle valve job, also referred to as a competition valve job. While some shops always perform this task, you need to ask for it to be sure. A typical bargain valve job consists of basic cleanup of the 30-degree top cut. The most common three-angle job utilizes the 30-45-60, which is a 30-degree top cut, 45-degree mid cut, and a 60-degree back cut. This helps transition the airflow to the valve with less turbulence. Once the valve job is complete, the rest of the bowl can be blended into the 60-degree back cut for further enhancement. Along with a three-angle valve job, Buick engines really benefit from a 30-degree angle back cut on the valves themselves. This little trick will increase the flow by improving the transition from the port to the cylinder. A 30-degree back

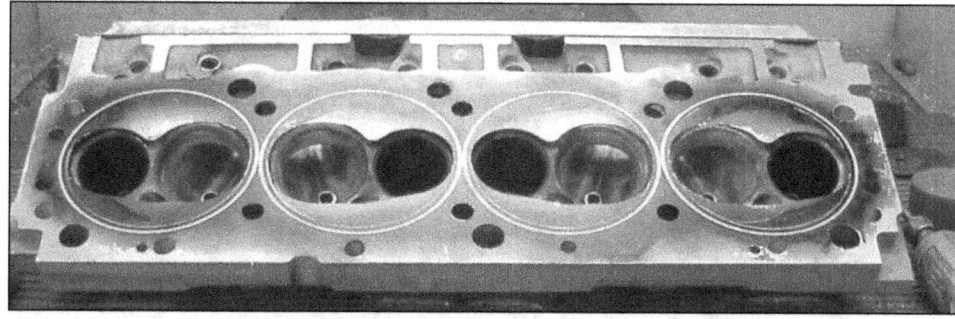
Blue machinist dye has been sprayed on these heads to aid in porting. This helps you see where you have cut and where you have not.

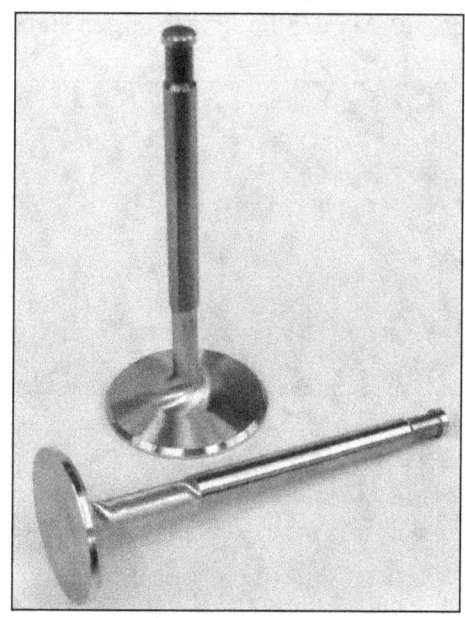
These stainless-steel Nailhead valves illustrate where the engine gets its name – they look like nails.

The Sunnen machine is set up to cut a three-angle valve job on this head. This step greatly increases the flow characteristics of the head and therefore should not be overlooked.

CHAPTER 5

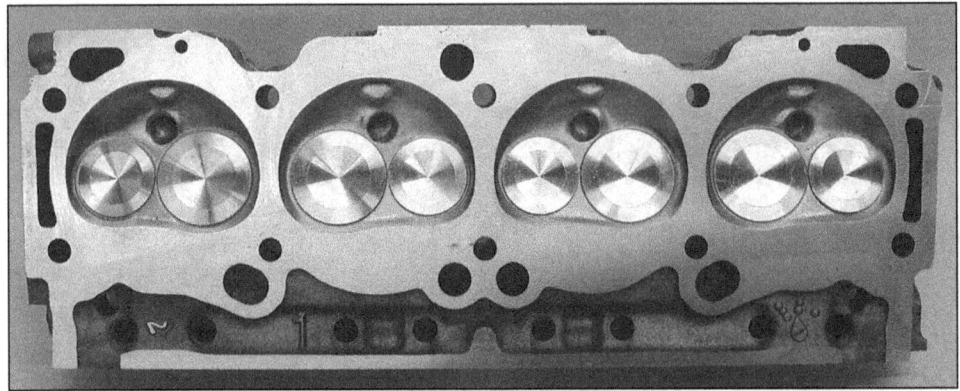

Installing larger valves in a 455 requires unshrouding the valves. This is a completed 455 head with larger Stage 1 valves.

The swirl-polished stainless-steel valves feature a 30-degree back cut. These valves are stock sizes (1.88-inch intake, 1.55-inch exhaust) for the 350.

cut makes the most difference in the low lift range — 0.100 to 0.300 inch — which is very important to the volumetric efficiency of the engine. Performing this modification to an engine that is using a smaller cam (less than 0.500-inch lift) is necessary and can add as much as 25 percent flow at the lower lifts.

Combustion Chamber Polishing

While this step is not critical for mild street engines, it will certainly make a difference in high-performance street and race engines. The goal of polishing the combustion chamber is eliminating the hot spots, which lead to detonation and eventually destroy the engine. The benefits serve not only race engines, but also the mildest street engine because a polished combustion chamber allows the engine to run higher compression at a lower fuel octane rating. This benefits the pump gas engine as the quality of gas is always on the decline. The higher compression aspect obviously benefits the racer: more compression equals more power.

The process is quite simple. Starting with a medium-grit sanding roll on a die grinder, the rough finish is removed from the combustion chamber. Progressively moving to finer grits, the chamber is smoothed until the metal has an achieved a bright luster. A fine Roloc conditioning pad gets the mirror shine that will resist carbon deposits. The key here: less is more. The less material removed from the chamber the better, as even minor removal of material in the combustion chamber increases the chamber volume, reducing the compression ratio.

Heat Crossover Vent Modification

Another cheap horsepower increase comes from blocking the heat crossover passages. This small hole in the center of the head on the intake side allows hot exhaust air to transfer to the intake, warming the incoming air, operating the factory heat stove for the choke. Simply plugging these holes will provide a moderate boost of 8 to 15 hp. The increase comes from cooling the

Polishing the combustion chamber reduces detonation by eliminating the hot spots. A series of sanding rolls accomplishes this task.

The exhaust heat crossover vents, while necessary for cold climate cars, creates a large amount of turbulence in the center exhaust runners flow. The simplest way to block this opening is to install 3/4-inch freeze plugs in the two holes at the back of the opening.

CYLINDER HEADS

The crossover vent on this head has been filled with aluminum and ground smooth.

intake and reducing the turbulence in the center exhaust ports. There are several ways to plug these holes.

Greg Gessler, of Gessler Head Porting, uses an old-school approach. Gessler recommends blocking the backside of the hole with a piece of copper and filling the hole with molten aluminum. In order to achieve a solid plug, the hole needs to be very clean. A grinder with a stone is used to clean the hole of any debris or corrosion. A sanding roll or flap-disc finishes off the cleaning, bringing the internal walls to a nice shine. Then a clean copper plate is laid over the backside of the center hole on the intake side of the head. Next, molten aluminum is poured into the holes and allowed to cool. Once the aluminum has solidified, each modified crossover hole is ground smooth and flush with the port. To finish off the job, the plate is removed from the other side and the aluminum is milled, ground flush or just below the intake surface. This technique provides the most benefit, while taking the most time to accomplish.

The other option is to use a much simpler technique, but it reduces the benefit because the holes inside the port are not filled. This technique reduces the turbulence, but not as much as the metal-filling process. To start, a die grinder with a small stone or carbide bit is used to open the hole just slightly. With the holes cleaned and slightly larger, it becomes easier to drive in a 3/4-inch freeze plug. The 3/4-inch plugs work for both early- and late-model heads in both 350 and big-block families.

These techniques work for any engine, street or race, and provide a modest gain. However, if the engine is to retain the factory heat stove choke, the passenger-side head should be left alone. Along with that, cars driven consistently in very cold weather should keep one hole on each head open. This helps the engine heat up faster and increases drivability over a completely plugged head.

Flow Testing

Flow testing typically determines the effectiveness of head porting, and this is done on a flow bench. These 350 heads gained 25 percent flow at 0.500-inch lift. Quite an impressive feat, considering we used stock valves. The trick when comparing flow numbers is to be sure to compare percentages as opposed to actual flow numbers. The same head can vary greatly on different flow benches.

Buick 350-ci V-8 Head Flow Chart

VALVE LIFT	STK IN. CFM	STK EX CFM	PORTED IN CFM	PORTED EX
.100	66	44	74	55
.200	119	93	135	110
.300	169	124	187	145
.400	198	128	241	167
.500	198	130	243	176
.550	N/A	N/A	251	178
.600	N/A	N/A	254	181

These are Buick 350 head's flow numbers.

CHAPTER 5

Several times during the porting process, the flow bench is used to check the progress of the job. The final numbers are impressive: 25 percent more flow than the stock head.

The stock shaft-mount rockers limit the ability to adjust the valvetrain. Adjustable roller rockers, such as these V-6 turbo units from TA Performance, allow the builder to set the valve preload.

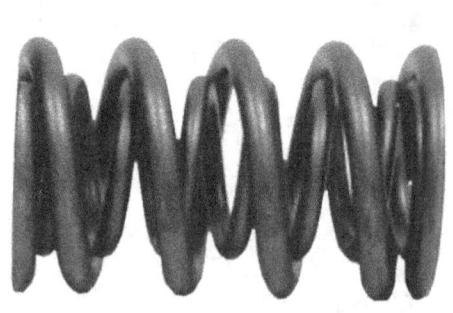

These dual-valve springs maintain much higher pressure compared to the stock springs. In order to use these types of springs, the spring perches must be machined to fit the larger-diameter springs, and specific retainers must be used, as well.

High-Performance Head Parts

To get the most out your heads, there are quite a few high-performance parts available. Porting and polishing the heads increases their performance, but using stock parts will limit the engine's ability to take advantage of the gains. While not flashy parts, the parts that make the head work are very important and should not be ignored.

Roller rockers provide substantial performance benefits. The original Buick design utilizes shaft-mounted rocker arms. While they do what they are supposed to, they certainly have a downside. The stock rockers are not adjustable, so the only way to adjust the preload on the valves is with the pushrods. On top of that, the rockers are kept in place with plastic buttons that are prone to breaking, creating a huge problem. The best solution is a set of shaft-mount roller rockers from manufacturers, such as Poston Enterprises. These rockers use hardened shafts, needle bearings, aluminum spacers to separate the rockers, and, best of all, they are adjustable. This gives the builder the ability to fine-tune the valvetrain. Roller rockers are available for 455, 350, and V-6 turbo engines.

Valve springs pull the valve back to the seat after it opens. When these break, bad things happen. Using a stock spring on a mild engine is just fine, but high-performance engines need better springs. For mild 455 performance engines, the 1-inch Stage 1 spring with 115 psi is a good place to start. Serious street and race performance engines need a little better spring when using high-lift cams and running at high RPM, so a dual spring should be used. Most dual springs, such as Poston's springs, require milling the head to accept the larger-diameter base spring, and require the use of specific valve seals and retainers. These valve springs can provide up to 130 psi of seat pressure, which is good up to 0.650-inch lift.

Chrome-moly "no wiggle" retainers are a valuable upgrade. As the valves move, the springs twist and slide. The stock retainers fail to control this movement, eventually leading to broken springs and dropped valves. Using a set of no wiggle retainers eliminates this problem by correctly controlling the spring movement. This is an absolute must for any high-performance Buick engine.

Stock valves are adequate for stock rebuilds, but high-performance engines need a strong valve that will resist the higher temperatures and increased stress. Stainless-steel valves resist corrosion and wear better than stock two-piece valves, and are necessary for any performance build.

Buick heads only use four bolts per cylinder, so the clamping force is especially important. A set of head studs will increase the clamping force, which provides a better combustion chamber seal. Head studs also make assembly easier and eliminate the possibility of installing the gaskets upside down. This is disastrous on the 350 because it would expose a water jacket, causing a serious leak. Installing head studs is simple. Thread each stud in the block using about 10 ft-lbs of torque. No sealer is required, as all Buick head holes are blind — they all have solid bottoms and do not enter the water jackets. When using the TA Performance Stage II heads, you must drill and tap four additional head bolts. TA sells a drill jig to make this easier.

Big-Block Heads

The 400 and 430 cylinder heads also have a place in high-performance applications, although there are a few caveats you should know before bolting a set on your 455. The 400 and 430 heads have an oil passage that sends oil to the rocker shaft pedestals. The 400 and 430 engines (as well as 1969 and earlier 350s) oil the rockers through the rocker shafts because these engines use solid pushrods. A small hole on each side of the block sends oil to the heads. These passages are no longer needed because the rockers will receive oil through the pushrods. Pushrod oiling is better because oil is pumped directly to the rockers, and the parts are much easier to find. In order to eliminate these, the holes need to be plugged at the head or in the block with freeze or pipe plugs. Any 400 or 430 can be made to oil through the pushrods by simply blocking oil passages and running hollow pushrods with matching oiling lifters. The 455 blocks also have one of these holes on the driver side, which should be blocked when using 400 and 430 heads. Jim Burek, of PAE, recommends changing any 400, 430, and 1969 and earlier 350 engines to the pushrod-oiling method. Running roller rockers also require this modification, as the rocker shafts are solid.

In 1973, Buick added a few more water passages to the heads. If you plan to use newer heads on an older block, these passages need to be eliminated; otherwise they will pour water directly into the lifter valley. These holes are located in the center of the head, flanking the center head bolt on the intake side of the head. A pipe or freeze plug will effectively block the holes.

The pipe-plug method involves tapping the holes for a 1/2-inch pipe plug. The pipe plug simply threads in and you are done. The freeze-plug method may be a little quicker, but there is a modicum of instability. To start, a small amount of high-heat epoxy, such as JB Weld, is wiped around the hole. Then a 3/4-inch freeze plug is pressed in the hole. While the freeze plug usually fits tight, the epoxy is there to ensure there is no leakage. The pipe-plug method is certainly more secure, but does require the ability to tap the block. A tap and die set is certainly worth the cost in this instance.

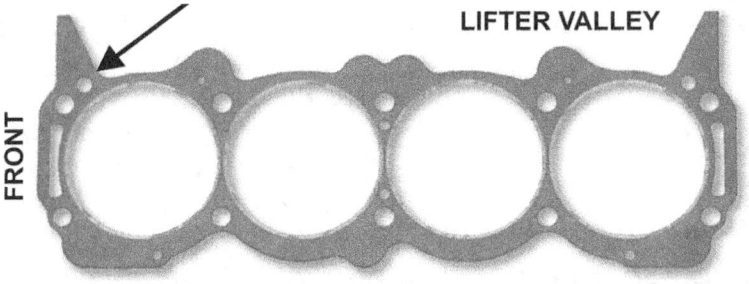

Mounting 400 and 430 heads on a 455 requires removing an additional oiling hole, which oils the rocker shafts. The pushrods oil the rockers on the 455. Switching the 400 or 430 to pushrod oiling simply requires hollow pushrods and plugging this hole. The 1969 and older 350s can also benefit from this mod. This mod is also required when using solid-shaft roller rockers.

CHAPTER 5

From 1973 and on, Buick integrated an additional water jacket in the cylinder to help meet emissions standards. These heads will fit an earlier block, but only if this hole is plugged. If not, water will dump right into the lifter valley. A 1/2-inch pipe plug or 3/4-inch freeze plug easily fills this jacket.

Big-Block Head Porting

Porting your factory heads is quite a task, but it's a great way to wake up your Buick and gain a lot of HP. But keep in mind, it is not the only solution. In the late 1960s through 1972, Buick offered the Stage 1 and later the Stage 2 option. The Stage 1 option included reworked heads, which added a good deal of power. While they only listed an advertised gain of 10 hp, the actual gain was much closer to 30–40 hp. The biggest difference in the engines was the heads. The valves grew to 2.125-inch intake and 1.75-inch exhaust; the chambers were unshrouded, meaning the iron was cut away from the valves. The process of converting a standard 455 head to a Stage 1 head is quite simple. The valves must be replaced with the larger Stage 1 valves. Then the combustion chamber is milled to unshroud the valves. The standard 455 chamber has a D-shape, and the Stage 1 chambers resemble a heart shape. Even back in the 1960s, Buick engineers knew a thing or two about head design — the heart shape is found on most modern high-performance heads.

Along with the Stage 1, Buick also offered the Stage 2 heads for $51.97 — a great price for the benefits. Produced from 1969 through mid-1972, the Stage 2 heads were primarily used for racing, with very few actually making it to the street. The Stage 2 package included a wild cam, 11:1 forged pistons, Stage 2 heads, custom headers, and an Edelbrock B4B intake manifold. The monster oval exhaust ports, which require custom tube headers, make these heads interesting. The ports are designed so the exhaust valves are exposed directly to the exhaust flanges with almost zero turn. Along with that, the intake ports are much larger than regular 455 heads. The combustion chamber on the Stage 2 heads is also 57 cc, much smaller than on the standard 455.

While there were only a handful of Stage 2 heads produced, some Buick specialists are reproducing the Stage 2 heads, including TA Performance. While there is nothing currently available for the Buick 350 as far as cylinder heads, all is not lost. Bulldog, one of the Buick aftermarket's best friends, is working on a cylinder head for the 350 that should be nearing completion by the time this book is available. Details are sketchy right now, but this head is expected to flow in the 250-cfm range, which would be capable of producing 480–500 hp with the right cam.

Nailhead Cylinder Heads

When it comes to heads, the Nailhead engine family has been left out in the cold. There are zero options, with nothing on the horizon, but things are not all bad. The castings started out the same but were machined differently, first for larger valves and then, in 1956, the combustion chamber was reshaped to fit the 4-inch 322 bore (264 was no longer made). These are the best heads for the 322 (never to be used on a 264), but the 1954–1955 heads can be machined to copy the 1956. The 1957–1958 head was basically the same as the 1959–1966 head but

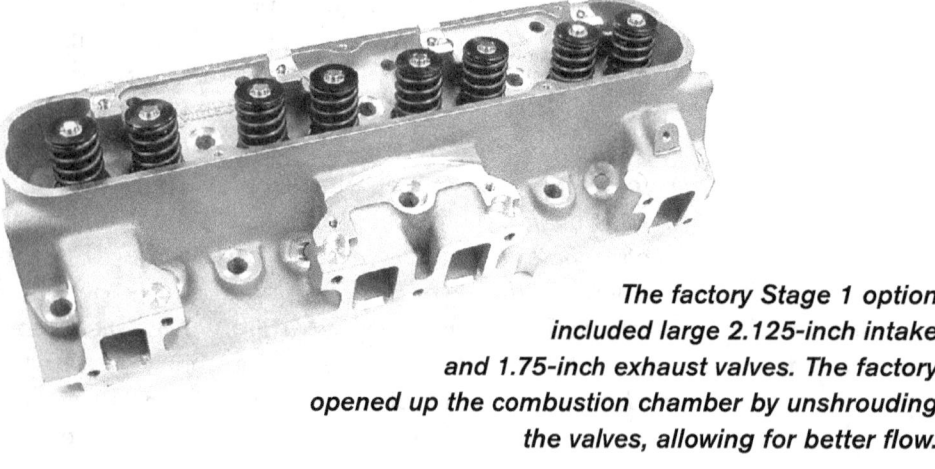

The factory Stage 1 option included large 2.125-inch intake and 1.75-inch exhaust valves. The factory opened up the combustion chamber by unshrouding the valves, allowing for better flow.

CYLINDER HEADS

While there were very few Stage 2 cars produced from 1969 to 1972, TA Performance produced its own Stage 2 aluminum cylinder heads. These heads offer much higher flow ratings, pushing 380 cfm.

TA Stage 1 aluminum head is offered in two levels: Street Eliminator and Track Eliminator. Each offers specific characteristics that make them perform better for their respective duties. The Street Eliminator is at home on any street 455.

In 1953, Buick introduced the 322, affectionately known as the Nailhead. It was named for its small vertical standing valves that looked like nails. While heads for all sizes will swap between each other, bolting the larger heads on the smaller engines requires expensive custom pistons. These reproduction valve covers from Kring really finish off a Nailhead engine.

These Stage 1 Track Eliminator heads support 500–800 hp and are well suited for any serious track motor.

with smaller valves. The combustion chamber size from the 1957–1966 heads is the same, and much larger than the 1954–1956 head, so putting the late heads on the 1954–1956 would cause a big compression drop without custom-made pistons. In addition, the intake ports are larger and would not fit the 1953–1956 intake. Log-style manifolds or injection would be a way to go with this swap. The intake ports are bigger, but so are the exhaust ports. The 1953–1956 heads have round ports; the 1957–1966 heads have rectangular ports. The 1954–1956 heads flow within 10 percent of the later model cylinder heads. Factory head swaps are nearly irrelevant. Russell Martin of NailheadBuick.com discovered that the 1954–1956 heads flow within 19 pecent of the later model cylinder heads. Factory head swaps are nearly irrelevant. The exhaust manifolds will bolt to any head, but will either leak or restrict flow.

Do not use bronze guides in a Nailhead engine; the stock guides are what you want, because bronze guides have a tendency to wear out quickly. The 1966 401 and 425 intake guides (which are already cut for seals) should be used on the intake and have special seals for them — do not use seals on the exhaust side.

CHAPTER 5

Stage 2, 3 and 4 Aluminum Heads

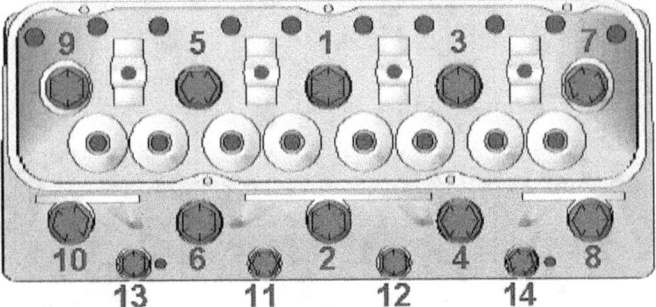

The additional four bolts added to the Stage 2, 3, and 4 heads from TA Performance are shown. While not required, drilling these bolt holes will increase combustion chamber clamping force.

Stock and Stage 1 SE Aluminum Heads

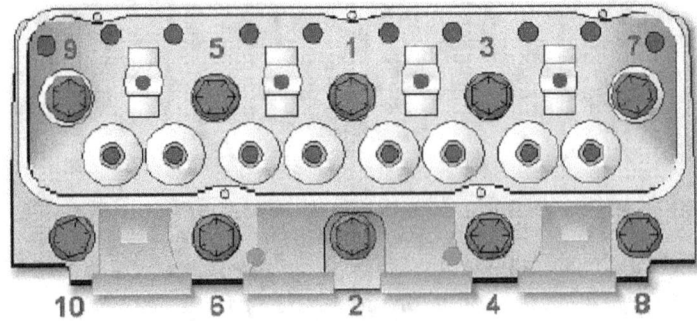

The TA Stage 1 and stock heads need to be torqued in sequence. This picture shows the number sequence for torquing the head bolts. The torque process should cinch up each bolt a little at a time and should take several loops through the numbers.

There are many different valves for the Nailhead engines. The 1953 had unique one-year-only valves. The 1954–1956 heads all had the same intakes but exhaust valves were different for each year. The 1957–1958 heads had their own unique intake and exhaust valves. The 1959–1966 valves were the same, except early valves (1959–1961) had tulip exhaust valves, although were the same size as the 1962–1966 valves.

Hardened valve seats are an absolute mistake for a Nailhead. There is simply not enough material available to install hardened seats, and the head will more than likely be ruined if you try to install them. There are only a select number of individuals who have the experience with Nailhead engines to properly install hardened valve seats. Do not let your local machine shop try it. For performance builds, the 1955 or 1956 exhaust valves (both the same size, larger than the 1954; the 1956 is tulip shaped) allow better breathing, and you will have new seats at the same time. If the seats are bad on the 1955–1956 heads, use 1957–1958 exhaust valves. The larger 1957–1958 intakes can also be used on the 1954–1956 heads. You can put 1959–1966 valves in 1954–1956 heads, but the smaller combustion chamber will only shroud the valves. The 1957–1958 heads will benefit from the 1959–1966 valves, or you can just swap to the later heads.

Buick 455 TA Stage 2 SE
with competition valve job and mild blending of the valve job

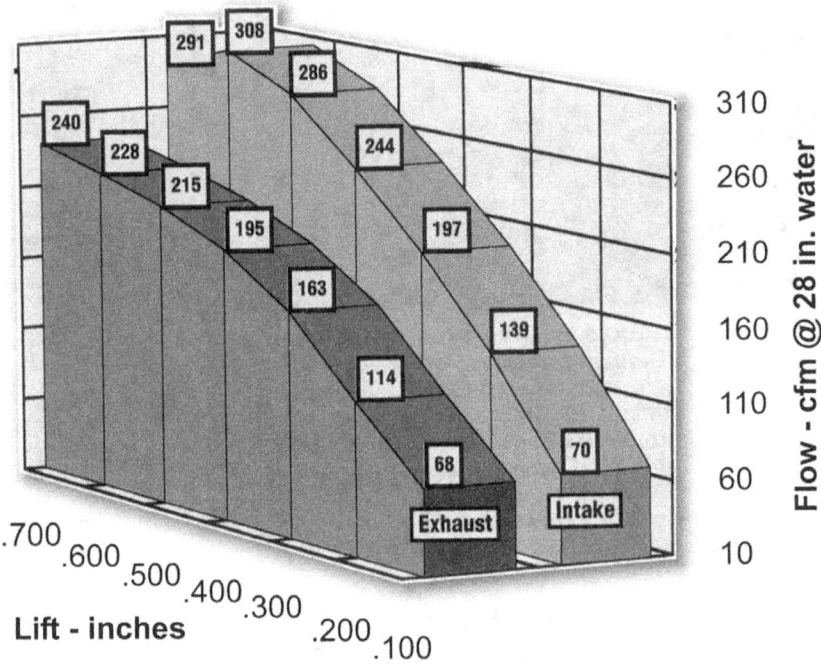

This flow chart shows what can be accomplished with a mild port job on a set of TA Performance Stage 2 SE heads.

Aftermarket Head Options

Few modifications for an engine can increase performance more than a set of aftermarket aluminum heads. Reduced weight and better design and flow characteristics simply

CYLINDER HEADS

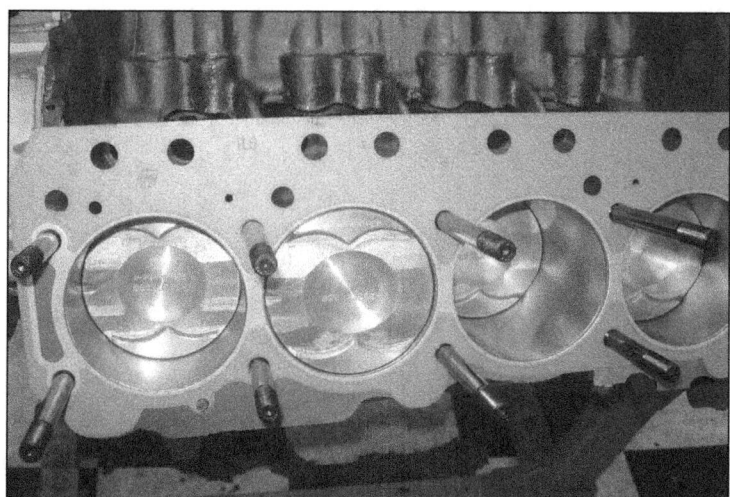

ARP head studs are always a good idea for a serious performance engine. These studs make installation easier (out of the car) and provide more consistent clamping force. If you have a car with A/C and/or a power brake booster, these might make life difficult if you need to remove the heads in the car.

The Edelbrock 455 aluminum head weighs a mere 34 lbs and accepts the more widely available small-block Chevy rockers, which is a nice touch.

The Loc Wire head gasket for the V-6 turbo uses an internal wire ring, simulating an O-ring right in the gasket. The Loc Wire gaskets require a groove to be machined in the head surface to accept the wire ring.

eclipse stock heads on practically any application. While the 350 and Nailhead engines have no support in this area, the 455 family enjoys a solid aftermarket, with several options in aluminum cylinder heads.

The choices range from mild to full-out race heads. Bulldog Performance makes 455 street-performance heads as well as 455 race and 350 street-performance heads, which will be released soon. Bulldog has not been around as long as Edelbrock, but it knows a thing or two about building heads all the same. Bulldog specializes in producing parts for the "undiscovered" engines, such as Buick, Cadillac, and Oldsmobile, where no other manufacturers really invest the effort. Currently, Bulldog offers the 455 street-performance head, which features large 2.190-inch intake and 1.81-inch exhaust stainless-steel valves. These heads accept all the stock-type parts, such as shaft-mount rockers (including roller rockers) and valve covers.

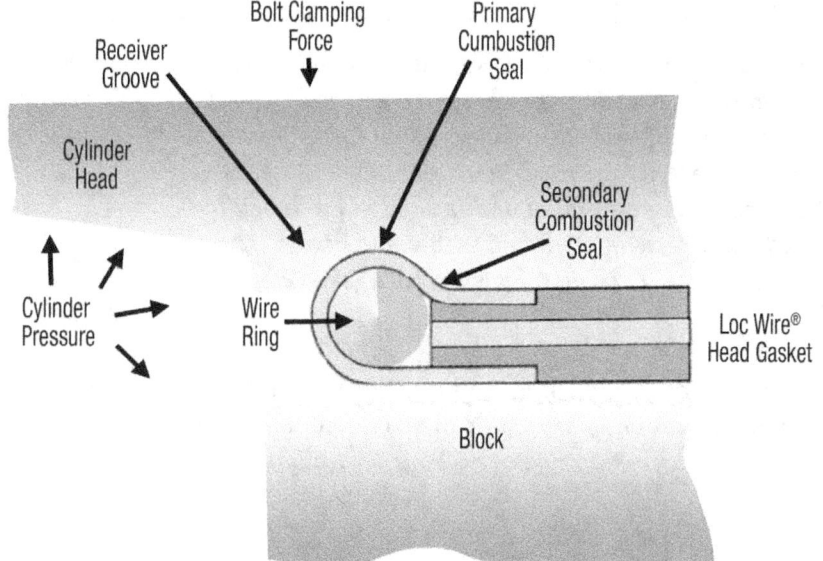

Loc Wire Performance Head Gasket Design

The heads flow over 293 cfm intake and 201 cfm exhaust at 0.500-inch lift, and have been ported to flow well over 340 cfm intake. Bulldog is working on a set of 455 heads that will flow over 400 cfm intake out of the box, and a set of aluminum Buick 350 heads that will flow upwards of 250 cfm intake. This will be the first-ever Buick 350 aftermarket head.

Champion Racing's GN1 3.8-liter V-6 turbo aluminum heads are CNC machined with 46-cc combustion chambers. Champion adds radii to the head bolt spot faces to reduce stress risers that lead to cracking. The CNC-contour-machined multi-angle

CHAPTER 5

	STAGE 3 Tall Port	STAGE 4 Tall Port
Intake Manifold	SP2, Custom	SP2, Custom
Exhaust Manifold / Headers	Oval Port Headers	Oval Port Headers
Rocker Assembly	Stage 3 Roller, TA Shaft Mount	Stage 4 Roller, TA Shaft Mount
Head Bolt/Stud Kit	Stage 2	Stage 2
Camshaft	Hyd, Solid, or Roller	Roller
Power Potential	600-900 hp +	700-900 hp +
Application	Hot Street / Race	Race
Valves Int./Exh. ①	2.250 / 1.800 ②	2.250 / 1.800 ②
CFM (base) Int./Exh.	300 / 230	325 / 230
CFM (max) Int./Exh.	385 / 270 ③	395 / 270 ③
Chamber CC's	58	58

	Street Intimidator SI	Street Eliminator SE
Intake Manifold	TA, Stock, BGC	TA, Stock, BGC ① Port Matched
Exhaust Manifold / Headers	Same as stock Heads	Same as stock ② Heads
Rocker Assembly	Stock, TA V1309SI Series	TA V1308 Series
Head Stud Kit	TA 1133A (8 bolt) TA 1133B (14 bolt)	TA 1133A (8 bolt) TA 1133B (14 bolt)
Camshaft	Any	Any
Power Potential	③ Will support up to 1000 hp ③	Will support 1500+ hp ③
Application	Street / Strip / Race	Street / Strip / Race
Valves Int./Exh.	1.940 / 1.600	1.940 / 1.600
CFM (base) Int./Exh.	211 / 166 .500" Lift	213 / 178 .500" Lift
CFM (max) Int./Exh.	247/195 @ .550" Lift	270/187 ④ @ .550" Lift 275/200 @ .650" Lift
Chamber CCs ⑥	46	46, 55 ⑤
Runner CCs Int./Exh. Base	156 / 72	163/ 73

The Stage 3 and 4 heads are for serious race engines, although they are capable of street duty, as well. Capable of well over 900 hp, these heads represent the ultimate in cylinder head technology for a Buick big block. Additional four-head bolts can be drilled and tapped in the block for increased compression clamping with these heads. TA Performance offers a drill jig for this purpose (see Chapter 9).

The TA Performance-designed Orange Crush head gaskets use a carbon-graphite core with two steel outer layers that are capable of holding 13:1 compression.

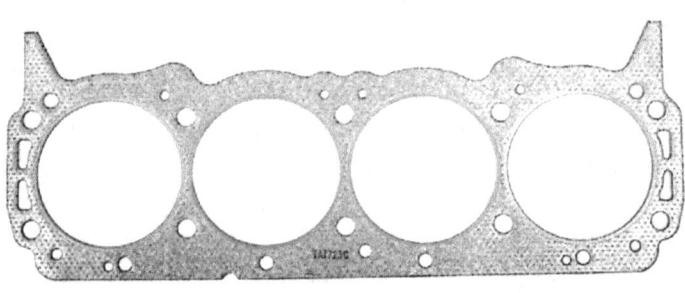

For the V-6 turbo crowd, these TA Stage 1 heads can handle 1,500-plus hp.

Finish off your heads with a set of cast-aluminum valve covers, like these from TA Performance.

valve seats provide superior geometry, roundness, and surface finish. The large 1.900-inch intake and 1.600-inch exhaust valves are moved closer to cylinder bore centerline to unshroud valves for more flow, while the spark plugs are moved closer to cylinder bore centerline for improved combustion. The Champion heads accept stock rocker arms and stock valve covers.

Edelbrock produces Buick 455 Performer RPM heads for the 400,

CYLINDER HEADS

FAST-Class 1972 Buick Gran Sport

Greg Gessler, owner and operator of Gessler Head Porting, is one of the most recognized authorities in Buick head porting. Not only does Gessler know how to port Buick heads, but he races them, too. In the one of the newest forms of drag racing, the FAST, or, Factory Appearing Stock Tire class, Gessler's 1972 Buick GS is at the top of the pile, having run 10.95 seconds at 126 mph in the quarter mile. The class requires its participants to run bias-ply tires and retain the complete stock look. This includes manifolds in place of headers, stock intakes and stock carburetors. What is inside the engine is up to each builder. However, the cam must sound stock. In this situation, superior cylinder-head prep is an absolute must.

Gessler has spent considerable time reworking the 1972 455 cast heads to the point of calling them "maximum effort" work. The heads have been fully ported and polished, and the crossover vents filled with aluminum and smoothed flush. Gessler also used a special welding technique to fill in the low-flow areas of the exhaust ports, greatly increasing low- and mid-range flow. The heads have been fitted with 2.16-inch intake valves with 11/32-inch valve stems while the exhaust valves remain stock at 1.75 inches. These heads flow over 300 cfm, and at 0.300-inch and 0.400-inch lift they really come alive, due to removal of the shrouding inherent to the heads. In order to save a little weight, Gessler removed some unneeded

Greg Gessler's 1972 Buick runs in the FAST-class drag racing series. In this class, cars must appear stock and use only factory available parts. Gessler's buildup and use of stock parts has produced incredible results. The GS runs high-10s in the quarter mile.

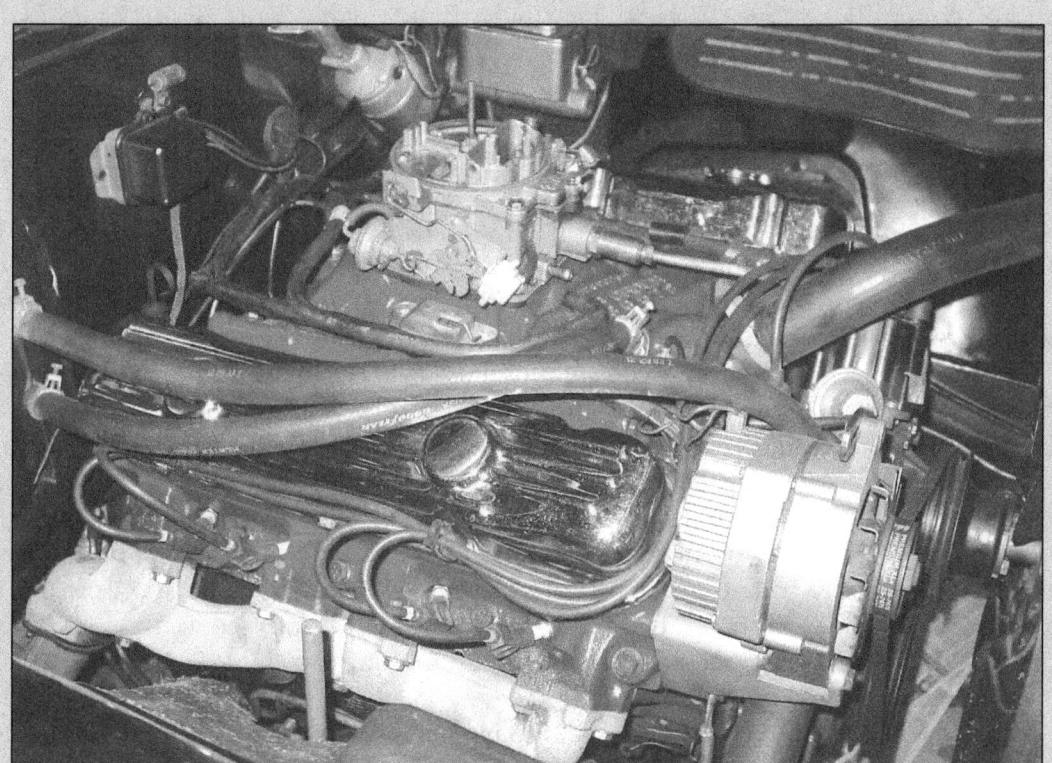

The 1972 455 heads are heavily ported — so much so that Gessler ruined several sets of heads finding a sweet spot for maximum flow, which is over 300 cfm. He went on to use some special welding techniques (which he's kept to himself) to add material in the exhaust port and further increase flow.

FAST-Class 1972 Buick Gran Sport *continued*

iron from a few secret places and lightened the heads.

The TA camshaft is a hydraulic unit with flat-tappet grind, 0.543/0.560 lift, and 234/248 duration at 0.050 inch on a 116-degree separation. To finish off the heads, a set of Comp Cams Magnum lifters with 0.015-inch pre-load were added to actuate the 3/8-inch TA Performance adjustable pushrods. The 1.6 ratio Kenne Bell roller rockers compress and release TA Performance dual valve springs. To support all this flow, the stock intake and exhaust ports were machined to increase flow and eliminate some of the dead-flow areas. The air and fuel is metered with a 1972 vintage 800-cfm Quadrajet, which has received its own dose of tweaks, courtesy of Stage 1 Automotive, Pompton Plains, New Jersey. Naturally, the rest of the engine has been heavily modified to increase power output. The engine is bored 0.038 inch for the Venolia flat-top pistons, moved by a set of Eagle H-beam rods and a stock crank. The crank is stroked from 3.9 to 4.15 inches – equaling 493-ci displacement – by Hansen Racing of Middlesex, New Jersey. The ignition system is comprised of a stock points distributor hooked up to an MSD 6 box running 12 degrees initial and 36 degrees of total timing with no vacuum advance.

Engine Equipment Package:

- 1972 455-ci block, bored 0.038 inch
- Venolia flat-top pistons
- Eagle H-beam rods
- Stock crank stroked from 3.9 to 4.15 inches, equaling 493-ci displacement, performed by Hansen Racing of Middlesex, New Jersey
- Heavily modified 1972 cast-iron 455-ci heads
- TA Performance dual valve springs
- 1.6:1 Kenne Bell roller rockers
- 3/8-inch TA Performance adjustable pushrods
- Comp Cams Magnum lifters
- TA hydraulic cam, 0.543/0.560 inch lift, and 234/248 duration at 0.050 inch on a 116-degree separation
- 1972 vintage 800-cfm Quadrajet, heavily modified by Stage 1 Automotive, Pompton Plains, New Jersey.
- Stock points distributor, 12 degrees initial, 36 degrees of total timing with no vacuum advance.
- MSD 6 box

430, and 455 Buick engines. These A356-T6 aluminum and CNC-machined heads have been dyno tested at 480 hp and 540 ft-lbs of torque from a 0.030-over bore 455 engine with an Edelbrock intake manifold, Crane hydraulic lifter cam, and 1-3/4-inch headers. They are available in bare or fully assembled form with high-quality Stage 1 sized stainless-steel 2.125-inch intake and 1.75-inch exhaust valves. The heads feature 215-cc intake ports and are CNC-gasket-matched for outstanding flow characteristics. The 68-cc combustion chambers produce 9.2:1 compression ratio with stock pistons. A unique feature to these heads is the rocker arms. Unlike every other Buick head on the market, these heads have been designed to use a standard small-block Chevy rocker arm, which adds adjustability and certainly simplifies locating parts, especially if a rocker breaks on a road trip.

TA Performance offers Stage 1, 2, 3, and 4 aluminum 455 heads. This company has long been a benchmark supplier for performance Buick engines, and its Stage-series aluminum heads are no different. Cast from 356-T6 aluminum, these heads offer the most potential of all of the aftermarket heads. Available from stock Stage 1 configuration to full-race 2.25-inch-valve fully ported versions, the TA Performance head adds a level of performance never before seen from out-of-the-box Buick heads. These heads use stock-type rockers and come drilled and tapped with all the OEM accessory holes.

Any of these heads will be at home on your high-performance Buick engine. There are, however, two questions you need to ask before you invest in a set. Are you planning to run a stock hood? If so, then the TA Performance Stage 2 heads are out. Will it be used for street, strip, or both? This is a very important question, because as most of these heads will work great on the street, but the Stage 2 TA heads and the Bulldog race heads require a large cam that might not have good street manners.

While you get better flow out of the box and reduced weight (aluminum Buick 455 heads typically weigh about 60 lbs less than stock), you will pay more for an exotic aluminum head. Typically, each head costs anywhere from $800 to $1,200.

CHAPTER 6

VALVETRAIN

Buick engines are similar to most pushrod-actuated engines. The valvetrain follows the traditional path of a single camshaft, which is timed with the crankshaft using a set of timing gears and a chain. The timing set is front-mounted underneath the timing-chain cover. The original Buick timing gears featured a nylon-coated cam gear that often failed due to breakage. Using aftermarket double-roller timing gears is recommended. All of the Buick engines used hydraulic lifters, which feature less maintenance than solid lifters. The 1968–1969 350, 400, and 430 engines use 3/8-inch ball-tipped pushrods oiled through the rocker-arm shafts. The 1970 and later 350 and 455 engines use 5/16-inch hollow push rods that are oiled via the lifters. All of the Buick engines have non-adjustable, shaft-mounted rocker arms. The 1968–1969 350 and big-block engines have cast aluminum 1.58:1 ratio rocker arms, while the later engines have stamped-steel 1.55:1 ratio rocker arms. The rocker arms open and close the valves.

Rocker Arms

All of the rocker arm shafts and stands are the same for all years of production Nailhead engines. There were several different rocker arms made for the hydraulic lifters. The 1953–1958 rocker arms were 1.5:1 ratio iron arms and are all the same, except for the oiling hole in the rockers that was moved to reduce oil consumption in 1956. Oil was running down the valve guides and into the combustion chamber, causing excessive oil consumption. The 1959 rockers are 1.6:1 ratio and are the last of the production iron rocker arms. The 1960–1966 are aluminum using a 1.6:1 ratio. By using the aluminum 1.6 ratio on all earlier Nailheads, you will be able to get a 10-hp increase. If you run stiff valve springs, the iron

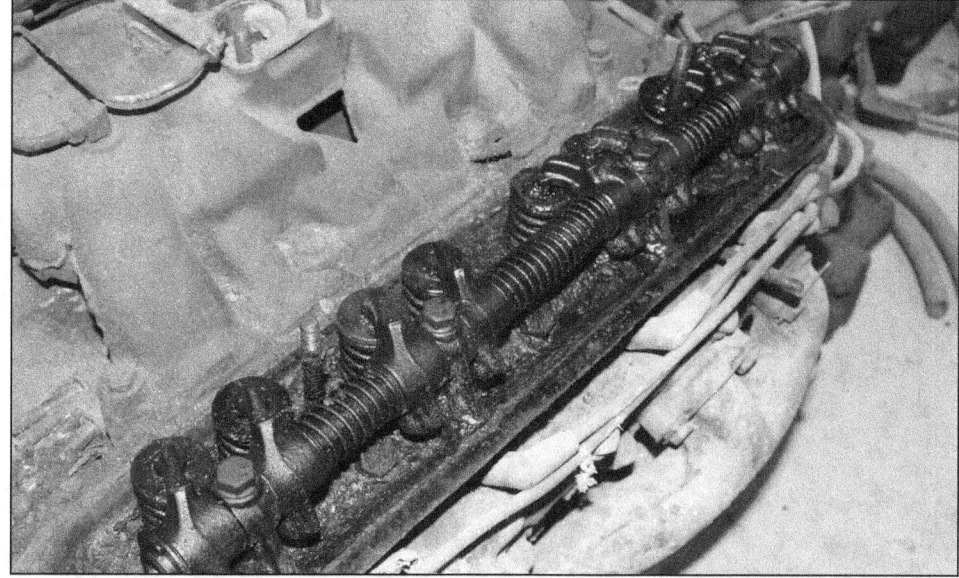

The Nailhead rocker-arm shafts and stand are the same for all years and sizes. Using the stock rocker with .0480 or more lift can result in shorter valveguide life.

ones are the way to go because they are bulletproof. These rockers are much heavier, so only use them if the aluminum rockers can't handle your valve springs. The TA1445STG2 springs, which have a 300-lb rate, are a good choice. The spring rates are as follows:

Stock outer is 43-49 at 1.6, and coil bind occurs at 1.030; 97-105 at 1.16; 110 at 1.1 (0.500 lift)

Inner 23-28 at 1.690 with coil bind at 1.190 (0.500 lift) 73-79 at 1.250; 78-84 at 1.190 (0.500 lift)

Both together 66-77 at 1.6 and 188-194 at 1.190 (0.500 lift)

Nailheadbuick.com offers three springs: the mild springs which are 87-95 at 1.6 and 125-130 at 1.1, and two more with higher pressures at 145/350 and 105/275.

Buick did offer adjustable rockers for racers. Called the Export Kit, these were made in two different versions. For the 1953–1956 engines, the rockers used a 1.5:1 ratio. The 1957–1958 rockers were 1.6:1 ratio. These are very heavy, ultra rare, and expensive rocker arms. If you are really pushing the high-performance envelope, aftermarket rockers are a must. There have been several available throughout the years, and all but one is eBay or swap meet search material. The Gotha rocker arms came in 1.5:1 and 1.7:1 ratios. These rockers were weak, needed a special pushrod, and did not stay adjusted with their interference fit adjuster. They might look cool on a shelf in your shop, but don't put a set on your Nailhead. The Thomas rockers were made of iron and had a 1.6:1 ratio. These are good-quality rockers but are very hard to find. Tom Telesco roller rockers are the last remaining set of aftermarket rockers that are still in production. By bolting on a set of these aluminum adjustable roller rockers, you can easily realize a 20-hp increase. They even feature a variable ratio, depending on pushrod length. Unless you are die-hard on building an old-school Nailhead with old parts, these are the rockers to use, high-performance or otherwise.

Using the stock rocker-arm assemblies for mid-level street engines is acceptable. The original rocker arms are strong but are non-adjustable, making them unsuitable for use with the larger camshafts now available. Most of the larger cams use a smaller base circle, so there will not be enough preload. This is in addition to the strength required by the more aggressive cams, with their faster lift rates and required heavier springs.

Using a set of aftermarket roller rockers on any serious performance engine is recommended. Roller rockers decrease friction in the valvetrain and help produce more horsepower. They are also more accurate because they feature improved geometry and are stronger than the stock pieces, allowing you to run higher-lift cam profiles. Most aftermarket rocker arm assemblies range from 1.6:1 to 1.7:1 ratio, depending on the set, allowing more output from a smaller cam. The aftermarket rocker arms are typically sold as assemblies, which is the best way because they are a perfectly matched set. Most aftermarket roller

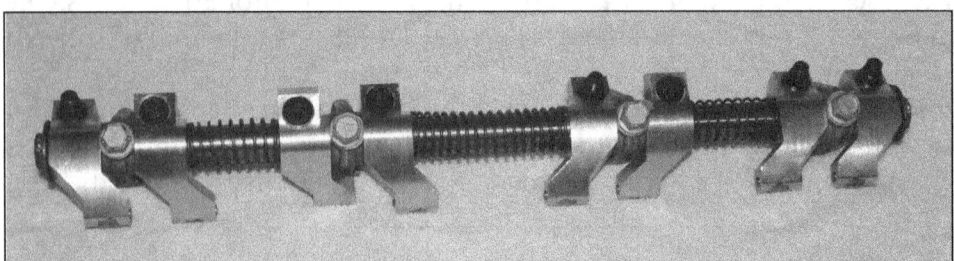

The Thomas Telesco roller rockers are the best bet for any Nailhead. These lightweight rocker kits feature a roller tip and roller-type fulcrums, which reduce a lot of friction.

The Telesco rockers are also adjustable, which is certainly a nice addition for any Buick engine.

VALVETRAIN

The stock 350, big-block, and V-6 turbo rockers are held in place with these little plastic retainers, which break very easily, so take care when working around these parts.

On the Edelbrock big-block heads, small-block Chevy rockers can replace the stock shaft mounted rocker system and open up a world of options.

This TA Performance roller rocker for a big block features the Torrington bearings in the shaft section.

Diagram A

1. Base circle
2. Mid lift
3. Max lift

This diagram shows the path of a roller rocker on the valve stem. It is important to have the rocker properly adjusted, or you will have erratic wear.

rockers are also adjustable, which makes adjusting the valves much easier than using adjustable pushrods.

If you choose to go with the roller rockers, you will need to use two gaskets under the stock valve covers to get the necessary clearance for the rockers. The alternative is to use aftermarket, aluminum, tall valve covers like the units available from TA Performance and Poston Buick. For the 3.8-liter turbo engines, the stock rocker arms are suitable for the street, and on up to 10-second drag cars. The factory rockers are quite strong and work well with a mild camshaft and stock valve springs. Installing a set of roller rockers never hurts because the reduced friction and rocker arm ratio equates to more HP and less heat (always good in a turbo engine). If you have the budget, these are a wise choice, although they are not absolutely necessary. In order to mount the roller rockers, the factory heads must be modified. Also, the stock rocker shaft towers must be ground for rocker arm clearance.

HOW TO BUILD MAX-PERFORMANCE BUICK ENGINES

CHAPTER 6

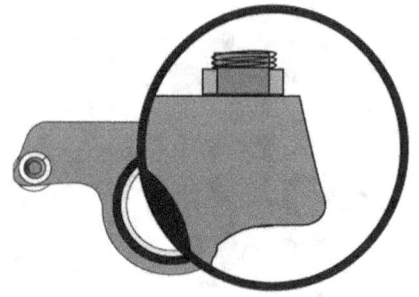

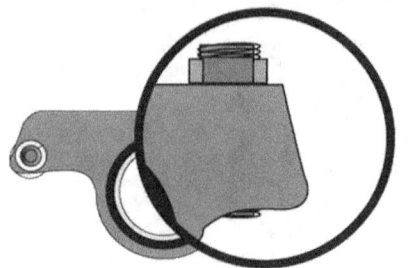

This rocker is being clearanced for large-diameter valve springs.

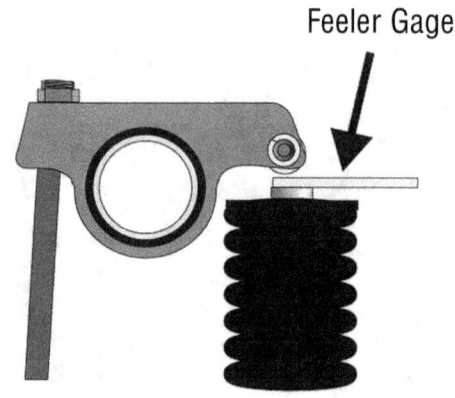

When adjusting roller rockers, slide the feeler gauges under the rocker and above the valve tip as shown.

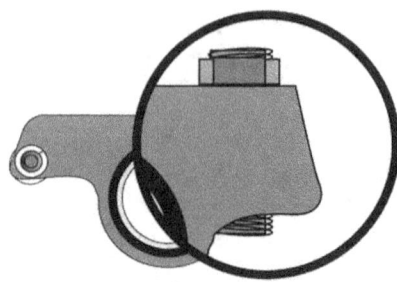

This diagram depicts three rocker arm adjustment levels, and the top two are acceptable. The adjustment shown on the top image is optimal; the adjustment screw is flush with the bottom of the rocker. The adjustment on the middle image is acceptable, but it will slightly affect the pushrod geometry with one thread exposed on the bottom. The adjustment on the bottom image is not acceptable; it will negatively affect the pushrod geometry.

When using roller rockers on the 350 and V-6 turbo engines, you may need to set clearance on the rocker stand for the larger rocker body.

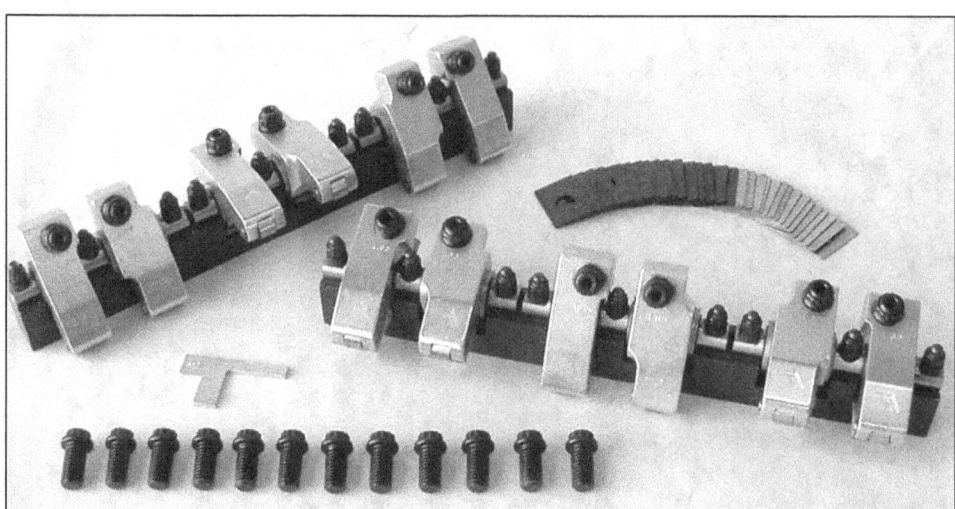

These V-6 turbo roller rockers are really only needed when running extreme performance engines, such as 0.500-inch lift cams, 275-lb or heavier valve springs, or 30-lbs of boost or more.

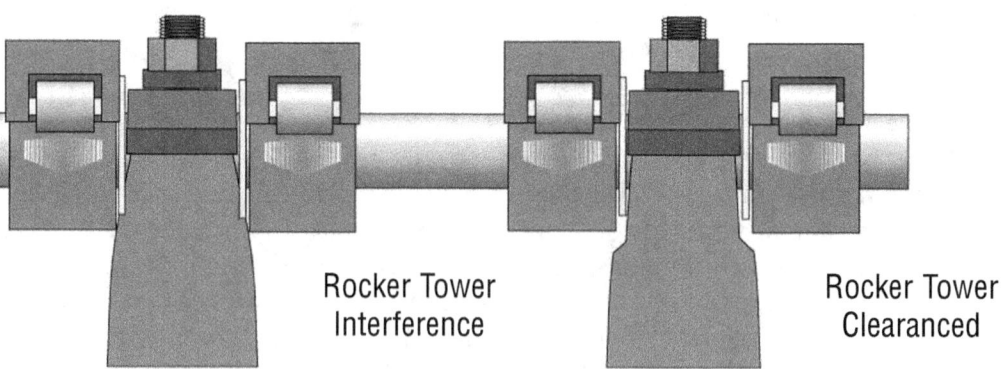

70   HOW TO BUILD MAX-PERFORMANCE BUICK ENGINES

Running large camshafts with more than 0.500-inch valve lift or more than 230 degrees duration at 0.050-inch lift, 30 lbs or more boost, or valve springs larger than 275 lbs pressure require roller rockers. The stock units simply cannot cope with the extreme levels of stress these situations put them under. Always consult the camshaft manufacturer; some cams that don't quite fit these prerequisites may still require roller rockers. Aftermarket cylinder heads should always be used with roller rockers.

Pushrods and Lifters

Since all of the Buick engines utilize non-adjustable, shaft-mounted rocker arms, adjusting the valves is a problem. A simple way to add adjustability to a stock rocker-arm engine is to use adjustable pushrods. These pushrods allow the builder to adjust the preload on the lifters without any other changes. The trick is turning them upside down and adjusting them in the lifter valley where you have lots of room. Because of the tight area at the rockers, they can be a real challenge to adjust the normal way. While you may not be able to adjust them on the fly without removing the intake, once they are set, you shouldn't have to mess with them for a while.

For the Nailhead, there are four different pushrod lengths by model year. These years are 1953–1955, 1956, 1957–1961 364-ci, and 1959–1966 401-and 425-ci engines. For lifters, there were two types, one for the 1953–1955 with the steel cam and one type for the 1956 and later cast-iron cam. The plunger is deeper on the 1953–1955 lifters so longer pushrods are needed.

When building a 264- or 322-ci engine, use the 1956 cam and later lifters with 1956 pushrods. The distributor gear must be changed, too, since the 1953–1955 gear is made for the steel cam, so the 1956–1966 gear must be used. With a little stiffer spring, the stock lifter works up 6,000 rpm, which is more than enough for a Nailhead engine.

Hardened or chrome-moly pushrods must be used if you are running roller rockers. The stock

Adjustable pushrods are an alternative to both custom-length pushrods and adjustable roller rockers. The 400-hp 350 we built uses the adjustable pushrods.

pushrods can flex — not good. For full-on, race-only applications, a 5/16-inch pushrod may be required. Pushrod length can change with several variables, such as how much the head and block is decked, base circle of the camshaft, etc. Any one of these things can throw off the requirements for your pushrod length. Follow the guidelines in the sidebar "Pushrod Geometry" for details on how to do this. It is advisable to use adjustable pushrods on all rebuilds when stock rockers are used.

Camshaft

To understand proper camshaft choice, we must first understand how a camshaft works. In Buick engines, the crankshaft drives the camshaft, which spins at half the speed of the crankshaft. The camshaft has separate lobes for each valve, 16 for V-8s and 12 for V-6s. The bottom or lowest point of each lobe is the base circle. To find the measured base

Buying the right pushrods is important for a properly built engine. Decked blocks and milled heads will affect the final length of the pushrod needed to achieve proper valve adjustment.

CHAPTER 6

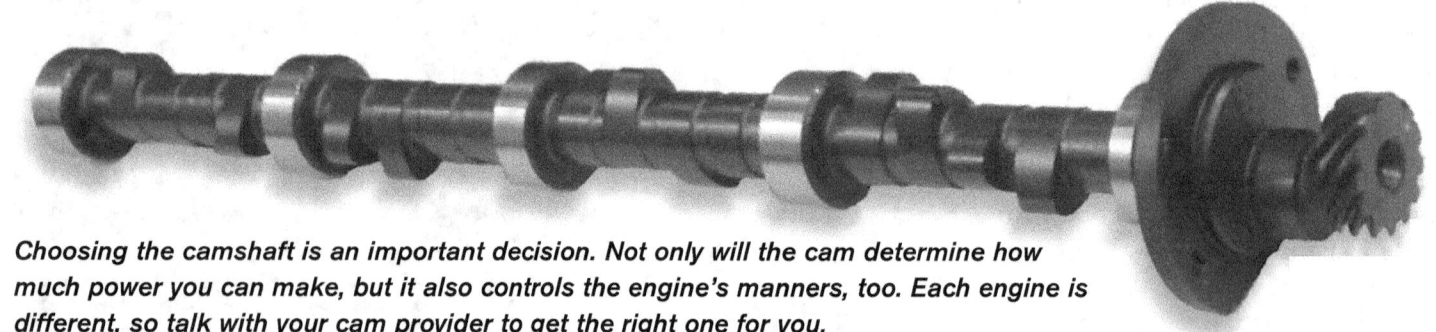

Choosing the camshaft is an important decision. Not only will the cam determine how much power you can make, but it also controls the engine's manners, too. Each engine is different, so talk with your cam provider to get the right one for you.

Always use pre-lube before installing the camshaft. If you don't, a cam lobe can easily be wiped out in the first few minutes of start up.

The V-6 turbo cam thrust plate from TA Performance eliminates cam bumper adjustment. This piece simply bolts in for easily setting the fore and aft cam positioning.

circle, take the radius of the base multiplied by 2. (The manufacturer can provide these specs.) This is where each valve rests closed, in the valve seat. This is also where you would make any valve lash adjustments. Rotating beyond the base circle, the lobes are machined with ramps that actuate the valves via the lifters and pushrods.

Valve lift is the amount that the valve is lifted off its seat. Measured in thousandths of an inch, valve lift is determined by multiplying the lobe lift (the measurement of the actual cam lobe above the base circle) by the rocker-arm ratio. As a result, a simple change of rocker arms, from 1.5:1 to 1.65:1, can increase HP because the valve lift is greater, thereby adding to the flow. Lobe lift is the amount that the cam lobe raises in radius above the cam's base circle. For example, a cam with 0.275-inch lobe lift yields 0.426-inch lift at the valve with a stock 1.55:1 rocker arm. Upgrade to 1.65:1 roller rockers, and the lift increases to 0.453-inch.

The duration of a camshaft is determined by the measured amount of crankshaft degrees that the valve is lifted off the seat. There are two standard notations for duration, advertised and duration at 0.050 inch. The advertised duration is measured when the lifter is raised more than the SAE standard of 0.006 inch off the base circle. The second type, duration at 0.050 inch, is measured when the lifter first rises 0.050 inch off the base circle to the corresponding measurement at the return to the base circle. These two figures offer an excellent guide for comparing camshafts, as two cams with similar lift and advertised duration numbers can have different 0.050-inch duration numbers.

Lobe-separation angle is another important factor to consider when choosing a Buick camshaft. Lobe-separation angle is measured in camshaft degrees, not crankshaft degrees (as in duration). To measure the lobe-separation angle, add the intake and exhaust centerlines, which are measured in crankshaft degrees, and then divide that figure by two. The camshaft spins at half the speed of the crankshaft, and therefore, the formula for this is:

(Int centerline + Exh centerline) / 2 = Total lobe separation in degrees

The centerline for each intake and exhaust lobe on a camshaft is the halfway point of the duration curve.

The intake centerline is notated in crankshaft degrees after top dead center (ATDC), while the exhaust centerline is notated in crankshaft degrees before top dead center (BTDC).

To calculate a camshaft with an intake centerline of 110 ATDC, and an exhaust centerline of 114 BTDC, use this formula:

(110 +114) / 2 = 112 degrees of lobe separation

Most cam manufacturers list the lobe separation in the catalogs along with the intake centerline. The intake centerline is used to notate where the camshaft sits relative to the rotating assembly. Some cam grinders choose to grind timing advance into the cam itself, so advancing or retarding the cam during the installation shifts the engine's torque curve. A cam with a smaller-than-stock base circle can provide more lift. An adjustable valve train is required with small-base-circle cams; be sure you check this spec with the manufacturer before you buy.

There are three different cam blanks for the Nailhead engines. The 1953–1955 steel cam, the 1956 iron cam, and the 1957–1966 iron cam. The 1953–1956 cam-bearing journals are smaller than the others, so no swapping can be done here. The Nailhead cams are fairly hot as far as factory cams go, and they are equal to about a 260/270-duration aftermarket grind. You need 218 duration at 0.050-inch lift or more to make it worth swapping to a bigger cam on the 1957–1966 engines, and about 210 degrees on the smaller 1953–1956 264 and 322 engines.. Lobe spacing has always been a problem because most cam grinders sell Buick cams with narrow lobe spacing. For Nailheads, the lobe separation needs to stay in the 110-114–degree range. For cams where lifts exceed 0.490 inch, a set of roller rockers should be on the build sheet. The stock rockers are very short, leaving guide wear a problem with high-lift camshafts.

If the crank is the heart of an engine, the camshaft is the brains. Therefore, choosing the right cam can make or break your engine. A high-lift, high-duration cam certainly sounds good, but often it is simply too much for the specific engine build. In fact, you can actually lose power by going with a larger cam. The cylinder heads must be able to take advantage of the increased lift in order to make the swap worthwhile. Buick engines are certainly no exception, and they prove the rule. The trick is figuring out what works with your combination. We have already discussed a few of the caveats you need to be aware of with big cams, particularly with roller cams (reinforcing the lifter bores is mandatory). There are many more considerations to be taken into account, as choosing the cam is one of the most important decisions to be made for every engine build.

Although most cam manufacturers have Buick cam grinds available, these profiles are basically Chevy grinds tooled up on a Buick stick. But this is not to say that all of them are lousy cams and won't work for your Buick. However, stick with Buick specialists who will certainly offer proven performance camshafts with specs that will work with just about any level of build. Both TA Performance and Poston Buick offer a full range of grinds from performance to all-out race. These cams are designed specifically for Buick engines, which makes things a little easier. The problem with non-Buick-designed camshafts is that a lot of high-performance camshafts are designed with a base circle different from the original factory cam. By reducing the base circle, the camshaft grinder is able to add more lift to a given cam. If you use a small-base-circle cam, you will need to be able to adjust the rockers or pushrods to set the lifter preload.

Whenever mechanical (commonly known as solid) lifter camshafts, either flat tappet or roller type, are used, the engine will require an adjustable valvetrain. This is required to maintain appropriate valve lash, but it must be checked periodically, leaving stock rocker arms out. In addition, flat tappet solid lifters require the use of high-zinc-content racing oil. The wear inhibitors in race oils provide the lifters with more protection; the higher spring rates and pressures involved with the solid camshafts really need the extra protection. If you use an inadequate oil, the cam will suffer greatly and be wiped out very quickly.

For the big cams — those with 230 degrees or more duration at 0.050-inch lift, vacuum will be significantly less than what is required for

CHAPTER 6

vacuum-operated accessories, such as power brakes and A/C valves. Vacuum canisters, electric boosters, or hydroboost units will be required to keep those accessories running.

Stock Buick heads do not flow well above 0.550-inch lift, so it is recommended to keep the lift under that mark with stock heads. Porting them will certainly increase the flow.

For the turbo set, choosing a camshaft is a little different. Due to the nature of turbochargers, any changes in lift and duration are amplified, showing larger increases in HP and torque than the same camshaft would show in a naturally aspirated engine. There are quite a few cams available for the 3.8-liter V-6 turbo Buick, but you need to be aware that it is quite easy to add too much cam to a turbo engines. There are many V-6 turbo engines that run in the 10s on the stock camshaft, so it's a good idea to be careful and conservative with your cam choice. Let the turbo do the work, and stick with cams that closely resemble the stock profile in all but the most extreme cases.

Lifters

Lifters transfer the rotation of the camshaft to the valves via the pushrods. There are two main types of lifters: hydraulic and mechanical. Within the two types, there are subsets. For mechanical lifters, there are flat tappet and roller lifters. The flat tappet features a flat edge of the lifter that rides along the camshaft. A roller tappet uses a rolling wheel to follow the camshaft. Roller lifters are less noisy, but are more strain on the lifter bores, as previously mentioned. The hydraulic lifter group has a few more subsets: flat tappet, roller, and high-bleed or anti-pump lifters.

For street engines, mechanical lifters are a little extreme because valve lash should be checked once a week. This level of maintenance is fine for race engines or weekend boulevard bruisers. However, stay away from solid lifters if you are building a street engine. If solid lifters are required, a set of roller rockers is needed to get the necessary adjustability.

With hydraulic lifters, the maintenance factor is practically zero. Set them once and they are good for the long haul. But there are some choices to be made. Flat tappet lifters are fine for most engines, but adding roller tips will certainly free up a little extra HP. However, adding roller lifters on a Buick requires strengthening the lifter bores, so keep that in mind. If you are adding a big cam and the engine is to be street driven, there is an option that provides a little cushion in the valvetrain.

Anti-Pump Lifters

Anti-pump lifters, such as the ones used in our 350 build-up from Rhoads, have a high bleed-off rate. At low RPM, they release pressure quickly, keeping them shorter than they would be if they were fully pressurized. This allows the engine to have a smoother idle and more vacuum at low RPMs because the valve lift and duration are reduced by 0.030 inch and 10-15 degrees, respectively. However, when the engine is up to speed — for our 350 this was about 2,000 rpm — the lifter is moving so fast it does not have time to bleed down, letting the cam run at full lift. With anti-pump lifters, you have two cams in one, making an aggressive strip cam more streetable. These types of lifters are available in different bleed rates, depending on your application. We chose the Rhoads lifters from Poston Buick because they have a proven track record and worked well with our high-lift, long-duration camshaft. These types of lifters tend to be noisy though, similar to mechanical lifters, which could be annoying in traffic.

Proper lifter preload is important — make sure you set it correctly. If you are using an adjustable valvetrain, 0.020 to 0.030 inch is perfect. With adjustable pushrods, this is

Roller lifters reduce friction and allow the cam grinder to run steeper ramps on the cam profile. The only caveat with these and Buick engines is that the big-blocks need lifter bore reinforcements before installing a roller cam.

VALVETRAIN

Double-roller timing chains increase reliability. This is a basic timing set for a 350.

This billet-steel double-roller timing set has nine keyways to really tune the valve timing. These sets are the best you can buy for a Buick.

The assembled 455 short block just needs the cam degreed.

A 30-degree mark was placed on the balancer for timing the engine. Once the timing mark is reading 4- or 6- degrees on the indicator at 2,200 rpm, you know you have 34–36 degrees of total timing.

about a 3/4 turn past snug; for roller rockers it is 1/4 to 1/2 turn. There are other methods of adjusting the valvetrain without roller rockers or adjustable pushrods, but they have no place in a high-performance engine build. Buy the right parts and you won't regret it.

Timing Chain

Double-roller timing chains should be used for all Buick engine builds. Timing gear drives are not available for any of the Buick engines.

The Nailheads share the same timing chain for all years,

HOW TO BUILD MAX-PERFORMANCE BUICK ENGINES   75

1953–1956 and 1957–1966, which have different sprockets. The 1953–1956 timing chains also have marked links to set cam timing.

For the 350 and big-blocks, there are three different timing chains available: stock, double-roller, and steel-billet double-roller. The stock is only suitable for stock builds. Double roller will get the job done, however the steel-billet unit has nine keyways, allowing for +/- 8 degrees of camshaft timing — a major benefit when building a high-performance engine. This eliminates most of the problems with degreeing the camshaft. When using a double- roller timing chain on the later V-8s, it may be necessary to clearance the fuel pump arm or run an electric fuel pump.

A factory tensioner is not used on the V-6 turbo with double-roller chain. In addition, all turbo builds should include a roller thrust button. This will reduce the wear on the timing cover and the block. This piece prevents cam walk, similar to the device we added to the timing cover for the V-8s. Only the V-6 turbo has the provision built in.

Retainers, Keepers and Springs

The Nailhead has two types of spring retainers: 1953–1958 type and 1959–1966 type. The later years take taller springs. The 1953–1958 springs were shorter; the 1959–1966 springs work well on the early heads. Adding excessive spring pressure on the Nailhead engines is not recommended, and it's risky because increased spring pressure is very hard on the seats, rockers, pushrods, and cam lobes. The Nailhead engine has lightweight valves and valvetrain in general; the heavy spring pressures are simply not needed.

On the 350 and big blocks, the stock retainers are strong enough for most street applications, depending on your camshaft choice. For more-serious HP engines, upgrading to chrome-moly steel retainers is highly recommended. These top-quality retainers control the lateral slide and twisting movements the valves want to make without chipping, flaking, or breaking (like aluminum retainers).

Using the better retainers typically require using dual-valve springs. The dual-valve springs are better suited to high-performance applications than the stock single springs. When choosing the springs, make sure you follow the suggestions of the camshaft manufacturer, with higher-lift cams requiring more spring pressure. The spring pressures can be adjusted using shims. The Poston dual springs have 110 lbs of pressure at 1.860-inch spring height out of the box, but by adding a 0.06-inch shim, the pressure jumps to 130 lbs at 1.80-inch height. This is enough pressure to handle a cam with as much as 0.650-inch lift. Be careful when purchasing cam kits built by non-Buick-specialist suppliers. These kits can sometimes be sold with Chevy springs, which won't work in a Buick. Stick with a Buick specialist supplier to get the right parts for the job. For drag-race engines it is recommended that you use a slightly stiffer spring, as the springs will be subjected to more strain on a regular basis than a mid-level street engine. Using the dual-valve spring may require the head to be machined to fit the inner valve spring and a smaller diameter seal. The keepers should always be hardened and never stamped. The stamped keepers will break with high-performance use.

The turbo engines should be run with the chrome-moly retainers, as well. The turbo engines can be used with Chevy old-style LT1 valve springs for mid-level street performance. Again, follow the cam manufacturer's recommendations on valve springs, they knows what the camshaft requires. Stock springs and retainers can be used, but if the engine is to see any real strip duty, then upgrading is an absolute must.

Since valve springs lose their tension over time, it is important to keep a minimum spacing between the maximum valve lift and the point where the coils bind. For turbo engines, 0.060 inch is the recommended spacing. This keeps the coils from losing tension due to the heat and being compressed to binding. The farther the spring compresses, the sooner the spring will lose tension. This is very important in a turbo engine because higher spring pressures are needed to overcome the higher cylinder pressures. If a stock spring (which has about 78 lbs of pressure) is used in a high-performance build, as the engine breaks in, the stock springs can lose as much as 10 lbs of pressure. With high-boost levels, the valve can only be opened against lower cylinder pressures. But as the engine revs higher, the valve will actually begin to float on the seats, contact the head, and eventually sink. This potentially catastrophic event reduces HP and performance. Simply stated, the stock springs are not strong enough to be used in a high-performance application.

VALVETRAIN

How to Determine Pushrod Length *by Comp Cams*

A large number of variables are involved in determining the correct length pushrod for your application. Pushrod length is affected by any one or all of the following:

- Block-deck height
- Head-deck height
- Head-stud boss height
- Rocker-arm brand/design
- Cam-base circle size
- Lifter design/brand/pushrod seat height
- Valve-stem length

Don't assume anything in determining the right pushrod for your new engine. A pushrod that fits one engine may not necessarily work in another. Any number of components can be different on your engine, requiring a different pushrod length. Following the steps below will streamline the pushrod selection process, ensuring that you get the right parts the first time.

1. Buy a Checking Pushrod

Do not buy pushrods when you buy the cam, lifters, and the rest of the valve train components. As much as we would like to sell you pushrods at this time, nobody can predict ahead of time what length a given engine needs, unless it is bone stock.

Instead, invest in a checking pushrod at this time. (They are on page 249 of the catalog.) They come in two different designs, and the more expensive of the two is easier to measure once you have it adjusted to the proper length for your valvetrain. Neither is particularly expensive if you consider time lost and freight costs when returning pushrods.

Other companies offer their own versions of pushrod length checking devices – funny little plastic things and such with a sheet of complicated instructions to calculate the length. The main disadvantage with these is that you have to order the pushrods and receive them before you know if your calculations are correct. With a checking pushrod, you can actually rotate the engine over and check the rocker arm/valve tip relationship as you adjust the pushrod length. When you get the correct geometry, it is a simple matter to measure the length and place an order. COMP Cams carries a large number of various length and diameter pushrods in stock. You can have them overnight if you want, and get the correct length the first time.

2. Determine Correct Valvetrain Geometry

What is the correct length pushrod for your application? The one that produces correct valvetrain geometry. What is correct valvetrain geometry? When the rocker arm roller tip rolls from the intake side of the valve tip, across the center of the tip (at approximately mid-lift), to the exhaust side of the valve tip (at full lift) and back. See Diagram A.

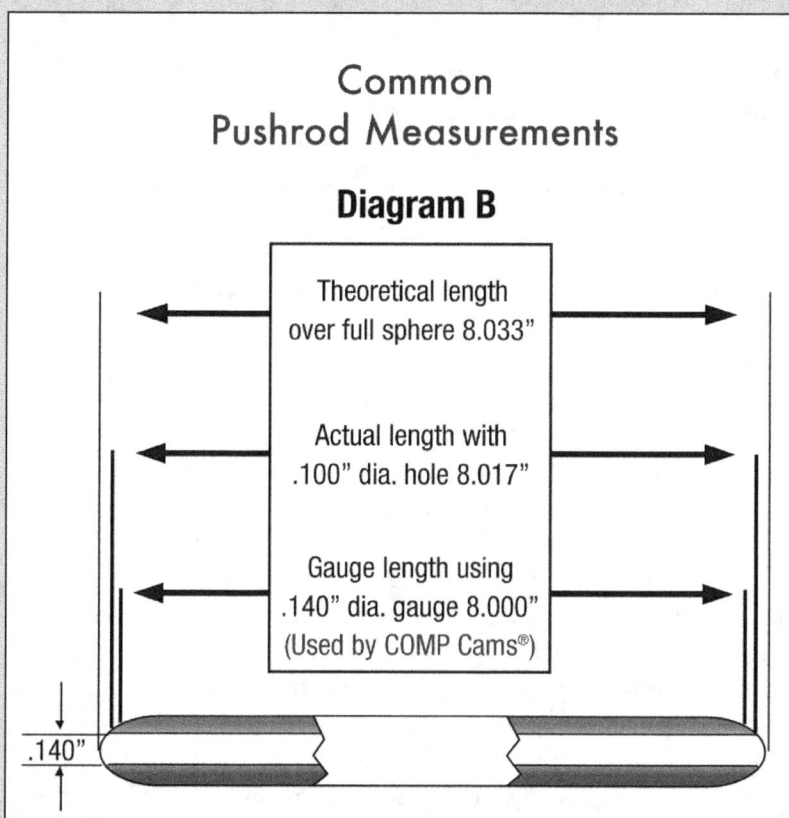

This chart shows the typical measurements used by most manufacturers.

How to Determine Pushrod Length *continued*

3. Measure the Resulting Pushrod

Measuring the length of a pushrod is really rather simple. The most important thing to remember is that different manufacturers measure pushrods differently. Not all pushrods of a stated length will measure exactly the same. The three most common pushrod measurements are shown in Diagram B.

Theoretical Length: This assumes that the pushrod has no oil hole in the end of it. Therefore, the radius at either end is complete, which lengthens the pushrod approximately 0.017 inch in the case of a 5/16-inch pushrod with 0.100-inch diameter oil holes, minimally chamfered.

Actual Length: This is what you would measure if you had a set of calipers large enough to measure over the oil holes at each end of the pushrod. This is the measurement that most people can relate to.

Unfortunately, this measurement is affected not only by the diameter of the oil holes, but also by the entrance chamfer for each oil hole.

Gauge Length: Although the most difficult to measure (it requires a special length-checking gauge), this measurement is the most reliable. This is because the oil holes and their chamfers are eliminated from the measurement. The only problem is that not all companies use the same gauge diameter. COMP Cams uses a 0.140-inch gauge diameter. All of the Magnum and Hi-Tech pushrods listed in this catalog are measured using this technique. See Diagram B.

4. Simple Measurement Techniques

The above was not meant to confuse you needlessly. We know that most people don't have access to the special gauge required for these measurements or even to a dial caliper large enough for most pushrods. We've developed two techniques to help you determine exactly how long the pushrod is – that you so diligently played with until the perfect valvetrain geometry was achieved in your engine.

Pushrod Measurement Techniques

Technique #1: This technique assumes that you have purchased one of our Hi-Tech pushrod length checkers. These are marked with a standard length stamped in them. This number represents the gauge length of the part (0.140-inch gauge diameter) with the two halves screwed completely together. Extending the pushrod one rotation lengthens the gauge 0.050 inch. For example, a pushrod stamped 7.800 screwed apart one rotation would be 7.800 inch + 0.050 inch = 7.850-inch gauge length. Therefore, you would order the part number from the catalog that matches this gauge length, since gauge length is how they are listed.

Technique #2: This technique assumes you have purchased one of our Magnum pushrod length checkers. Once fixed, you don't need to have an expensive gauge or a pair of calipers to measure it. You just need a pushrod of a known length to compare it to (a standard). Then use a pair of common 6-inch calipers to measure the difference between the standard and yours.

Final Tips on Pushrods

It is always a good idea to buy a few spares when purchasing a set of custom length pushrods, and stick them in your toolbox. If one ever fails at the track and you need a replacement, it would be nearly impossible to borrow one from a fellow racer.

Another tip involves cup-end pushrods. Measuring them for length is especially difficult, no matter which technique you choose to use. The size and shape of the cup end varies greatly from manufacturer to manufacturer, so measuring from the ball end to the cup end over the cup surface is a dangerous practice. The best strategy is to drop a 5/16-inch diameter steel ball into the cup end, and do all your measuring over this ball, subtracting the 5/16-inch diameter (0.3125 inch) to figure the length.

VALVETRAIN

How to Degree a Camshaft

In order to ensure proper valve timing, the camshaft must be degreed. There are several ways to do this, but using the intake centerline method is the simplest. You should purchase a camshaft degreeing kit when you purchase your camshaft.

The degree process starts by positioning the center of the number-1 intake lobe with Top Dead Center (TDC) of the number-1 piston. The intake centerline method is not the most exacting method, but requires accuracy to be correct. Place the supplied dial indicator on the number-1 intake spring retainer; this will take into account any deflection that may occur in the pushrod and rocker arm, making the process as accurate as possible.

With the camshaft and timing set installed, align the timing marks on both the camshaft and crank gears, as instructed by the manufacturer. Refer to the cam card for the recommended intake centerline. Then install the rocker arms, lifters, and pushrods. Adjust the valve lash on the number-1 cylinder. For the number-1 intake lobe, adjust the intake lash to zero; do not preload the lifter. After verifying the lash, adjust the number-1 exhaust lash to zero and check that both pushrods roll easily with your fingers.

Mount the supplied wheel pointer (or a solid piece of wire) to the block, then the degree wheel to the crankshaft. Always rotate the crank by hand, bringing the number-1 piston at TDC and verify both the intake and exhaust valves are closed, then set the pointer to zero (or TDC) on the degree wheel. Turn the crankshaft counter clockwise to approximately 15–20 degrees. The piston should be lowered enough to allow the TDC-plug to be installed in the spark plug hole. Thread in the plug until it touches the piston. Rotate the engine the same direction until the piston comes back up and touches the plug. Mark the degree wheel at the number the pointer is on. Spin the crank clockwise until the piston reaches the piston plug. Mark this number from the pointer with the pen. Remove the piston plug and rotate the engine to the center point between the two marked numbers. This is the engine's TDC for the number-1 cylinder. Adjust the degree wheel (not the crankshaft) to read 0 at the pointer.

Mount the dial indicator to the dial indicator mount. Set the tip to contact the retainer of the number-1 intake valve. Make sure that the indicator plunger is parallel to the valve stem. Any difference in the angle will produce errors

Example Installation of 4 degrees advanced is circled on diagram.

Degreeing a camshaft allows the builder to verify the proper valve timing in relation to the crank timing. For the advanced builder, a nine-way cam gear offers timing advance or retard adjustment at the camshaft itself and offers a range of tuning options.

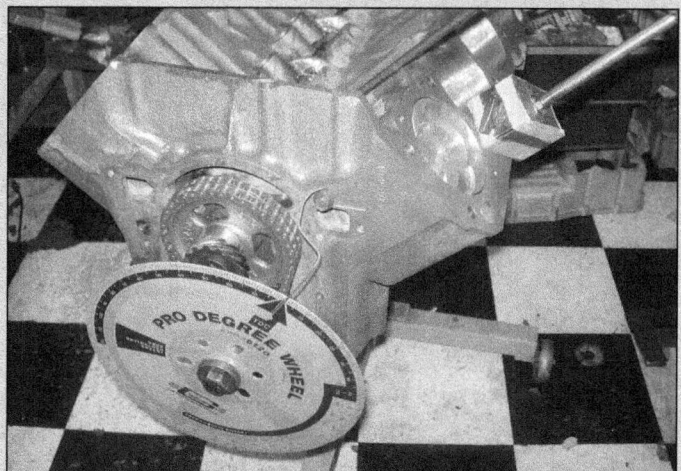

The degree wheel is bolted to the crank, and the engine is rotated until the number 1 piston is at TDC. A piece of wire is used to mark TDC on the wheel.

HOW TO BUILD MAX-PERFORMANCE BUICK ENGINES

CHAPTER 6

How to Degree a Camshaft continued

in the lift measurements. Rotate the engine clockwise until you've reached maximum lift. Maximum lift is notated when the dial indicator changes direction. Reset the dial indicator to zero. Again rotate the engine in the opposite direction until the dial indicator reads 0.100 inch. Then the engine is turned clockwise until the indicator reads 0.050 inch before maximum lift. Mark this number on the degree wheel. Continue to rotate the engine clockwise until the indicator goes past the zero setting to 0.050 inch on the closing side of maximum lift, and then mark this number in the wheel. Add the two 0.050-inch numbers and divide by two. This number is the location of maximum lift of the intake lobe relative to the crank and piston: the intake centerline.

Verify the settings with the cam card. The cam card provides a lot of information, but the numbers you need for the degreeing of the cam are at the bottom of the card. In the box reading "Cam timing at 0.050-inch Tappet Lift" (or rise) are the degree readings that the degree wheel should show for the intake opening side of the

Rotating the crank and measuring the intake valve gives you the 0.050-inch timing. This spec can be checked against the cam card for accuracy.

lobe and the intake closing side of the lobe when the dial indicator is at 0.050 inch of lift. Compare your readings for the intake to those on the card. If the readings are within a degree, the camshaft is installed in the correct position.

If the cam is off, the timing gears have multiple keyways to allow cam-timing adjustment. This is why it is important to buy a nine-keyway timing set; it offers greater adjustment.

Air Ride Buick GSX

Bret Voelkel is an avid Buick enthusiast and president of Air Ride Technologies. Voelkel built this 1970 Buick GSX to showcase the Air Ride Technologies' muscle car products. This is a serious street car, and Voelkel has put over 20,000 miles on the car since finishing it in 2004. The car gets track time at occasional industry track events – like the Year One show and Goodguy's events – competitively racing about six times a year. Voelkel bought this car off of eBay and built it at his home shop. While most people think of air ride as being for rods, customs, and lowriders, Air Ride Technologies has busted that myth with one swift blow.

Engine Package:

- 455-ci V-8 538 hp at 6,000 rpm; 550 ft-lb at 5,400 rpm with 10:1 compression ratio
- TA Performance Stage 1 Street Heads
- TA Performance 2-inch mid-length headers
- TA Performance SPX intake with EFI nozzles
- Big Stuff 3 EFI system
- Lunati rods
- TA Performance TA412 cam, 0.500/0.516-inch lift, 234/244 duration at 0.050 inch
- Petersen belt-driven oil pump

Transmission Package:

- Tremec TKO600 with McLeod shifter, hydraulic clutch, and throwout bearing

Chassis and Suspension Package:

Front
- Air Ride Technologies StrongArm tubular control arms

HOW TO BUILD MAX-PERFORMANCE BUICK ENGINES

Air Ride Buick GSX continued

- Double-adjustable ShockWaves Musclebar swaybar with Posi-Link end links

Rear
- Air Ride Technologies StrongArm tubular control arms
- CoolRide air springs
- Vari-Shock double adjustable shocks
- MuscleBar swaybar

Equipment Package:

- LevelPro compressor system with two compressors, three-gallon tank, auto-leveling computer and ride height sensors

- Rear end: DTS 12 bolt w/ Eaton Tru-Trac and 4:11 gears
- Brakes: Wilwood 14-inch rotor, six-piston caliper front and 12-inch rotor; 4-piston internal park brake caliper in rear
- Wheels: Billet Specialties 18- x 9.5-inch with 6-inch backspacing in rear, 18- x 8-inch with 5.25-inch backspacing in front; custom-painted centers and GSX logo center caps
- BF Goodrich KDW tires, 275/40-18 in rear; 245/40-18 in front

The 455 was built to exacting specifications using TA Perfromance Stage 1 heads, headers, intake, and cam. The Big Stuff retrofit EFI system produces 538 hp and 550 ft-lbs of bone crushing torque.

Not all Buicks are hot rods or drag cars. Brett Voelkel, president of Air Ride Technologies, puts his 1970 GSX through its paces to demonstrate the performance of his company's products. A stock-suspension system would flex hard and have more body roll than the GS shows in this hard corner.

CHAPTER 7

IGNITION AND FUEL SYSTEMS

A proper ignition and fuel system is critical for any engine to run properly. While a couple of components are Buick-specific, the majority of ignition and fuel system components are non-Buick, opening up the vast aftermarket to Buick engine builders. However, there are engine-specific parts, mostly the distributor and mechanical fuel pumps. The front-mounted distributor is one of the most exclusive aspects of the later-model (1968 and later) Buick engines. Most GM engines use rear-mounted distributor units, while the Buick put it in front, and it's direct-driven off the camshaft. The 400/430/455, 350, and 3.8-liter V-6 turbo engines share the same basic distributor; the only difference is the drive gear, which is replaceable. This is a real benefit for the 350 because the extensive aftermarket support and popularity of the 455 and 3.8-liter V-6 turbo makes for better ignition components availability for the 350. Whether you choose stock points, HEI, modified stock or aftermarket components, it is key that the ignition system matches or exceeds the output capability of the engine. You wouldn't want to run stock points on a 500-hp 455, but spending $600 on a high-performance digital distributor for a stock rebuilt 350 is overkill. The same goes for the fuel system; a stock mechanical fuel pump is not good for much past the stock output, but a 220-gallon-per-hour electric fuel pump may actually cause problems if your engine is stock or mildly built.

Distributors

The Nailhead engines use a rear-mounted distributor that runs off of a gear on the camshaft. The 1967 and later Buick engines have the distributor mounted in the front of the engine. The distributor is driven via a non-replaceable machined gear on the front of the camshaft. The 1978–1983 turbo engines ran with a distributor-based ignition, while the 1984–1987 3.8-liter turbo engines feature distributorless ignition. The ignition is controlled via the ECM unit located in the passenger-side kick panel inside the cars.

All Nailhead distributors interchange, but the 1953–1955 units need the distributor gear for the steel cam if the steel cam is used. The 1956–1966 gear is made for the iron camshaft. They have different advance curves in different years. The 1953–1956 had the early type without external point adjustment, and the 1957–1966 had an external point adjustment through a window in the cap. When running points, buy the best available: BorgWarner, Delco, etc. The cheaper points float at very low RPM. The high-rev points are too stiff, and they need to rev to 6,000 rpm; the ones that go to 7,000 or 8,000 rpm wear out shaft bushings and breaker plates in short order.

There were several aftermarket distributors made, but most are not any better than the stock iron unit. Mallory was the first with the old-dual-point waterproof cap. Later on, it made electronic units. The Spalding/Grant Flame Thrower, DuCoil, and Roto-Faze were all dual-point/dual-coil distributors and are scarce at best. If you find one for a Chevy, it can be adapted to the Nailhead because they both have a clockwise rotation. This stuff is for the retro hot rodder; so don't expect big power increase, just cool-points.

IGNITION AND FUEL SYSTEMS

For the high-performance Nailhead engine, MSD offers a Pro-Billet unit that is a drop-in for the Nailhead. This fully electronic distributor requires only three wires to hook up and is a stand-alone unit, so it does not need a separate timing box, although it can be used with one for more versatility. The MSD distributor has a mechanical advance that can be tuned with additional weights, which are supplied with the unit. The distributor also has a vacuum advance canister for fuel economy. This unit is an excellent choice for the early muscle cars, in which a little extra power is needed.

If you are building a retro dragster, a magneto would certainly look the part. Joe Hunt and Vertex have made magnetos for Nailheads for years, and there is also a look-a-like magneto/distributor. Pounden, another magneto builder, made a few units for the Nailhead. Running a magneto on the street is not recommended because it requires special tools and knowledge that is just not worth the limited benefit. In addition, magnetos require narrow plug gaps and cannot be tuned with vacuum advance. This might not affect power, but it certainly helps fuel economy and promotes longer plug life. But for a nostalgia dragster, a magneto would be right at home.

There are two types of distributors for the 1968 and later Buick 350 and big-block engines: points and HEI. The early engines all had points distributors, which, when set up properly, are reliable and suitable for mild-performance engines. The HEI units, available in 1974 as an option and standard in 1975 (available for 3 years for the 455, for 6 years for the 350), are better than points units because they are more reliable and maintenance free.

The stock HEI units lack the ability to control spark above 4,500 rpm, and lose performance above 5,500 rpm. This would not work for a serious performance engine, but there are fixes for those problems. Recurving the HEI distributor and upgrading to a high-performance ignition module under the cap will provide more than enough spark to supply the engine to the higher RPM range. As a side note: if you are running a GS and want to use the ram-air air cleaner, the HEI will not fit. The cap is too wide and too tall; you must use a points-style cap.

Finding a Buick HEI distributor can be tough because most of the cars with these distributors went to the crusher a long time ago. Upgrading a stock points distributor is a more common upgrade and will surpass the HEI's abilities. The most common upgrade is adding a Pertronix Ignitor or Ignitor II to the

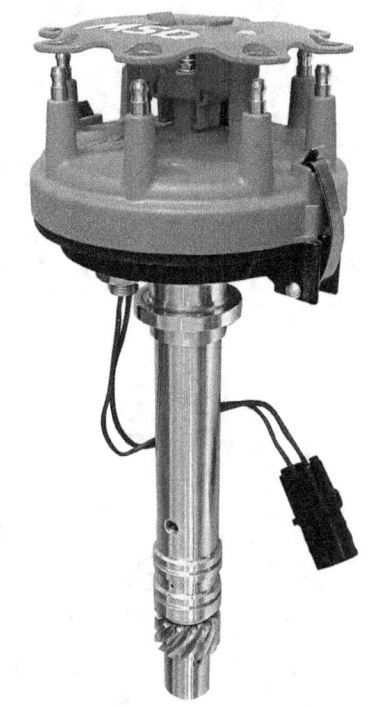

MSD has a few Buick distributors of its own. This low-profile model is an excellent choice for running the ram-air air cleaner on a Buick Gran Sport (GS); an HEI and some taller units will not clear the ram-air air cleaner unit.

This Mallory Nailhead distributor fits all of the 1953–1966 Nailheads. Swapping gears is the only modification that can be made, which depends on the year of the engine and the cam material.

For racers and nostalgia hot rodders, the magneto is always a unique option. These distributors are very difficult to set up properly and do not offer the best fuel economy.

CHAPTER 7

The stock points system works well enough for a basic street engine, but serious performance engines are better off with something else.

GM began offering the HEI distributor in 1974, and it is a good choice for a budget-oriented performance engine. In order to make one of these units work for high-powered applications, the module should be replaced with a high-performance unit that produces spark above 5,500 rpm.

For the 350 and big block, Mallory offers the Comp 9000 series distributor in both stand-alone and ignition box-controlled models. These units are substantially better than the stock points units.

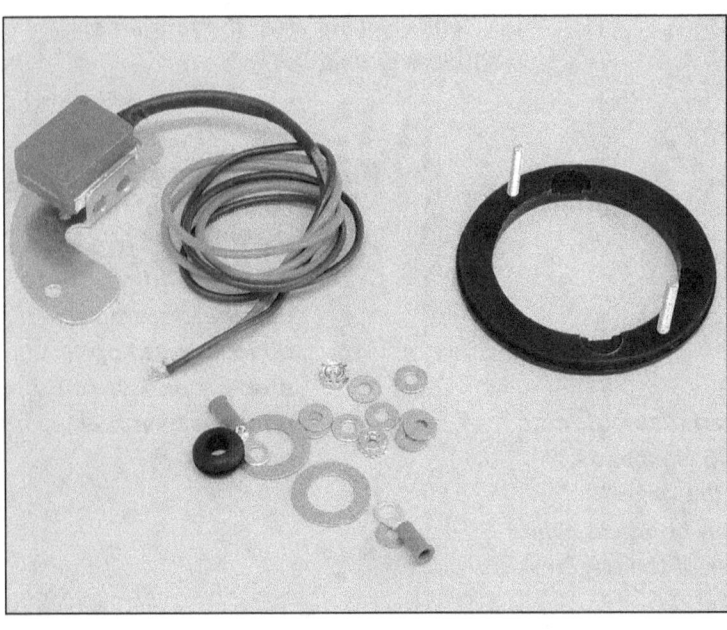

The Pertronix Ignitor II unit converts the points unit to a breakerless distributor with just a few hand tools. This is the complete kit here. We ran the original Ignitor version in our 350 for over 7 years without an issue and never had to worry about points.

stock points unit. The process is simple and can be done in a couple of hours. The Ignitor unit replaces the points and condenser under the cap so the distributor looks stock, but it is actually a high-performance unit inside. Crane also offers a retrofit unit, the XR-1, which features a built-in rev limiter — nice to have.

Aftermarket distributors are available from almost every major ignition supplier. For the 400-hp 350 built for this book, a Mallory Comp9000 electronic distributor was used. These do not require external control boxes, although they can be used with one.

The big-block distributor will interchange on the 350 with a simple gear swap. Therefore, most aftermarket ignition manufacturers make a big-block distributor unit that will

IGNITION AND FUEL SYSTEMS

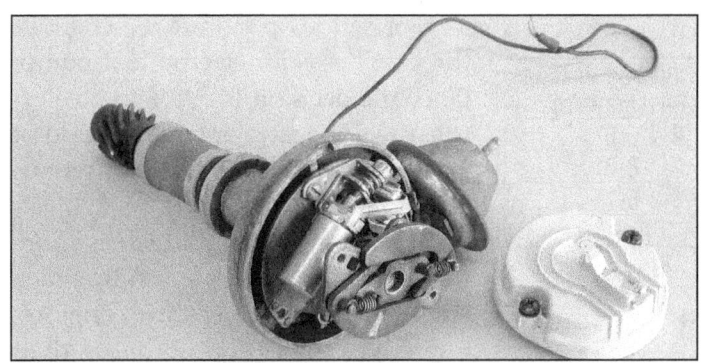

Any 350 distributor can be swapped into a big-block or vice versa with a simple gear change.

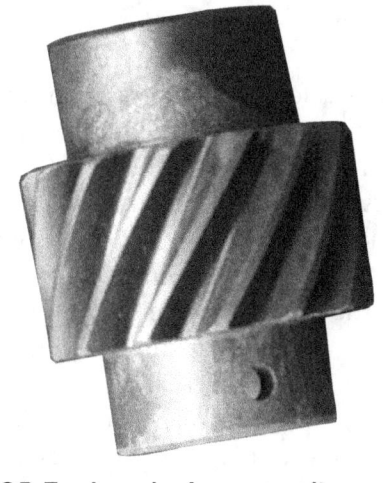

BOP Engineering's composite distributor gear is another option. The composite gear performs like the bronze gear, but it does not wear out. It lasts the life of the engine, and it does not leave metal shavings in the oil.

Cam timing is important. Since the timing tab is cast into the timing cover, painting the cover and then painting the timing marks on the indicator is a good idea.

fit the 350. BOP Engineering offers a composite distributor gear, which is a safe alternative to the bronze gear.

V-6 Turbo

The stock ignition system on the 1984–1987 turbo engines is suitable for engines running low 8-second quarter-mile ETs. The key is modifying the Eprom in the ECM, which is located behind the passenger-side kick panel. This upgrade is probably the most common modification to a turbo Regal or Grand National you will find. There are thousands of different tunes you can purchase, and you can have a custom tune made specifically for your car. Every chipset is different and has its own requirements, so be sure to check those out before buying a chip.

For a street-driven Buick turbo, it's important to have the ability to change the state of tune from mild street to full race. Systems such as the UltraChip, from Poston Buick, are the ticket. These plug-in units have multiple, progressive ignition curves built in, allowing you to go from economy to stock, on up to full race literally at the flip of a switch. For about the price of two chips, you can have seven ready-to-go tunes.

For 1983 and older cars, the best bet for any performance build is to rebuild the stock HEI distributor, upgraded with a performance ignition module and a high-voltage cap. It is recommended that these cars get an aftermarket control box to increase the efficiency of the stock ignition system. A performance-upgraded HEI distributor is capable of supplying the hot-air turbo engines with the spark they need.

Electronic Timing Boxes

For serious performance engines, an electronic ignition control box is the way to go. These aftermarket boxes allow your engine to fully combust the fuel mixture in the cylinder, yielding more power and better fuel economy. If you upgrade to an electronic box, make sure you buy a unit with a rev limiter. For a high-performance Buick engine, over-revving can be disastrous. Keeping the Buick under 6,000 rpm is advisable for anything less than an extreme-performance race engine. An aftermarket

Electronic timing boxes, such as this Mallory unit, give more control over spark and increase fuel economy.

CHAPTER 7

Firing Orders

Engine Size	Firing order	Bank Numbering LH (Driver's)	Bank Numbering RH (Passenger's)
400-430-455	1-8-4-3-6-5-7-2	1-3-5-7	2-4-6-8
300-340-350	1-8-4-3-6-5-7-2	1-3-5-7	2-4-6-8
401-425	1-2-7-8-4-5-6-3	2-4-6-8	1-3-5-7
198-255 V6	1-6-5-4-3-2	1-3-5	2-4-6
231-252 V6	1-6-5-4-3-2	1-3-5	2-4-6

This chart shows the correct firing order for all the Buick engines.

This MSD 6AL ignition box features a plug-style rev limiter. This important function prevents Buick engines from revving over 6,000 rpm and suffering catastrophic failure.

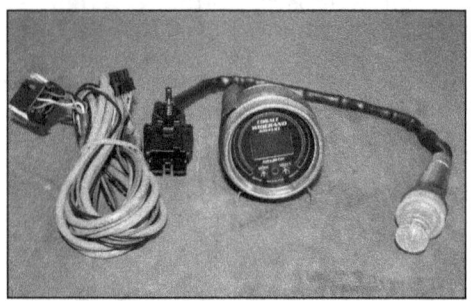

A very useful tool in engine tuning is this wideband O^2-sensor gauge from AutoMeter. Although it's not absolutely necessary, it certainly is easier to measure the O^2 levels in the exhaust, so you see the results of your tuning right away. A wideband sensor monitors the air/fuel ratio from idle to wide open throttle (WOT). A narrow band sensor (found in most computer-controlled vehicles starting in the early 1980s) only measures at idle and checks for an air/fuel mix of 14.7, which is ideal for street engines. The wideband feature gained widespread factory use in the 1990s.

ignition box is also a must if you are using any significant amount of nitrous. Anything over a 150-hp shot of go-juice will require the timing to be retarded slightly.

Fuel Systems

Getting fuel into the engine is always a primary concern. For the average street-performance engine, a mechanical fuel pump will do the job. A stock fuel pump is capable of feeding a 350-hp engine, but pushing beyond that will require a high-performance unit. There are a few aftermarket mechanical fuel pumps available for all of the Buick engines. TA Performance offers several pumps for all the engine families, while Carter also makes a Buick 455 pump. The TA Stage 1 pump for the 455 supports about 450 hp, while the street/strip mechanical pumps will feed up to 500 hp.

Mechanical fuel pumps are reliable, cost efficient, and work on demand from the engine. This TA Performance unit supports up to 500 hp.

For serious performance engines, the best bet is an electric fuel pump. Once the decision is made to go electric, the floodgates open to a world of options. Barry Grant makes a serious electric fuel pump that flows 220 gallons per hour (GPH), which is more than enough to feed a 1,000-hp Buick engine. For most street/strip engines, a rate of 110–130 gph is more than enough. The internal regulator is easy to set up and use, as the pressure is regulated inside the pump at a predetermined level — typically around 6–8 psi. This level is suitable for street driven applications, while 12–14 psi is necessary for high-horsepower strip engines. This is the most commonly used style for street engines. If you need the ability to tune the fuel pressure, an external regulator is ideal. Engines with power adders such as nitrous, superchargers, or turbos require more fuel pressure to ensure they do not run lean, which would destroy the engine in short order. Electric fuel pumps are not only more efficient; they also remove the mechanical connection to the engine,

Barry Grant makes this 220-gph (gallon-per-hour) electric fuel pump. It comes with an adjustable regulator and has enough capacity to feed a 1,000-hp engine. This unit is described as a street model, but it is probably too aggressive for the street.

IGNITION AND FUEL SYSTEMS

Proper fuel filtration is also an important component of any efficient fuel system. This canister-style unit from Barry Grant can support just about any level of performance.

which reduces friction and will increase horsepower. Although it's not a huge increase, it's an increase nonetheless. Therefore, all Buick engines can benefit from an electric fuel pump.

Engine Cooling

Keeping a high-performance engine cool requires a clean and efficient cooling system. The radiator is just one part of that system; the water pump and fan also play important roles in maintaining engine temperature. The stock radiator is typically sufficient for most street applications if you are running the same size engine: a 350 radiator for a 350, a 455 radiator on a 455, etc. If you are swapping the engine or building a custom, then the radiator must be of sufficient size for the engine. Using an aluminum radiator over a copper radiator has long been a staple for high-performance engines, though a copper radiator is not all bad. The stock copper radiators actually conduct heat better than aluminum. The difference is that aluminum allows the radiator to be fit with more cores and rows than a traditional copper radiator, which increases the cooling factor.

There are quite a few options for aluminum radiators; all you need to do is pick any speed-parts catalog and you will find hundreds of radiators. Model-specific units fit right into a Buick GS or Riviera, and universal radiators will fit a non-traditional or custom ride. Some builders recommend only using a custom-fit radiator, such as the TA Performance aluminum models. These units are excellent and certainly offer a simple installation. The universal-style units from companies, such as Griffin are excellent, too, and cost about half as much. As long as you measure correctly and don't mind modifying a couple mounts, you can have a great-looking and performing aluminum radiator.

The water pump is the other major key to the cooling system. While replacement-style pumps are readily available from the parts store, these pumps are not suitable for serious performance engines. Any engine pushing out 500 hp or more needs a high-performance water pump. TA Performance offers a couple of different options for the Buick engines. The first pump is a newly built unit that uses bearings instead of bushings. This reduces friction and increases the efficiency of the pump. TA will soon be introducing a new high-performance pump that will increase both the flow and pressure of the coolant system, allowing you to control the engine's operating temp.

When replacing your water pump, it is important to match the pump with the engine. The year and model of vehicle (the original vehicle for the engine) determines the style of water pump needed for your engine. The older 1968–1970 350 (through 1971 for the Jeep) used the short water pump body. The 1971–1972 350 Skylarks and LeSabres used a medium length pump body, while the 1973–1987 V-6 turbo and 350 use the long body pump. The big blocks, the 1967–1970 full-size cars, 1967–1972 A-body, and 1971–1976 full-size cars (without A/C), ran the short body pump. The 1971–1976 full-size cars and the 1973–1974 455 A-bodied cars ran the long body pump. The 364 and

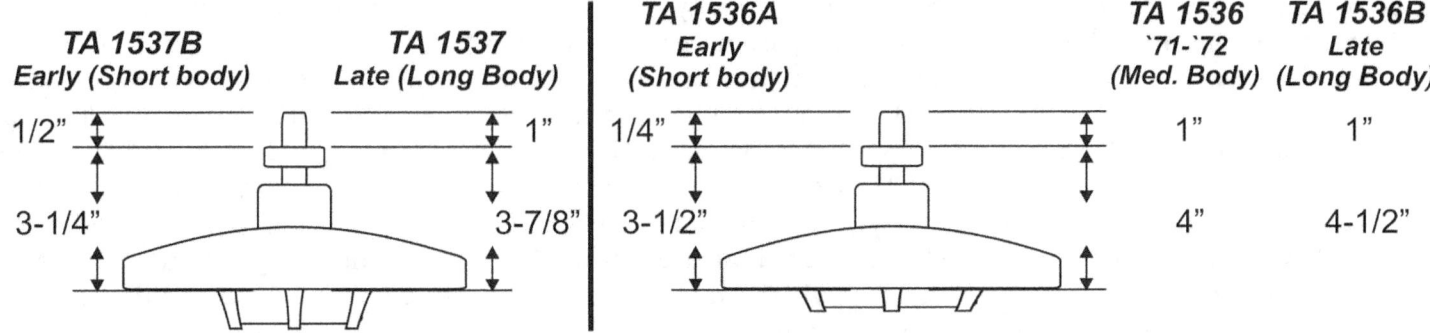

There are five different water-pump bodies for 1968 and later Buick engines. The big-block has two, while the 350 and V-6 turbo share three styles.

CHAPTER 7

Using an electric water pump on the street can be a little scary. As long as you have a heavy-duty unit like this one from TA Performance, or Meziere, combined with quality gauges and components, there should not be any issues.

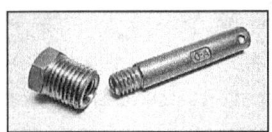

When aluminum components are used in the cooling system, install one of these anodes to the cooling tanks on the radiator. With an unprotected system, the electrolysis process leaches electrons right out of the aluminum, causing pits and eventually leaks. The anode releases its electrons to save the rest of the system.

Electric fans reduce strain on the engine and free up as much as 15 hp. They are also required if an electric water pump is used. Buy, or fabricate, a fan with a full shroud to cover the radiator. This will make the fan efficient as possible.

401 Nailheads from 1959–1961 cars without A/C have a specific pump, while the later 1962–1966 401 and 425 use another. When performing a big-block engine swap into a 1964–1972 A-body or 1978–1987 G-body, the short body pump works best. If you are using a 1971–1976 full-size donor engine with a long pump, the water pump pulley must be swapped to an early 1967–1970 full-size or 1967–1972 GS400 or 455 short nose pump pulley. These are available online used and new in billet aluminum from March Performance and TA Performance.

Then there is the electric water pump. There are a lot of differences of opinion when it comes to electric water pumps. If you are building your engine for a daily driver, an electric pump is probably not a good idea because they simply do not last long enough to justify the small increase in horsepower. High-quality units, such as the Meziere heavy-duty street pump (available for big blocks, 350, and V-6 Buicks), have a 2,500-plus-hour life expectancy. If you drive your car two hours a day, every day, then you can expect the pump to last about 3-1/2 years, while a belt driven unit should easily last 10–15 years under the same duty. If you are building a weekend cruiser, a heavy-duty electric pump will do fine on the street; just make sure you install a precision water temp gauge. For a track application, however, an electric pump is commonly used. Keep in mind that an electric water pump needs current to operate. If your alternator or battery goes down, the electric water pump (6–7 amps) will probably stop pumping before the ignition system quits, letting the engine overheat. Switching to an electric pump requires the switch to electric fans because the belt-driven fan runs off the water pump-pulley.

The last major player in the cooling system is the fan. A belt-driven clutch-style fan will keep the air flowing through the radiator. This style should keep a mid-performance street engine cool, although they are not perfect. Engine-driven fans rob the engine of HP, sometimes as much as much as 15–20 hp. Keeping a belt-driven fan on a street engine requires a couple of things: a functioning hydraulic clutch unit, and a fan shroud. If you are doing an engine swap and leave off the radiator fan shroud, the fan is not really doing anything except whipping the air around it. The fan needs the shroud to focus its air draw through the radiator. The clutch is important because it allows the fan to spin slower than the engine at start up, letting the engine come to operating temperature faster than if the fan was running at full tilt.

Switching to electric fans is an option for engine swaps, custom builds, and just about any other application that can benefit from the switch. There are those who feel that electric fans are not as efficient as belt-driven fans, and that is true to an extent. If the electric fans are not installed correctly — with an electric fan shroud — then the fans will not be able to draw air through the entire radiator. As long as they are correctly installed, then there really is no issue. The added benefits of an electric fan system can actually add efficiency to the engine. The electric fan can operate even when the engine is off, cooling the coolant in the radiator. This helps keep the engine in its optimum temperature range when on cruise nights, or just during general driving and parking for short terms. In addition, the electric fan does not run directly off the engine, freeing up HP that was eaten up by the mechanically driven fan. When shopping for an electric fan, make sure you purchase one designed for high-performance engines and one that has a fan shroud, to maximize efficiency.

CHAPTER 8

INTAKE, CARBS AND EXHAUST

Many engine builders tend to choose induction-system components that are excessive. Installing a carburetor that is larger than the engine needs is one of the most common issues. The engine will then stumble on the line or sputter at part throttle. Most importantly, performance suffers dramatically and fuel economy takes a dive. This has long been a problem for most GM engines, particularly the small-block Chevy.

Buick engines are a little different, and thankfully so. Buick ports feature a tall, skinny profile that is relatively small in volume, but develop a high port velocity. This means that the engine can take in a lot of air and fuel quickly, which pushes the low-rpm power through the roof. This is why Buick engines are known as torque monsters, and they tend to have much higher torque numbers than their corresponding-sized and horsepower-rated competing engines.

Buick engines take a much bigger carb than most people would say is necessary. If you were to follow the advice of a Chevy builder, you would end up with a 600-cfm carb on a 350 and maybe an 850 cfm on a 455. However, a 350 Buick saddled with a 600-cfm Holley will be starved for air, and top-end performance will suffer. For the Buick 350 built for this book, a Barry Grant Speed Demon 850-cfm double-pumper was the carburetor of choice. While this would be excessive for most other 350 engines, the heavily worked Buick 350 can take all it has to offer. For the 455, an 850-cfm double-pumper is enough for a street engine, but when stepping into the realm of serious drag racing, more is needed. A 1,000-cfm range is not unheard of for these high-horsepower engines.

Carburetors

Nailhead

For the Nailhead engines, the carter AFB is an excellent choice for a stock-bodied Buick. Rivierice and some GS models 1959–1966 401 and 425 engine intakes swap across each other. The 1966 intake works with the Quadrajet, and the AFB/4-Jet Rochester intake accepts the newer Edelbrock carbs; however, the stock steel shim gasket must be used or the exhaust

This Kring brand 1x8 intake for Nailheads uses Weber 48 IDA-based carburetors or throttle bodies. Find this new and unique-looking intake at milrproducts.com.

warm-up holes (these two holes come up from the exhaust and help warm up the carb in cold weather) must be plugged just below the intake carburetor base flange with 1/4-inch pipe plugs or 7/16- to 1/2-inch set screws after tapping. If you live in a warm climate, these holes can be tapped and plugged, which is the best way to go, but if you plan on any cold-weather driving, this mod is not recommended. If you are planning on using a Dynaflow transmission or the stock 1964–1966 kick-down switches, you are going to have to adapt different linkage to the new carburetor to get proper transmission performance.

CHAPTER 8

The Demon 98, a unique two-barrel carb from Barry Grant, offers modern carburetor technology with a vintage look. Builders usually install it in singles or triples. This setup works well on a classic Nailhead 2x3 intake.

Since the Buicks like big carbs, a 500 cfm on the 322 using an adapter is adequate. For the larger engines, a 600–750 cfm on a 364 is good, while the 401 and 425 engines like 750–850 cfm. For the hot rodders, which is where most of the Nailheads live, multiple carbs are commonplace. Whether you have dual-quads or a three two-barrel set up, getting the right CFM is important. While the Buicks like more air, stuffing a 322 with 1,500 cfm is going to be too much air.

When dual four-barrels are the desired carburetion, the small WCFB Carters are perfect on the 322. While the Carter WCFB is no longer manufactured, these can be found at swap meets, junkyards, or on eBay. These 400-cfm carbs work very well when rebuilt and were put on practically everything in the 1950s. Holley carburetors are too long for the dual-quad intakes, so keep that in mind. The 364 should get a set of 500-cfm carbs.

Mechanical secondaries or double-pumpers for multi-carbed street engines dump too much fuel in the system and just are not needed when running multiples. The 401 requires dual 600-cfm carbs, while the 425 needs a pair of 650–750-cfm units. For those who like the look of a three two-barrels, there are several old-school carbs to choose from, plus a new unit from Barry Grant. The typical carb of choice for a triple-deuce setup is either the Holley 94 or the Stromberg 97. Finding these old carbs is becoming increasingly difficult and expensive. Barry Grant offers their Demon 98, a 205-cfm carburetor, in either primary form with choke and idle-mixture adjustment or secondary form as a basic carb without a choke or idle-mix adjustment. They are designed to bolt together in groups of three. What makes this carb perfect for a performance Nailhead engine is its modern design with retro look. If you simply must have the traditional hassle of old carbs, by all means buy a few old carbs and rebuild them, but you can eliminate a lot of hassle by purchasing a new one.

Small-Block 350 and Big Blocks

As stated earlier, these V-8s like a lot of carburetion, too. The stock 650- and 750-cfm Quadrajets are adequate for mild-performance builds; later-model Quadrajets or aftermarket carbs are needed for true high-performance engines. GM made millions of Quadrajet carbs. To be sure, checking the codes is

For our 350 build, we chose a Mighty Demon 850 double-pumper. The Buick engines can take more carburetion than similarly sized counterparts. This carb is sold without a choke, so you have to purchase the choke parts separately for street use.

This specialized Holley carb is the ticket for supercharged engines. The trick is a modification of the internal power valve.

INTAKE, CARBS AND EXHAUST

Instead of a standard power valve, the carb uses this vacuum line to draw air from the manifold. Since supercharged engines operate under boost, a standard power valve reads boost levels, not vacuum, which does not affect the engine load.

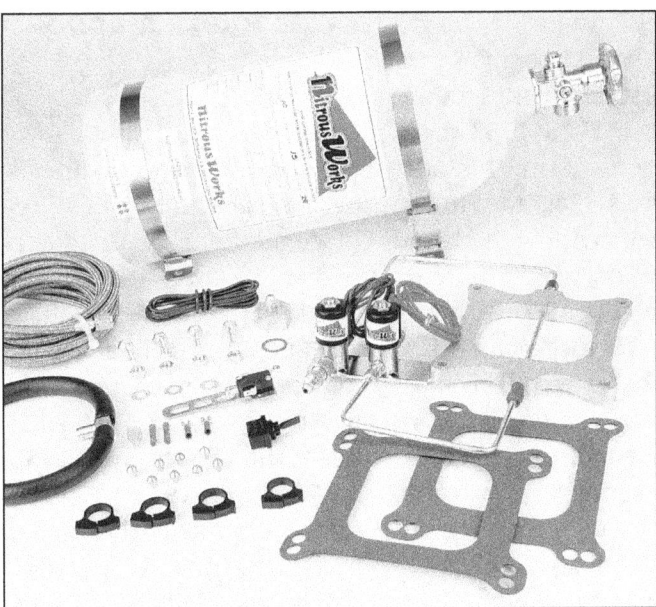

Installing nitrous oxide to an engine always gives you power on demand. If you are going to spray your Buick, use up to a 125-hp shot on cast or hypereutectic pistons, or run forged pistons.

required. There are entire books dedicated to the Quadrajet, so we will leave that to them. The Q-jet provides enough flow for 350 small blocks up to 350-hp, and for 600-hp or less big blocks. In turn, an aftermarket carb is needed for serious performance engines, such as 350-plus-hp 350 small blocks or 600-hp or more big blocks. The Quadrajet is a great carburetor, but for serious performance, an aftermarket carb is the way to go.

Depending on the application, the style of carburetor you run is up to you. While those who compete in the Factory Appearing Stock drag races must use the factory carburetor, most engines will benefit greatly from an aftermarket carb. If you are using the stock manifold, you could swap to a spreadbore carb or use an adapter plate, but the intake would need some extensive port work to make it capable of supporting serious HP. Once you have decided to use an aftermarket intake, any one of the hundreds of aftermarket carbs will be right at home on a Buick. The key is getting the CFM selection right for your application.

An 850-cfm carb with vacuum secondaries pumps enough fuel for 350-plus HP 350 small-block, while the 750-cfm carb works well on a 350 producing 350 hp or less. A quality rebuilt 850 Quadrajet will do just fine on a 350-hp or less Buick 350. If you are planning on stepping up your game and running with the big boys, the 400-plus-hp 350 engines need a little more flow. An 850-cfm double-pumper is perfect, though getting into the 500-hp range would require a little more work. When supercharging a Buick 350, even a stock engine requires much more, as a stock 350 with a Roots-style blower should get 950-cfm minimum (there will be more about supercharging later). The big blocks need more cfm, with a mild build needing a minimum of 750 cfm with vacuum secondaries at the least, but 850 would be better. For a 455 with an aftermarket intake and ported or aftermarket heads, 950 to 1,000 cfm is not out of the question for serious drag-race engines.

This blow-through carburetor from Barry Grant is perfect for custom turbo and centrifugal supercharger applications. The hat and carburetor make designing these types of systems much simpler.

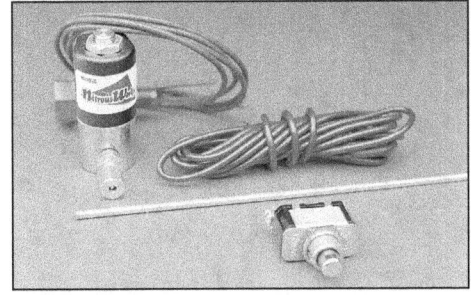

A purge kit is necessary for clearing nitrous kit lines. This kit ensures you have liquid nitrous in the lines and not just vapor.

V-6 Turbo

The V-6 turbos were manufactured with two styles of induction: carbureted for the 1978–1983 models, and fuel injection for the 1984–1987 engines. Upgrades to the fuel-injection units will be discussed in Chapter 10. For the carbureted models, there really are not many options. The stock intake base is a unique design that uses a three-bolt mounting base for a pipe that connects to the separate carburetor plenum that mounts to the turbo. The 1978–1979 V-6 turbo engines used a heavy cast-iron intake, but the 1980 and later models had aluminum intakes that shed about 20 lbs off the engine. The 1980 intake is aluminum and exactly the same for the 1978–1979 engines, while the 1981 and later engines used an ECM. If you want to swap an aluminum intake onto a 1979 engine, look for a 1980 model or buy the entire intake setup because the placement of the carb pad and other fittings changed. The aluminum intakes are not compatible with 1978 heads and do not have a provision for the knock sensor.

The carburetor mount on the V-6 turbo looks like this. This very interesting piece ties to the up-pipe, which runs to the intake.

Intake Manifolds

Nailhead

There is not much swapping to be had with the Nailhead engines because as the engines grew in displacement, they also got taller and wider. The 1953–1956 four-barrel is a good intake and will bolt right onto the 264 and really add some performance. There are two main intake designs made for the smaller Nailhead: the 1953 to mid-1955 version, and the mid-1955 to 1956. The difference is the later intake has an exhaust passage to put heat on the base of the carburetor for better winter driving and uses a different carb base made of cast iron. The 1953 to mid-1955 is a cooler-running intake, which is better for performance. For the bigger engines, the 1957–1961 364-ci 300-hp engine has a nice four-barrel intake, but this intake will not work on any other engine. They are fairly rare because they came only on the 1957–1958 Century and Roadmaster, and the 1959–1961 LeSabre with the high-performance option.

The 401 and 425 used the same four-barrel intakes from 1959–1966. There is an early (1959–1962) and late unit, but they swap freely through the years. The best factory intake came on the 1966 Riviera. These 425s came out with the first Quadrajet carb and are an excellent choice for 401 and 425 engines. A few of these intakes also came on the high-performance option for the 1966 GS Skylark. The last of the performance intakes are the dual quads from the 1964–1966 425. They came from the factory on the 1965 and some 1966 GS Rivieras, but the Super Wildcat (as Buick called it) could also be ordered on Electra, Wildcat, and Riviera from 1964 to 1966. These came with two 625-cfm Carter carburetors on a cast-iron intake with a recurved distributor, a chrome air cleaner with dual snorkels, and a pair of aluminum valve covers. It was rated at 360 hp from the factory.

There were many aftermarket intakes made for the Nailhead, but some were only good to bolt carbs onto the engine and made little increases in (or reduced) performance.

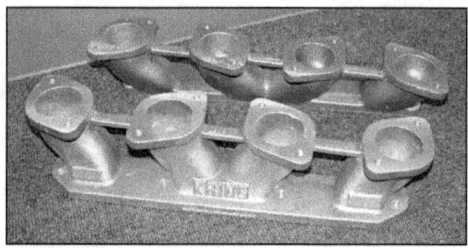

This Kring intake comes in two pieces and bolts to each head.

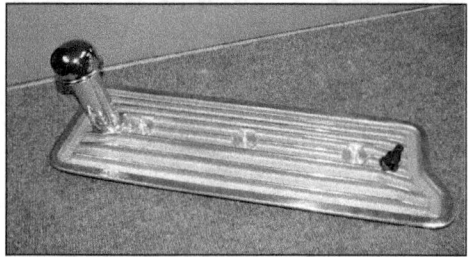

The Nailhead's bridge-style design needs a valley pan cover. This reproduction unit from Kring is right at home on any Nailhead.

Offenhauser makes a few Nailhead intakes. This dual-quad piece is perfect for nostalgia drag racers.

INTAKE, CARBS AND EXHAUST

Offenhauser manufacturers this unit for the three-deuce group.

The TA Performance SP1 intake is an open-plenum intake designed for high-HP Buick big blocks.

For extreme performance, the TA Performance SPX is a max-flow, open-plenum intake that's capable of over 800 hp.

The Edelbrock B262 is the winner in the old-school performance-intake category. Max Balchowsky built a few three two-barrel intakes and a four-barrel intake. He preferred six two-barrels on his race cars. These classic 1960s intakes can occasionally be found on eBay and at swap meets.

For new aftermarket intakes, Offenhauser makes several intakes for the Nailhead. A high-rise triple-deuce set up would be perfect for the hot rod, while the Offy dual quad would be a fitting topper for a nostalgia dragster. These new units are not cheap, though; prices start at around $450. The Offenhauser intakes are not known for making power — they can actually rob over 50 horses from a Nailhead — so they are really only for the street rodders who don't care about big power.

Small-Block 350 and Big Blocks

There are not very many aftermarket intakes available for Buick engines. The 350 has two: one from TA Performance (although rumor has it there is a true high-performance model coming soon), and one from Poston Buick. These intakes are suitable for mid-level builds, but not for serious performers. For the 350 built here, the Poston intake was used. The engine could seriously benefit

The Edelbrock B4B intake was part of the original Stage 2 factory package. A very popular intake in the early 1970s, GM reintroduced it in 2007 due to the resurgence in popularity of the Buick engines.

from a better intake, as these aftermarket units were not designed to support 400-plus hp, but they are all that is available.

The big blocks have a few more options that certainly flow better. Both TA Performance and Poston Buick have their own offerings, as well as Offenhauser with a dual-quad dual-plane intake, in either square or spreadbore application. Edelbrock makes a performer series (stock replacement, slight performance

This dual-quad big-block intake from Offenhauser offers the hot rodder a different look for the big block.

Based on the SPX, TA Performance offers this bolt-on fuel-injection kit. This ready-to-run system comes complete with computer and wiring.

CHAPTER 8

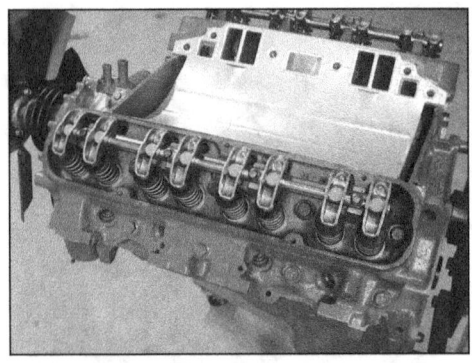

The 350, big block, and V-6 turbo use a stamped metal valley pan cover that controls oil splash and keeps oil off the bottom of the intake. It also prevents sludge and debris from falling back into the engine. These units, however, are not very good gaskets, which they are intended to be.

This fuel-injection intake for the 1984–1987 V-6 turbo engines eliminates the poor flow conditions that plagued the stock intake.

If you want to use a higher-grade intake gasket, which is always recommended, you will need to modify the stock gasket. Trim the intake gasket portion of the valley cover along the marked line shown here. This will allow you to reuse the lower portion and get a better seal from a high-performance gasket.

Unlike the Chevy engines, the Buick powerplants require the use of the little rubber intake end seals. If you place a thin bead of silicone on here, you will get a leak. There is simply too much gap here, about 1/8 inch, much more than a Chevy.

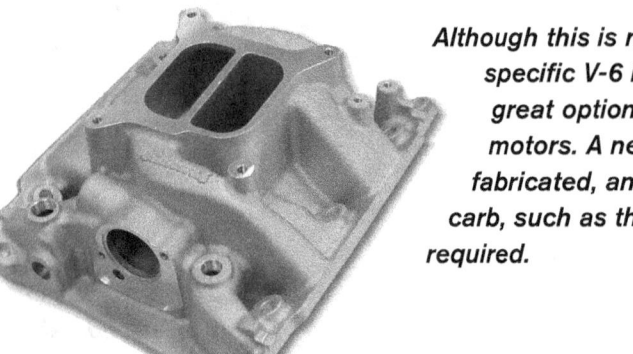

Although this is not a turbocharger-specific V-6 intake, it is certainly a great option for carbureted turbo motors. A new up-pipe needs to be fabricated, and use of a blow-through carb, such as the Barry Grant, is required.

increase) and a Performer RPM series called the B4B, which is the exact same intake Buick used for the 1972 Buick GS Stage II engines. The B4B is a very popular intake and works quite well with the Edelbrock heads. The TA Performance SP1 single-plane intake is the most popular for the Buick big block, designed to run on the stock heads on up to the TA Performance's Stage 3 heads. For serious high-RPM drag racing, an open-plenum (single-plane) intake is the best choice.

Sheet Metal Intake Fabrication

For the 350 crowd, extreme output 455 racers, and anybody wanting to add a Roots-style supercharger, there is only one real option: a sheet-metal intake. Don't let the exotic sound scare you off; it is not that difficult to build your own custom intake manifold. There are some cheats you can use if you are not up to task of building the entire manifold, or you can go for the gusto and build the whole thing right in your garage. There are a few things you need to consider before building your own intake. The right welding equipment is required. In order to get a good seal, your welder must have adjustable settings and have enough amperage to weld 1/4-inch steel plate or be a TIG unit for aluminum. Do you have the necessary welding skills and experience? If you can't weld a solid stitch, you might want to tap somebody else for the welding side of things.

You need to determine if the intake is for a basic carb or forced-air induction system. A naturally aspirated intake requires more attention to details, such as flow characteristics,

INTAKE, CARBS AND EXHAUST

When building a sheet-metal intake, the first step is to make the intake plate. You will create a perfect template by using the stock gasket and tracing it on a piece of 1/4-inch plate.

At this point, you need a plasma cutter. We used an Esab Handyplasma 380 to cut our parts. With a steady hand and some practice, you can produce very clean cuts that require little clean up.

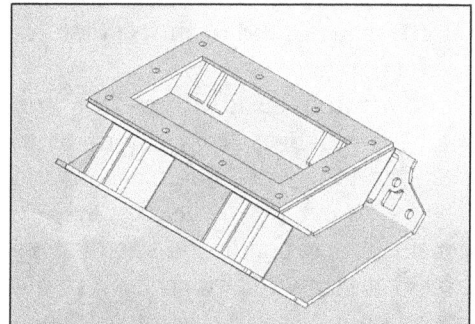

The sheet metal intake for the supercharged 350 was designed in Solidworks, a 3D modeling program. We used the program to model the intake, and then we sent the file to the local steel supply company that cut it out on its CNC-plasma machine. It does not have to be done this way; it's just easier and cleaner. We also went through the process of hand-cutting the parts.

The intake plate was cut out, and the ports, bolt holes, and water jackets were torched out, as well.

The angle for the intake bolts is unique, so we used the original intake as a drill guide to get the right angle we needed for the holes to be perfect.

than a super- or turbo-charged induction system. A supercharger forces the air and fuel through the intake, which makes them more tolerable to turbulence and flow restrictions. Hood clearance must also be considered. In most instances, a sheet-metal intake is *not* going to clear the stock hood, especially on a Buick GS or Skylark.

Once those issues have been settled, the design of the intake can take place. The first step for any intake is to set the engine on a stand, torque down the heads and remove the factory intake. The old adage "measure twice and cut once" certainly applies here, as the measurements are crucial for a correctly built intake. Measure the base of the intake, which will be the area above the lifter valley side to side and front to back. This area is not square front to back; the driver side of the engine sits back slightly. The general shape of this piece will be a parallelogram (two sets of equal-length parallel sides, with non-right or 90-degree angles). Make sure you have this piece cut a little long so you can trim it to fit. This piece can be made of

This CNC plasma part is much cleaner than the hand-cut parts, and it's a perfect fit.

The intake bolts sit at an arbitrary angle that does not match anything. We had to use some spacers to bolt the plates to the engine.

The valley pan plate was placed on the engine and aligned to the edges. By building your own intake, the rubber end seals won't be needed.

1/8-inch plate. The head flanges need to be made of 1/4-inch steel or thicker (if using aluminum), as will the two upper plates for the plenum.

The rest of the intake can be built with 1/8-inch plate-steel or aluminum. Measure the height and width of the head intake flange. These plates will need to be cut down around the edges. Have the metal shop cut these for you in rectangle strips. For the intake built here, eight 4-inch long, 1-3/4 x 2-inch 14-gauge rectangle tubing was used for the runners. Since this is a forced-induction intake, plain rectangle tubing is fine. If this were a carbureted intake, we would want the runners to start out rectangular, then narrow down as the runner reaches the flange. Rectangular tubing can be used here, too; it will just need to be pie-cut and bent together on both the width and height of the runner, where the length is measured from the plenum to the flange.

With the basic pieces cut and ready, the flanges need to be cut to shape and the ports, water jackets, and bolt holes cut in. The easiest way to get the correct shape and size of these holes is to copy the intake gasket onto the plate itself using a marker. Then with a plasma cutter (you really need a plasma for this, unless you have access to a water jet or laser cutter and a CAD program), cut out the pattern drawn on the metal. You could use an oxy/acetylene torch, but you might want to buy a few extra flange plates because it might take a few tries to get it clean and straight. If your metal shop has a CAD-operated plasma or water jet, you could give them the dimensions and the old intake gasket and they can draw up what you need and cut it on their machine. This usually costs extra, and at $50 an hour or more, the price racks up quickly. TA Performance does offer a set of pre-cut intake manifold plates for about $150, which is another option.

INTAKE, CARBS AND EXHAUST

With a silver welding pencil, we traced the shape of the block to the metal pan, so it can be trimmed for a professional look.

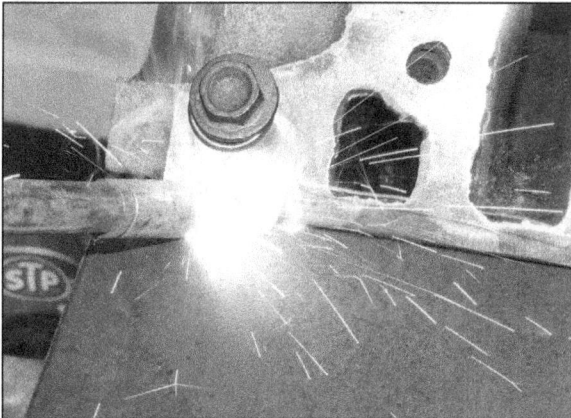
The pan was tack-welded to the intake plates. Don't do this on a ready-to-run engine. This is a mock-up engine, and it will be rebuilt before it is run again.

Spot weld the plate every two inches. TIG-weld it later on.

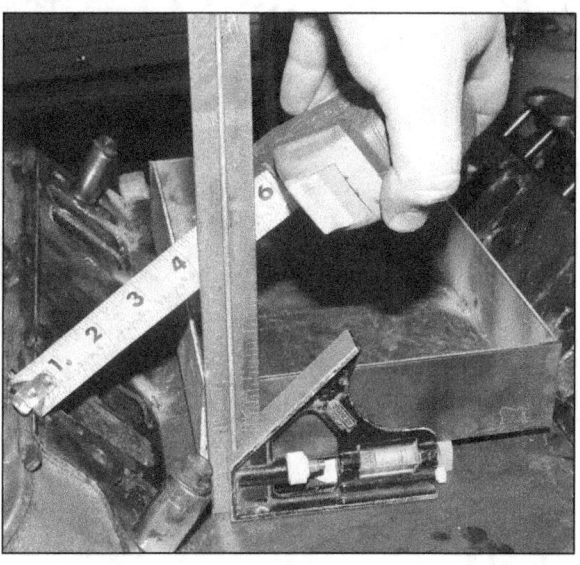
Using a square, we measured for the runners. The runners need to be as straight as possible, so we kept the tubing square.

Once the flanges have been cut, the base plate is laid onto the engine and the flanges are placed on the heads. The Buick intake mounting holes sit at an odd angle, so you will need some small tubing as a spacer for the bolts. Cut off a short piece of tubing (about 1/2 inch), slide it over the intake bolts, and thread it into the head. Mark the angle with a marker on the tubing. Remove the tubing and cut it off at that angle. Reinstall it over the flange and tighten it down. Don't weld this on yet; you may need to adjust it to fit the runners. Bolt down the rest of the flange bolts, making sure the intake flanges sit down on the base plate. Once everything is tightened, place a few rags in the intake ports if you will not be rebuilding the heads later, and tack weld the flanges to the plate. Do not place tack welds under the intake ports at this time. Now would be a great time to add a 1/2–3/4-inch hole with a corresponding pipe to a clear location in the base plate for the PCV valve.

The crankcase still needs to be vented, so don't skip this step. Pair up the eight pieces of rectangular tubing. Using a clamp, square each pair on all sides and clamp them together. Tack-weld each pair along the length of the joint — do not weld on the open ends. Next, place

HOW TO BUILD MAX-PERFORMANCE BUICK ENGINES

Eight pieces of tubing were cut 4 inches long and tack-welded into pairs.

Each pair was placed on the intake flange and positioned.

Using a magnetic square (available from most hardware or welding stores), the runners were held in place for welding.

The runners were tack-welded in place.

each pair one at a time on the intake flange and square it up with the intake ports. Take notice of the bolt holes, as you might have to clearance a spacer or modify a runner to get appropriate clearance. Place tack-welds on each side of the runner to the flange. Using a magnetic welding clamp helps make positioning these runners easier.

With all of the runners welded in place, the entire assembly needs to be welded together using stitch welds along every joint. Keep the flanges bolted down so nothing moves with the heat from the welding. Go slow and take your time. Cool the part about every inch of stitch. Make sure you weld the entire joint — leaks here are bad. Once the runners and flanges are welded together, we can start designing the plenum.

Building the Plenum

The plenum is where most of the magic happens. This is where all of the runners are fed, and the volume of the plenum is important. The minimum volume for the plenum needs to be at least 1.5 times the displacement of a single cylinder. As stated in Chapter 2, the cylinder displacement is calculated using this formula.

Cylinder = (Bore x Bore x Stroke x 0.7854)

For a Buick 455 this would be:

(4.313 x 4.313 x 3.9 x .7854) = 56.97 ci

Then plenum volume must be a minimum of:

56.97 x 1.5 = 85.45

INTAKE, CARBS AND EXHAUST

The plenum was finished off with a plenum ring that had been drilled and tapped. The supercharger will be bolted to a separate same-sized plate, and the assembly will be bolted to the finished intake.

The water jackets were a little troublesome, so we decided to weld in pipe fittings. Hoses will run from the fittings to a separate water neck box for proper water flow. These runners have been TIG-welded, too.

The plenum was built to match the supercharger and the engine in relation to the pulleys. The two sets of runners were tack-welded to a separate plate to keep them from tweaking while being welded.

This means for a 455, the plenum must be a 10 x 3 x 3-inch. Since this intake is for a supercharger, it will be a good deal larger, more in the neighborhood of 12 x 6 x 3-inch H, plenty of volume for what is needed. You can see how the intake was built for a single-base carburetor and the runners were angled toward the center. However the plenum could become a little cramped.

The next step is dependent on the application and the measurement of the nose length for the supercharger. Some units do not have the ability to be adjusted, so make sure you check the distance from the pulley to the base and factor that into the build process. Since the distributor is front-mounted, you need to make sure that the nose does not interfere with the distributor, especially if you are running a particularly tall distributor, such as the unit from MSD. With the nose length of the supercharger noted, the plenum can be fabricated, keeping in mind how far forward or rearward the supercharger needs to sit on the plenum. For this intake, there is a definite width and length that is needed. The supercharger is bolted to a plate that bolts to the top plate of the plenum, so there needs to be a little room to access the bolts. With those measurements in mind, the width between the lower edges of the runners is measured. Then the overall length of the plenum is added in and the bottom of the plenum is sized.

The second sections, the two plates that will cover the runners, need to be measured. Depending on how you build it, these can be wider than the runners or the same width, and cut in three sections: front, middle, and rear. Either way is acceptable, the latter being a touch more difficult to weld, but probably more accurate and easier to create than cutting out holes in a single plate for the runners. The upper section of the plenum is basically the same length as the middle section, but shorter and solid. This piece does not need to be very tall, but by adding 1/2 to 1 inch, the airflow will be greater at the top of the runner and will smooth things out inside the intake.

At this point, hood clearance is not a factor, so you might as well add a little height for better flow. These pieces should be tack-welded in place as you go so that the measurements do not change, and everything is in the place where it needs to be. Don't finish welding it at this point. The ends or front and rear plates of the intake need to be fabricated. The easiest solution to this problem is to use a piece of cardboard and create a template for both the front and rear sections. This makes sure the piece of metal you cut is going to fit. At this point, the ends should resemble half of a stop sign, with five separate sides. The ends should be tack-welded in place and the entire intake should be welded solid. You can weld it from the inside or the outside; welding both sides would certainly ensure a good seal.

The two upper plates for the plenum should be constructed of 1/4-inch plate steel for strength. This is a little heavy, but should not weigh more than the stock unit, which tips the scales at over 65 lbs. This is where the supercharger bolts to the engine, so it is important it does not flex. The top plate of the plenum should be measured to fit and welded just like the rest of the intake. The upper plate needs to be just a basic ring, following the perimeter of the plenum. It needs to be open in the center. A width of 3/4 inch should be sufficient for most applications. Depending on your application, there needs to be several threaded holes for the supercharger plate to bolt to. There are two ways of achieving this. The first is to simply drill the holes in the plate (before welding to the plenum) and either tap them for 1/4-20 grade-8 bolts *or* welding grade-8 nuts to the underside. This works, but could lead to a leak around the threads. The other way, which certainly takes a little more work, is to use 5/16-inch tubing, cut to length, tapped for 1/4-20 threads, and welded inside the plenum and to the holes in the top plate. Either way will work, whichever method you choose.

With the intake buttoned up, the supercharger plate can then be drilled to mount to the intake and the supercharger. This plate should be cut open in the center to match or be slightly larger than the opening in the base of the supercharger. This will reduce turbulence and obstructions. You do not want to hamper the supercharger's ability to force air into the engine.

Constructing the Water Jacket Crossovers

The last step in building the intake is to build the water jacket crossovers. For the rear of the engine, you could simply weld two pieces of 1/2-inch pipe to the flanges and use a piece of heater hose to transfer the

The Magnuson MP112, based on an Eaton OE high-helix twin-screw supercharger, produces about 40-percent more power at 10 psi.

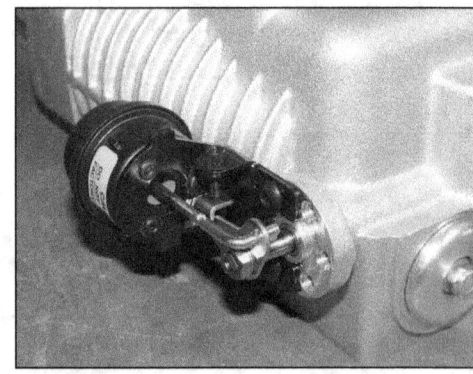

The Magnuson units come with a factory-set pressure valve that controls the boost.

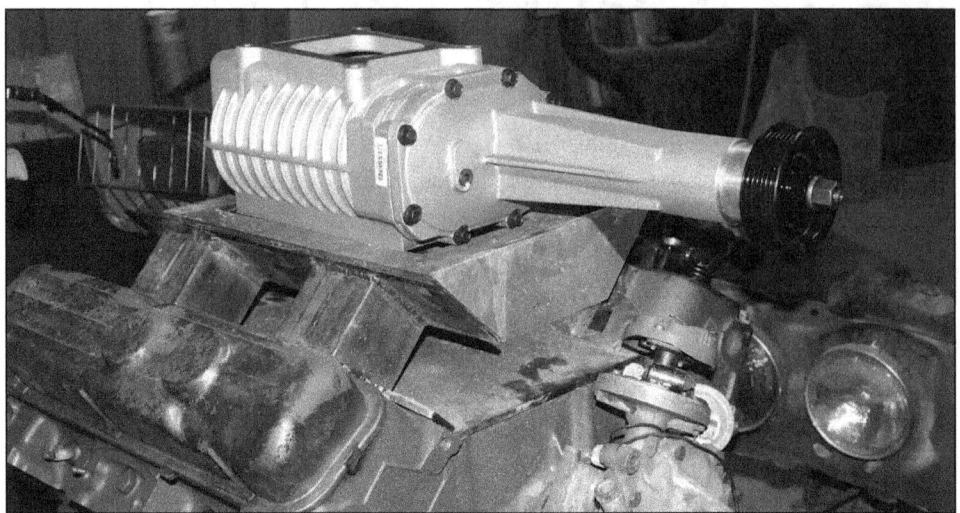

The Magnuson MP112 supercharger on the intake should be capable of producing about 350 to 400 hp on a stock low-compression Buick 350. This intake design can be used for a supercharger or for carburetors, depending on the top plate.

INTAKE, CARBS AND EXHAUST

water to the other side, but the better looking and lower maintenance way would be to weld a straight piece of 1/2–3/4-inch square tubing to either side. The front water jackets are a different story. These need to be built in such a way that the water neck can be bolted on and the feed line to the water pump can be added. Depending on your application, you could simply build a link between the water jackets with rectangular tubing and cut the hole for the water neck, or you could weld on two correctly sized pipes and attach the hose directly. For a street-driven car, using the factory water neck would make it simpler to utilize a thermostat, so that is what was done for the intake on the 350 build.

If you do not want to hassle with building the entire manifold, and fabricate the water supply, there is another option. Simply purchase an aluminum intake for the engine you are building. Take it to a machine shop (or, if you have one, put it on the mill) and fly-cut the carburetor pad off the top of the intake. Continue cutting until you have enough space to mount the supercharger. Make sure you remove any obstructions on the inside of the intake that may become a problem. Then cut two top plates from aluminum, similar to the previous intake build. Drill and tap the lower plate for the upper plate, and TIG-weld the lower plate to the intake. Then drill and tap the supercharger plate for the supercharger. Bolt it all together and you are done.

There are advantages and disadvantages to both styles. The modified aluminum intake is quicker, simpler, and easier to build in some respects than the full custom builds, but it does not have the same flow characteristics. The second version also is not as forgiving in reference to placement of the supercharger itself. It is also more expensive, with the cost of the machine work, aluminum plate, and new intake; this unit could easily reach $700–$1,000—not cheap. The full custom unit takes more time, more design work, and a little more head scratching. If it is built from steel, it could be made with materials costing less than $75, and most shops are equipped with decent gas-shielded MIG welders, which will do the job. Neither one will fit under a stock hood, so that is out on both styles. The full custom intake will certainly flow better than the modified unit. For those of you who are thinking about modifying a stock cast-iron unit, it will work if you can find someone who can competently weld steel plate to cast iron (not a simple task) and keep it from breaking off. It has been tried and most times it fails, which could be dangerous if it fails on the strip or street. Either way, you should have the new intake pressure-tested for leaks. Most machine shops can handle this task for a nominal fee, and it is important to do so, because a little leak in an intake will create more confusion and frustration than almost any other engine gremlin.

Headers, Manifolds and Exhaust Systems

Nailheads

The Nailhead manifolds have pretty decent flow with the stock manifolds. The first engines to have factory-type iron headers, they can be swapped only from 1953–1956 and from 1957–1966, because the early models have round ports, and later engines have rectangular ports. In small hot rods, like early Fords, the left-side manifold for the 1953–1955 or 1956 with single exhaust work great and will bolt on the right side. They tuck in close to the block. The 1957–1966 exhaust manifolds were made in several forms. The left-side manifolds came in a front, center, or rear dump, so there are plenty to choose from when swapping engines into different chassis.

There are a few headers for the 1957–1966 engines: block hugger headers and long-tube styles made for the 1965–1966 GS, and others. Header flanges are available from Headers By Ed for all Buicks. Ed

The stock exhaust manifolds on the Nailhead are adequate for many applications. Make sure you find a set with the right dumps for what you want.

makes them any thickness, and his ports line up right. Headers can be fun to make and sometimes are the only way to get what you want. For performance, do not use large tubes. Only the hottest Nailheads can use 1-3/4-inch tubes, typically 1-5/8 inch for the 364, 401, and 425; the 322 would be even smaller at 1-1/2-inch. The block hugger-type headers are not going to perform much better than cast-iron manifolds.

Small-Block 350 and Big Blocks

The later V-8s have decent-flowing exhaust manifolds. They are not great, but will be sufficient for any mid-level street build. With worked exhaust ports on the heads, the factory cast-iron manifolds can achieve some decent performance when they are ported. If you are running a 350 in stock appearing drag racing, the manifold requires serious port work to get the flow where it needs to be. For serious performance, headers are needed.

As with most items, there aren't many header options for either of the later V-8s. Hooker makes headers for both the 350 and the big blocks. These headers are 1-5/8-inch tubes with 3-inch collectors and are designed to fit the 1968–1972 Buick Skylark and GS cars. In most cases these headers fit fine, but with cars that have modified suspensions that sit lower to the ground, these headers tend to scrape the ground. Both TA Performance and Poston Buick offer headers for the V-8s. These are custom designed to fit the 1968–1972 A-bodied cars, as well, and are available in several tubing sizes from 1-5/8-inch up to 2-1/8-inch tubes (TA Performance only).

Any performance V-8 needs to have at least 2-1/2-inch exhaust. If you are running a high-output (500-hp or more) engine, you can probably get away with a set of 3-inch pipes. You just don't want to go too big because you want a little back-pressure to keep the flow even. Thus, avoid the monster pipes for most performance street engines. Without getting into too much theory, the scavenging effect — in which the negative pressure wave from the previous exhaust pulse travels back to the port from the collector — creates a vacuum on the exhaust port. This helps draw more fuel into the combustion chamber during the overlap period in the valve timing. As back-pressure drops, the exhaust gasses tend to stall in the pipes; there is less force to push these out and, in turn, fewer negative pressure waves.

In reality, running a slightly smaller pipe is actually better for a street car than running pipe that is too large. What gains in high-rpm performance can be had with running large-diameter exhaust are not enough to

In order to accommodate the Chevy 350 six-rib pulley, we made an adapter to bolt the three-bolt pulley to the Buick six-bolt crank pulley. Converting the Buick to a complete serpentine drive system is another option, which can be done with a few parts from March Performance and a junk yard. You need a crank and water pump pulley from March Performance, an alternator from an 86 TPI Camaro, 3/4-inch spacers for the alternator bracket, and a water pump for a 1973 or newer 350 or 231.

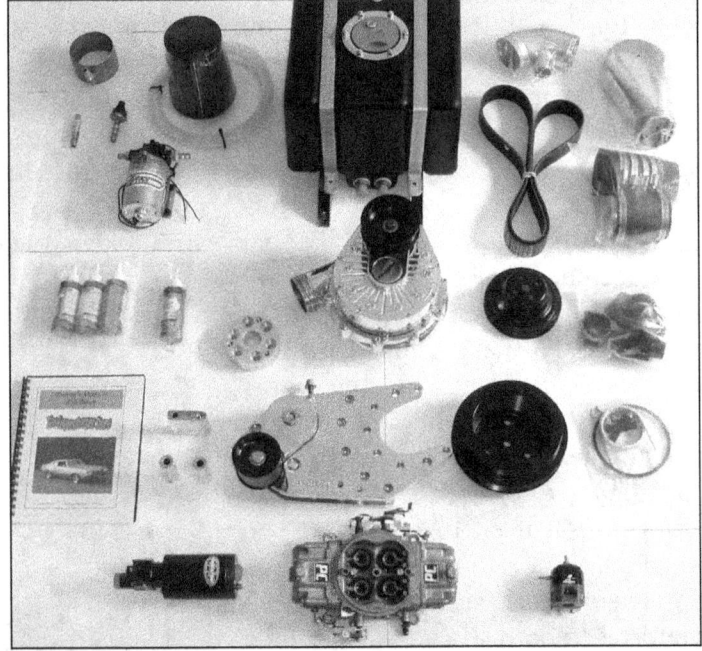

The Procharger system from TA Performance is one alternative. To adapt the Chevy pulley to the Buick, the aluminum disc located at the lower left of the supercharger is needed.

INTAKE, CARBS AND EXHAUST

The 350 we built was bolted together with a set of Hooker Super-Comp Cermakrome headers. These headers ride a little low to the ground, but fit between the GM A-body frame rails.

Headers and Buick engines have a few issues. The oil dipstick must be unbolted from the block before mounting the headers, or a flexible unit needs to be used.

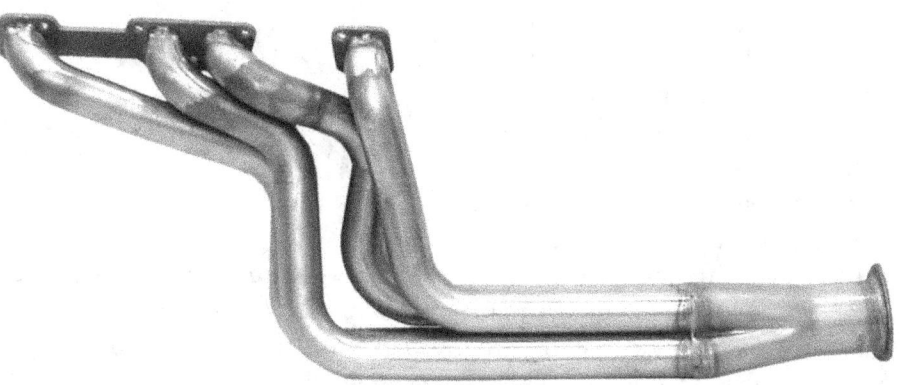

TA Performance offers these split-flange headers, which eliminate the problem with the dipstick tube.

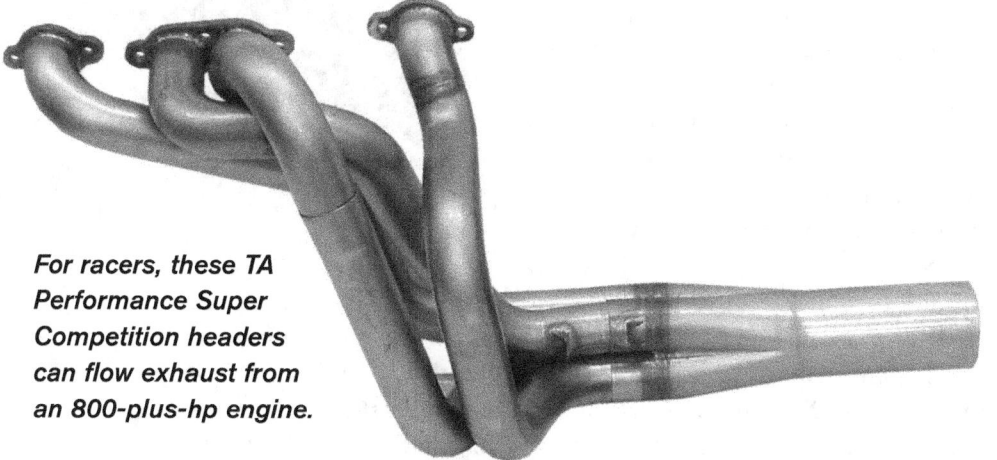

For racers, these TA Performance Super Competition headers can flow exhaust from an 800-plus-hp engine.

These ARP header studs are nice, but don't work very well for the Buick application. With our 350, the passenger side front tube hits the stud, and the driver side won't fit with the dipstick in place. The bolts were used on the passenger side, except for the front bolt, and the driver side needs a different dipstick. They make hanging the headers much easier.

HOW TO BUILD MAX-PERFORMANCE BUICK ENGINES

CHAPTER 8

The stock 1978–1983 V-6 turbo manifolds provide capable performance, which is good because it's the only one available. However, you can convert to the later-style turbos and piping.

This 2-1/2-inch exhaust kit from PYPES is a perfect fit for the Buick A-body. The cutouts are designed to flow directly with the headers, and not on the curve like most other brands.

overcome the lost torque in the lower RPM range. Several companies offer kits for the Buick muscle cars, predominantly the 1968-1972 A-bodies (Skylark, GS). Pypes has an excellent kit that comes with mufflers and an X-pipe, which will increase the scavenging effect and equalize the pulses of the exhaust, resulting in more horsepower than dual pipes alone. TA Performance, Hooker, Pypes, Torque Tech, and quite a few others make quality kits for Buick muscle cars. Torque Tech is owned and operated by a Buick enthusiast, so it specializes in Buick exhaust kits.

V-6 Turbo

The 3.8-liter turbo engines have special exhaust requirements because the turbo is tied into the exhaust system. The factory 1978–1982 manifolds do not have very good flow, which increases backpressure. The 1983–1987 engines have factory tubular headers, though they are not mandrel bent, which created a few flow issues. The stock later-model headers are good for low-12 quarter-mile runs, but going faster will require an upgrade. Switching to a set of mandrel bent headers will not only reduce the backpressure as much as 1/3, but they also have as much as 25 percent more flow, which is a significant increase. When looking for a set of headers, go for the ceramic-coated units. They cost a little more, but the ceramic coating reduces the heat transfer, which helps keep the engine compartment cooler. Heat is the enemy of any engine, and turbo engines are notorious for creating excessive heat. Nothing kills a turbo like too much heat.

Upgrading the stock exhaust is a quick way to boost HP. There are quite a few systems available, which means you must decide what you want. For all but the most extreme engines, a 2-1/2-inch exhaust system is sufficient. Depending on your application, which for the majority will be G-bodied cars (Grand National, Regal), there are prefit systems. If your engine is being built for swap, then the system will need to be custom made. The 2-1/2-inch free-flowing system will support just about anything the V-6 turbo can throw at it.

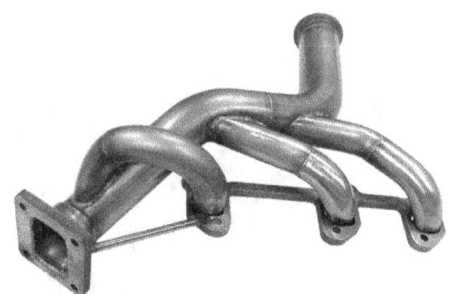

For the V-6 turbo, these specialized headers can handle about any power level, but they do not fit stock downpipes.

When running open headers, these header baffle inserts from carchemistry.com make a big difference in sound volume, while not drastically affecting performance.

CHAPTER 9

RACE ENGINES

There are high-performance engines and then there are race engines. A full-bore race engine requires meticulous attention to detail and a few extra precautions. Some of the basic rules are the same while others will change. Each system is once again broken down into groups and examined with the hard-core racer in mind.

Block Preparation

For the extreme-output engines, the foundation of the engine must be carefully chosen, because any weakness here will surely end in catastrophe. *Always* have a race block sonically tested for material thickness. The big blocks of the late 1960s up to 1972 have more core shift issues than any others. The 1972 and later blocks are much better but can still have some problems. The main focus on these engines is cylinder wall thickness and lifter bores. There have been engines that were in service that had obvious visual core shift, and the outer walls of the lifter bores were half the normal thickness. While this may be suffi-

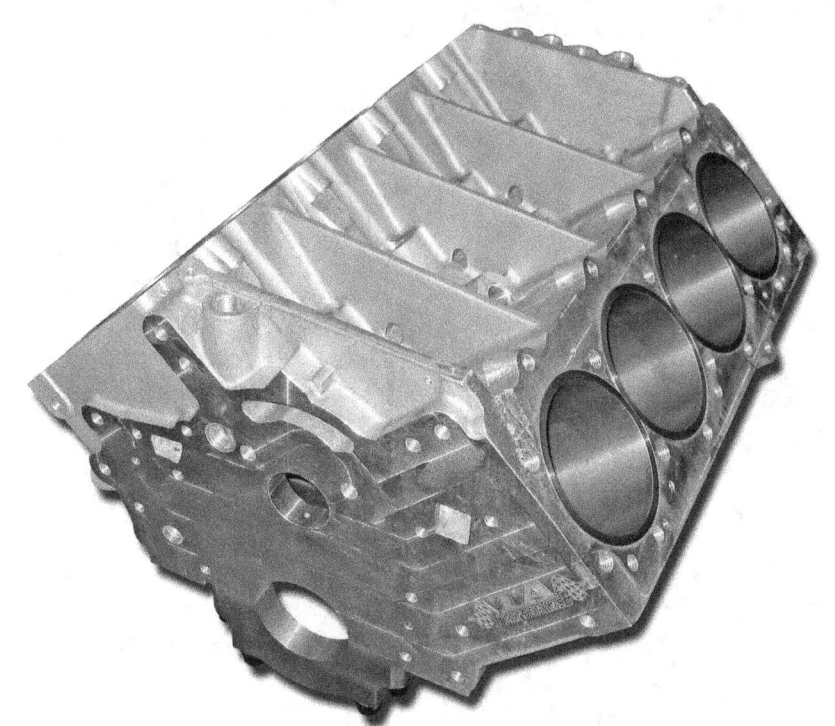

The block is the foundation of any race engine. TA Performance's new aluminum 455-ci block is a true game changer. The block is available in three versions: stock replacement, raised-cam block, and raised-cam tall-deck version. All the weak areas of the stock block have been fixed, and the new block even features a dual transmission bellhousing bolt pattern.

cient for a stock street application, any serious stress on these lifter bores — like that from a radical cam profile — and they are going to break, taking out the rest of those expensive parts.

Using a new cast block will alleviate all of the inherent problems facing a Buick racing engine. There are some options when choosing your block. The 455 block — the more popular V-8 — has two after-

CHAPTER 9

The four-bolt mains in a Bulldog block are an important feature. A modified stock block is capable of making over 1,500 hp, while this high-performance aluminum block should be able to handle well beyond that.

market block suppliers. Bulldog Performance is the first to market, with its 455 cast-iron and aluminum blocks. These blocks have none of the issues surrounding the original casting and can use stock parts. TA Performance will soon have its own version of the big Buick called the Tomahawk that's built for racing applications.

For the turbo group, in 2006 TA Performance released an all-new aluminum V-6 turbo block. This block eliminates all of the oiling issues with the original block. In addition to those upgrades, the new V-6 turbo block is built to make serious power, to the tune of 2,000 hp. The block comes with steel-billet main caps with six main bolts, four vertical bolts, and two horizontal, with the front main cap having two vertical and two horizontal bolts. The block is drilled and tapped for 14 head bolts, which offers the head more holding power and the ability to bolt on a set of 14-bolt heads without having to drill and tap the holes. The head bolts are like every other Buick; they are dry holes, meaning they do not enter the water jackets.

The TA V-6 turbo block also has dry-sump oiling provisions, which allows the builder the ability to provide a competition-level oiling system without the extra machine work. Another unique feature of the block is the dual-transmission bolt

The new TA Performance aluminum block is capable of handling more than 2,000 hp thanks to upgrades, such as splayed four-bolt main caps and added material in the weak spots. Even though the new block is aluminum, it is only 12 pounds lighter than the stock cast-iron block, which is a testament to how much more material this block has in it.

The stock block's weak main webs need some serious reinforcement for revving over 6,000 rpm or putting out 600 hp, and a block girdle is the solution. There are two types: girdled oil pan and fully machine-fit girdle. The machine-shop-assembled version (shown here) features a girdled oil pan. For high-output street engines, the girdled oil pan should be sufficient, but for serious drag engines, the fully machine-fit girdle is the better choice.

RACE ENGINES

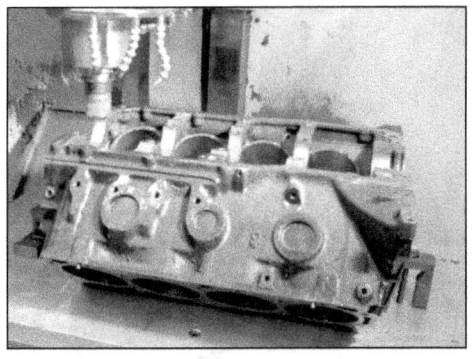

Here, the block is machined to accept the TA Performance block girdle. Once installed, the girdle becomes an integral part of the block.

For 900 hp or more, the halo girdle is recommended. This additional piece further strengthens the tops of the main caps. It requires a fabricated oil pan, and probably won't fit a frame car.

pattern. The block has both the B-O-P (Buick-Olds-Pontiac) pattern as well as the Chevy pattern, which opens up the possibilities for transmission choice. The block also has a clutch-linkage provision — a nice touch.

There are some more options for adding strength to the weaker big-blocks if you choose to forego an aftermarket block or are racing in FAST-style events in which the factory block must be retained. Adding a block girdle will not only increase the block's strength, but it eliminates the flex in the main caps. A block girdle is an absolute must for any 600-plus hp, 6,000-rpm applications, or use of an aftermarket steel crank. The original main webs are only 3/8-inch thick, which are sufficient for stock builds, but adding any serious power causes the caps to twist and flex, resulting in failure.

The TA Performance girdle is made from 1-inch thick, high-tensile-strength ductile iron, which is stronger than the iron used in the block itself. Installation of the girdle must be performed by a qualified machine

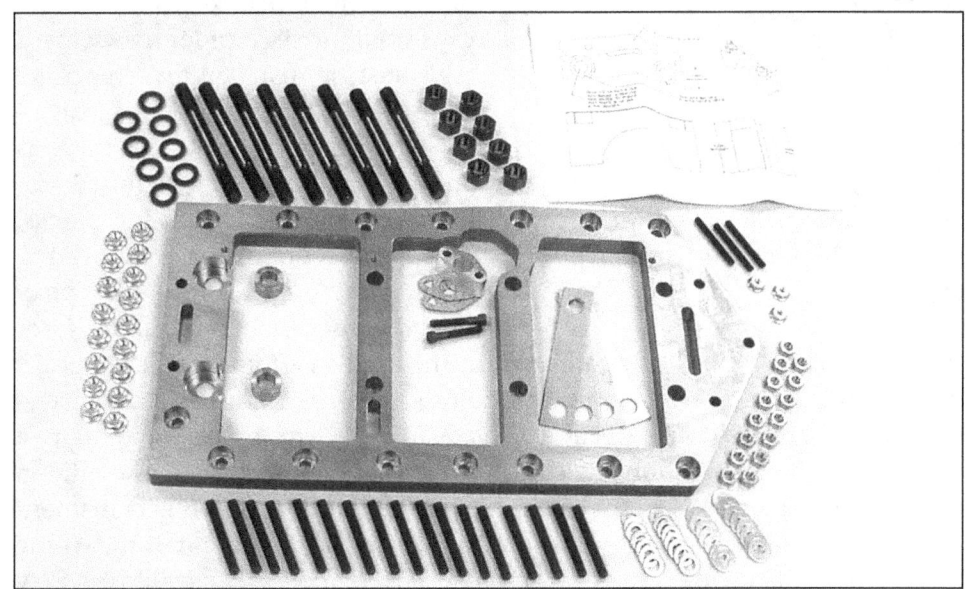

The V-6 turbo girdle should be used on 600-hp applications, and it installs like the big-block unit.

The lifter bore girdle is an absolute must for any race engine running high-lift roller cams.

HOW TO BUILD MAX-PERFORMANCE BUICK ENGINES

If you are not running a girdle, switching to billet main caps is a good idea. These caps eliminate cap walk, which is very common on these engines.

shop because the girdle becomes a part of the block. The main caps must be machined to fit inside the girdle, and then align-honed to the block. The oil pan bolts to the girdle. The TA girdle will help prevent blocks from distorting, cranks from breaking, main webs from cracking, and permit the use of a stock or deep sump oil pan. The girdle is machined to clear the starter and the crank counterweights. TA recommends that this is the only way to properly prep your big-block Buick for racing, but there is also another option from Poston Buick.

The Poston Buick girdled oil pan is a simple bolt-on piece that adds preload to the main caps. This piece would work well on engines in the 600-hp range. For 900-plus-hp engines, TA recommends using their halo girdle to supplement the TA block girdle for additional strength. The halo girdle requires the use of a fabricated oil pan (usually dry sump type) and is intended to fit tube-chassis cars, or cars with heavily modified stock engine cross members; this will not fit a stock car.

The 3.8-liter V-6 turbo builders also have an option for the stock block. The TA Performance block girdle is recommended for any turbo engine building 600 hp or higher, and it's available for both the 20-bolt oil pan blocks (1986 and 1987) and the 1985 and earlier 14-bolt oil pan blocks. The block keeps the main caps from moving under heavy loads and must be installed by a machine shop, just like the big-block girdle.

Strengthening the lifter bores is another modification required for building race-only Buick big blocks. This can be done two ways: fitting metal plates and using the epoxy method discussed in Chapter 4, or using the TA Performance lifter girdle. Both have their advantages and disadvantages. The epoxy method is a do-it-at-home method that requires a little patience and some craftsmanship. There is the potential that if the block is not perfectly clean, the epoxy will not hold, which could result in pieces breaking off. This is not likely, but is a possibility. Also, the block should be warm when the epoxy is applied, which will help with adhesion. The advantages to this modification are that is cheap, simple to do, and efficient. The drawbacks are potential for debris falling in the engine if not correctly done, and there is no adjustability for preload.

The TA Performance lifter bore girdle is another option. Similar to the block girdle, the lifter bore girdle requires machine work to fit and install the unit. This is both a drawback and an advantage because it is difficult to install, but the piece becomes a part of the block, with no possibility of becoming separated.

Stroker crankshafts are an easy way to get more HP from a Buick engine. These billet-steel cranks are available in strokes up to 4.40 inches, equaling 523 ci, and put out some serious power. Do not opt for a crankshaft that offers too much stroke for your application. A longer stroke places additional stress on the cylinder walls and pistons, which must be considered.

RACE ENGINES

This TA Performance balancer fits the stock pulleys and timing cover. It's externally balanced and SFI approved, which makes it the best choice for a race motor.

JE Custom Pistons makes these units for TA Performance. Available in custom compression ratios, you can get what you need for your race motor.

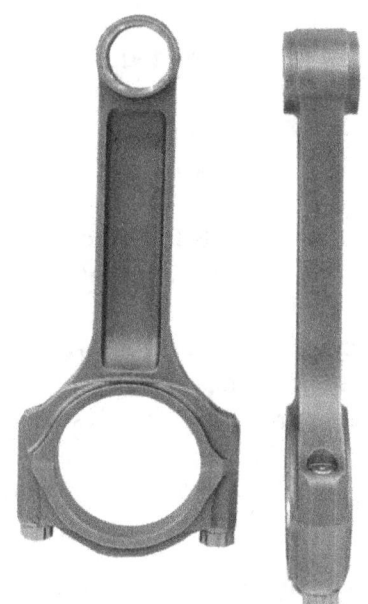

These billet-steel rods are the strongest rods available for Buick big blocks. These are the ideal choice for a race engine.

The lifter-bore girdle also has the ability to adjust the preload on the lifter bores, which adds flexibility later down the road. If you are building a race engine, you will be using a high-lift cam and possibly a roller cam, both of which require this modification. Which one you choose is up to you. The TA girdle is more expensive and requires machine work, but also has adjustability and might add some peace of mind. For a small-block 350, the only choice is the epoxy method.

Rotating Assembly

Race engines require more strength in the bottom end than a street engine. The stock crank can handle up to 600 hp, but beyond that, an aftermarket steel crank is needed. A forged-steel crank is suited for the stock 3.9-inch stroke or stroker applications. A billet-steel crank is in order for any engine making 900 hp or more. Since the Buick engine uses the crank as a stabilizer for the thin cast block, the stronger the crank, the stronger the engine.

The rods should be up to the task for any engine, but even more so for a race engine. The stock rods are not up to par for anything with over 500 hp — they simply are not strong enough. For engines putting out 500–800 hp, a forged rod is required, but there are a lot of options here. Chevy and Chrysler rods can be modified to run on the Buick crank, which adds quite a few off-the-shelf options from practically every rod manufacturer. The problem with this is that these rods then require additional machine work, which costs a good deal more. With the options available from Buick-specific manufacturers, Buick-specific rods are the best choice. TA Performance offers the Sportsman rod, which is a bolt-in, IHRA- and NHRA-approved, forged-steel connecting rod that requires no other modifications to fit the big-block Buick. These rods can be safely revved up to 7,000 rpm.

Billet rods are necessary for any engine running more than 800 hp or a stroker crank. The choice between aluminum and steel depends a lot on price. Billet-steel rods cost more than aluminum. They are equally strong, with the aluminum versions being larger in size than a corresponding billet-steel rod. Any race engine running heavy boost or large amounts of nitrous should be built with billet rods.

Pistons for race Buicks must be custom ordered. Each application is different, and the piston must be ordered for the specific application. Obviously, any race piston is going to be forged. One feature that a race engine should have is floating wrist pins. One of the benefits of a floating pin is less friction. Less friction means less heat, and that produces more power. The main drawback that most people talk about with floating pins is the possibility for a pin lock to break, which would allow the pin to slide out, scoring the cylinder walls. This potential issue can easily be resolved by using spiral-style locks. These locks twist in like a spring, and in the event of a failure, will still keep the pin in place.

The bearings for the rotating assembly should be of the best possible materials. Using top-quality bearings is very important for a race engine. Depending on the block and application, using a solid bearing would be more appropriate for a drag-strip-only engine since the bearing will support more thrust. Grooved bearings would be more important for a road course engine for oil supply in long sessions. The key to building a race engine that will last is in the tolerances.

An all-out drag engine can have slightly looser tolerances than a street engine. This is because the engine will not see the kind of daily start-and-stop stresses. A drag engine only sees short bursts of heavy stress, allowing for looser tolerances. Running slightly larger clearance will slightly reduce friction, pushing the power output up. A max main bearing tolerance of 0.004 inch is acceptable for a race-only engine. The rod bearings need to be in the 0.0025-inch range. These numbers are for the factory block because the block has so much flex on the engine. For the new blocks, this won't be an issue and normal tolerances should be sufficient. A race engine always gets set up a little looser; running 0.003 inch for the main bearings should be good with a new block.

Camshafts

For race engines, the camshaft type is just as important as the profile. A hydraulic lifter cam is not going to yield as much output as a solid lifter cam. With the Buick's inherent lifter bore issues, the cam choice will determine whether or not you need to reinforce the lifter bores. Extreme-lift cams (.650-inch or more) and roller cams will absolutely require the lifter-bore reinforcement. There have been reports of other issues with running extreme-lift camshafts. The issues arise with camshafts that have either a wider base circle than the rest of the lobe or in small-base-circle cams. The problem is that the lifter hits the opposing lobe at the base circle or the radius at the bearing journal. This is mostly with camshafts that were not manufactured by Buick specialist shops. Make sure you ask the manufacturer about this before purchasing your cam.

The other issue with high-lift camshafts is interference with the piston itself. At 0.550-inch lift, a stock head will get very close to hitting the piston. Make sure your valves will clear the piston at maximum lift in your engine. Do not just assume it will all fit together because the guy who sold the parts said it would. When a set of heads is rebuilt, they are almost always surfaced, which could mean the difference between clearing the piston and not.

With any solid lifter camshaft, roller rockers must be used, as this is the best way to add the adjustability needed to change the valve lash. In addition, roller rockers reduce friction, which will increase output, as well.

Heads

Choosing heads for a race engine all depends on the application and the power goal. If you need to run stock cylinder heads for FAST-class racing, then the heads will require significant porting. Greg Gessler, of Gessler Head Porting, is considered by many to be the best Buick head porter

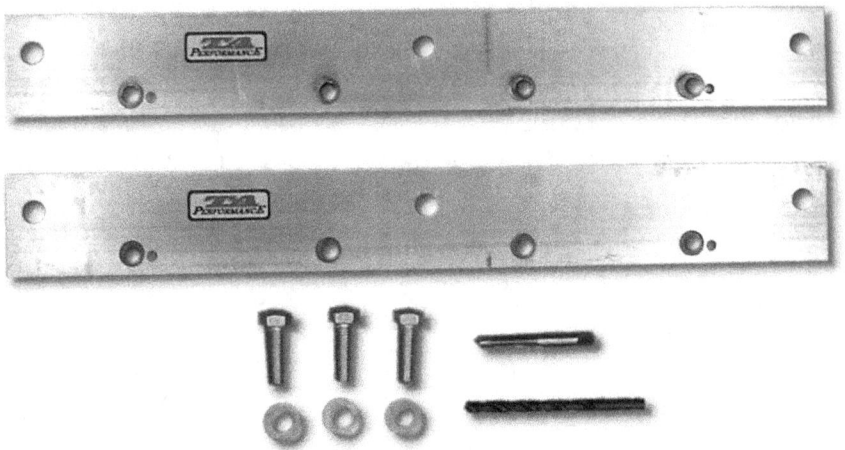

Higher compression means more opportunity for the head gaskets to blow. Adding these four extra bolts to the block when using TA's Stage 2 and up heads will add the extra clamping force needed to contain the combustion forces. This drill jig will make adding these holes a simple task.

around. Gessler has run 11-second flat quarter-mile times with his iron-headed 455 Buick.

For those racers who do not live under the stock head requirement, aluminum heads are the ticket to faster time slips. The key to making big power with a Buick engine is in the heads. There are quite a few aftermarket heads available for the big-block Buick; choosing the right one for your application is important.

The TA Performance Stage 4 head is the top dog in Buick cylinder head technology. Based on the Buick Stage-2 design, this head takes things to the highest level. These heads are capable of 395 cfm at high lift with large valves and some port work. These are the absolute top performers in the Buick cylinder head world and are capable of supporting over 900 hp. Using these heads requires Stage 2-style headers (the exhaust ports are D-shaped, not rectangular) and will not clear any stock Buick hood. These heads also require an SP2 intake or custom-designed intake.

Many times, race cars need custom-designed headers. These TA Performance header flanges make building custom headers much easier.

Induction

Race engines need more air and fuel to make the power. The stock intake simply is not up to the task. While FAST-class racers like Greg Gessler have 11-second cars that run the factory 75-lb iron intake, massive amounts of porting have taken place to make that happen. There are many hours of research in a well-ported intake; time is not the kind of thing that most weekend racers have a lot of. There are two options when it comes to race engines and intakes for the Buick: build (or buy) a sheet-metal intake, or buy an aftermarket cast-aluminum unit. For drag racing, an open-plenum intake, such as the TA Performance SPX, is the best bet for an off-the-shelf intake. Once out of the box, the intake should be gasket-matched to the heads, which will increase flow. This intake is capable of supporting 800 hp.

A custom intake is a must for a Roots-style blower or 900-plus hp engine. As described in Chapter 8, building a sheet-metal intake is not that difficult, though it may take a couple of tries to get it just right. For centrifugal superchargers or turbochargers, the intake's ability to flow air is modified with the introduction of force. A stock intake would support much more HP if the air and fuel were being forced in. That is not to say that you would not benefit from an aftermarket intake. Adding a more free-flowing, better-designed intake will allow the engine to breathe even better, so keep that in mind when choosing your intake for a forced-induction system.

When using forced induction, the compression ratio is important. While these things can be pushed to the limits for race engines, the basic guideline is 9.5:1 max compression

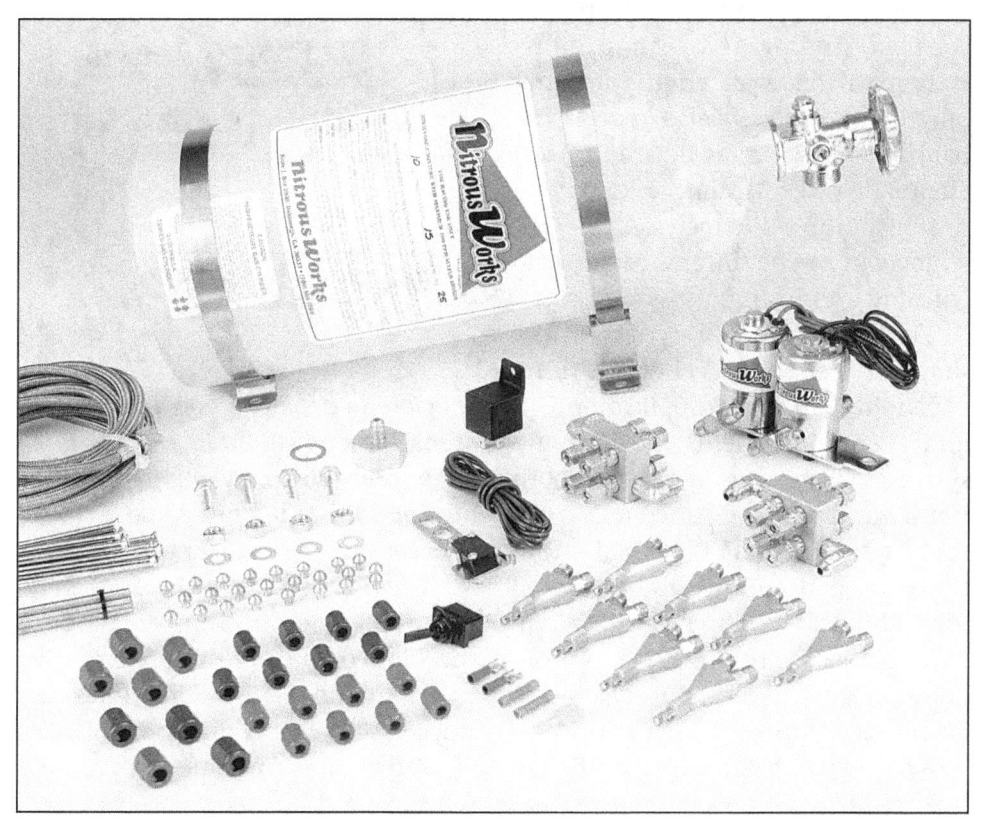

Nitrous oxide is the great equalizer. This fogger system from Nitrous Works adds up to 500 hp at the push of a button.

CHAPTER 9

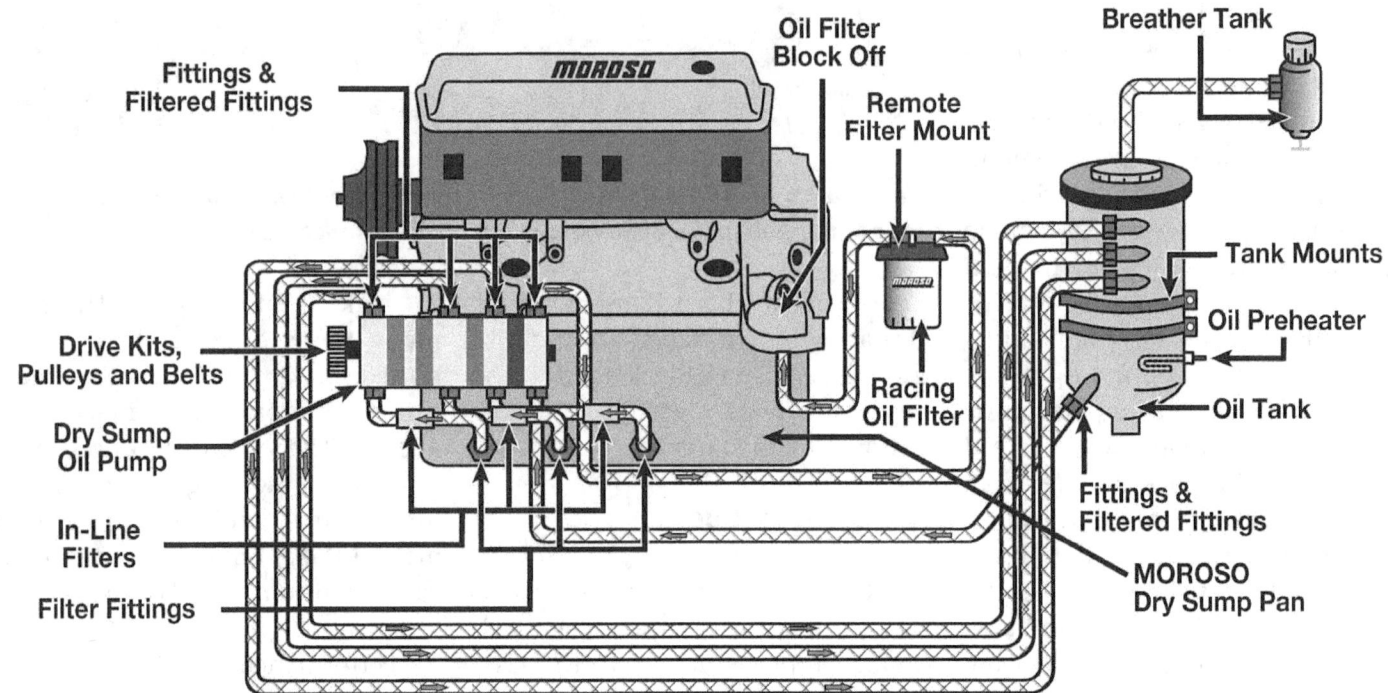

Dry sump oiling systems are expensive but are the best way to keep oil flowing at all times. This diagram from Moroso shows the oil flow pathways in detail.

ratio for a supercharged engine. Increasing the compression will increase the chances of detonation, which could kill the engine. Running 8.5:1 compression will allow you to run much more boost, which will allow for much more power than running 10:1 and 1/3 the boost.

Adding nitrous to the mix really brings in a whole other realm of issues. While some have been touched on here, there simply is not enough space to cover how to properly tune a nitrous-fed engine. Just be sure to follow all the basic guidelines and keep the engine from going lean. For more information on nitrous, I recommend *How To Install and Use Nitrous Oxide Injection Systems For Maximum Horsepower* from CarTech.

Oiling System

The biggest issue facing any Buick builder is the oiling system. For racers, there are other factors to consider. Adding a dry-sump oiling system will give an engine a better oil supply and will also reduce the parasitic losses associated with engine-driven oil pumps. Removing the oil pump will free up some HP, which can be the difference between winning and losing.

There are several types of dry sump systems to choose from, depending on your application. To understand the benefits of a dry sump system, you need to know how both wet and dry systems work. A wet sump system stores oil in the bottom of the oil pan and distributes the oil throughout the engine by the pump mounted in the timing cover. An oil-pump pickup, mounted to the block, extends to within 1/4 inch of the bottom of the pan to suck up the oil. You can make the stock oiling system work for a race engine, but this requires larger capacity oil pans and

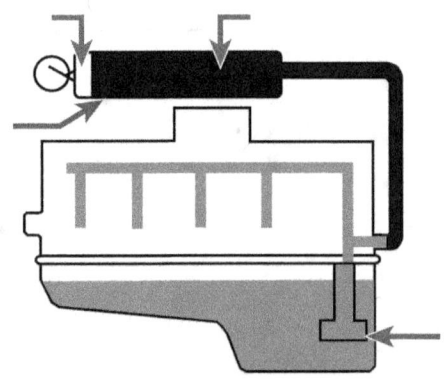

This image depicts an oil accumulator at rest. The oil stored in the tank is under pressure and waiting for the pick-up tube in the pan to be uncovered.

modifying the oil pump to produce the kind of pressure needed to give the engine longevity. Sometimes, the stock system just is not enough.

A dry sump system stores oil in a separate tank, using a very small oil pan without a sump. The oil pump is externally mounted. These pumps

112   HOW TO BUILD MAX-PERFORMANCE BUICK ENGINES

RACE ENGINES

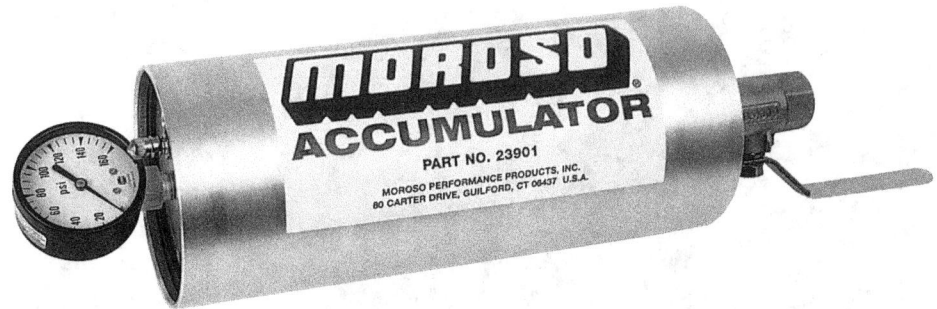

This Moroso 1-1/2-quart oil accumulator is compact, simple to install, and costs a lot less than a full-blown dry sump system.

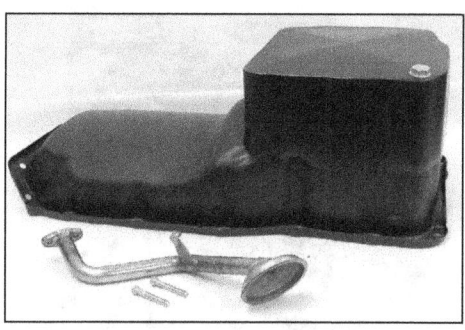

Modified oil pans, such as this one, are an easy way to add an extra quart of oil capacity to a Buick, and it's the only option for a 350.

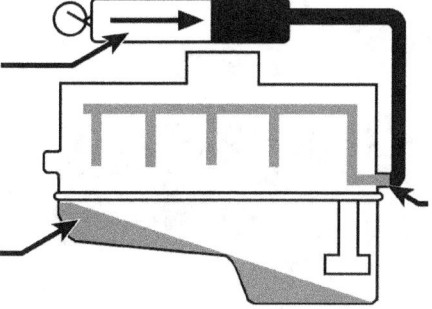

As soon as the pick-up tube is uncovered, the sudden drop in pressure causes the stored oil to rush to the engine and save it from oil starvation. When the pick-up is again submerged in oil and the pressure returns, the excess oil is pumped back into the reservoir.

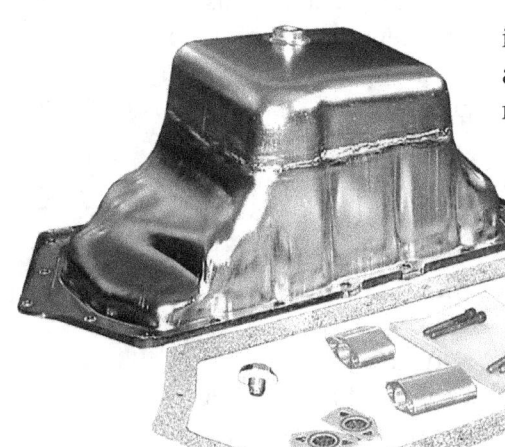

This deep sump pan for a V-6 turbo holds plenty of oil and is baffled, as well.

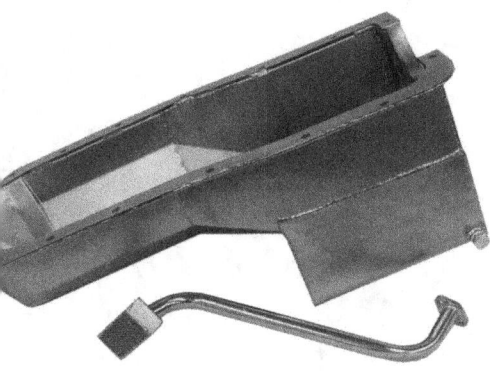

This fabricated TA Performance unit for big-block Buicks not only holds an extra quart of oil, but it is fully baffled on the inside and keeps a constant supply of oil over the pick-up tube.

come in at least two and as many as four stages. The pump uses plumbed lines to pull oil from the pan, send it to the storage tank, and finally back through the engine. In a typical setup, all but one of the stages is used to scavenge oil from the pan. A single pressure stage is used to return oil from the tank to the engine.

The main advantage of a dry sump system is its ability to make more power. With very little oil in the pan, the rotating assembly is not subject to windage, the parasitic process where oil is slung onto the crank, creating drag. Ring seal is also increased as the external pump creates extra crankcase vacuum, which results in more power. By using a dry sump oil system, you will also have increased oil capacity, more consistent oil pressure, and easily adjusted oil pressure; adding remote oil coolers is much simpler, too. Also, the oil pan does not have to be nearly as large because all of the oil is stored in the external tank. Most dry sump systems also allow the oil to sit longer before being recirculated through the engine, which gives the oil time to degas — release the air bubbles that are drawn into the system during the pumping process. This reduces foaming and sustains better oil pressure.

One of the biggest benefits from a dry-sump system is the constant oil flow. The design of the system is such that the engine will never be subjected to periods of no or limited oil pressure. In race cars, these situations typically come up during hard cornering or acceleration and in drag cars when the front end lifts beyond 4 inches off the ground. The problem is that at these times the oil pump pick-up tube can become

HOW TO BUILD MAX-PERFORMANCE BUICK ENGINES

Here is shot of the baffling inside the oil pan. The trap door allows oil to enter but not exit, keeping the pick-up tube submerged at all times.

Race engines typically use electric water pumps and require electric cooling fans. These custom-fit radiator fans come with shrouds to maximize efficiency.

uncovered, resulting in loss of oil flow and pressure. This also happens to be one of the most crucial load periods the engine will face, making things all the worse. A dry sump system is not needed on a street car, unless it is subjected to regular track duty. The biggest drawback for a dry-sump system is the cost; these units can run well above $2,000, which can make them cost prohibitive for the budget racer. For the serious racer who needs the added protection of a constant oil supply, there is another option.

An oil accumulator mounts in the engine bay and plugs into the main oil galley of the engine. These units typically hold 2–4 quarts of oil and use engine pressure to pressurize the tank piston. In the event the oil pick-up becomes uncovered, or there is any sudden oil pressure drop, the accumulator forces its oil into the engine, keeping the pressure up and saving the engine. When the pick up-tube begins pumping again, the engine's oil pressure forces the oil back into the accumulator, keeping the extra 2–4 quarts off the crank and keeping the engine from pushing out gaskets. This is the in-between step from a wet sump to a dry sump. An oil accumulator is not a band-aid for a poorly functioning oiling system, however. When installed properly, these systems will provide years of use and add life to any race engine. At around $200, an oil accumulator certainly costs much less than a full-on dry sump system.

High-compression engines need serious starters. This gear reduction starter is perfect for race engines and even weighs less than a stock starter.

This billet-steel flywheel is much stronger and lighter than the stock cast-iron flywheel.

For the manually shifted cars, a lightened flywheel makes a lot of sense and saves up to 30 lbs. This reduced weight lightens the rotating weight, letting the engine spin up faster.

Strengthening the Block

Using water jacket filler is one of the most important modifications that should be made to a stock block used for racing. Water jacket filler is a cement-based compound that is poured into the water jackets and, once cured, adds a good deal of strength and stability to the engine. There are several fillers available, with the most common being Hard Blok. There are several different ways to fill the block and the amounts depend on the intended application. Drag race blocks can be fully or partially filled, whereas circle track, road course, and street engines should only be partially filled. The reason for this is the filler takes up the space for the water to cool the engine. Where drag engines do not need a large amount of water running through the block because they are only run in short bursts, a street engine or road-course engine needs to maximize the cooling effect while also adding strength to the block. Hard Blok recommends a "Tall Fill" kit for 350-ci and larger engines and the "Short Fill" kit for a partial fill. Always add the filler before any machine work is done; the filler expands slightly and you do not want to ruin all that nice machine work.

There are several ways you can fill an engine block, but they all start with cleaning. A good fill requires the block to be very clean. You can have the block washed at a machine shop or, to get the absolute best clean, use acid.

To acid-wash the engine, seal up the block using a head and gasket along with rubber expansion plugs. Next, set the block on its end with the front of the engine up. Then fill the block with a mixture of muriatic acid and water (always add the acid to the water, never the other way around). Let it sit for at least 24 hours. If the solution quits bubbling before that, drain and refill. Once the acid is drained, the remaining acid needs to be neutralized. A mixture of baking soda and water is poured into the engine and allowed to sit. Once it stops foaming, drain the baking soda water and rinse the engine once again with plain water. The water jackets should be cleaner than they were when the engine was cast. Do not let any oil, lubricant, or other non-water based cleaner get in the water jackets; this will just nullify the acid wash process and the filler won't stick.

When it comes time to actually fill the block, there are a few things you need to remember. If there is any particular area you do not want filled, it needs to be filled with something else, like wax or clay. Important areas such as the water passages to the timing cover and the water jackets to the cylinder heads are important, so don't fill them up. If you are going to partially fill the block, try to work the filler around the cylinders, particularly around the thrust side to maximize the effect while minimizing the reduction of the water jackets. Also, the freeze plugs must be installed if the block is getting a tall fill. There have been street engines that have had good success with

The Hardblok in position in the water jackets is shown in this cutaway image. This will not only reinforce the block and stabilize the casting, but it will increase the life of the engine components.

Strengthening the Block *continued*

Setting the engine level on a stand is the first and most important step. The block must be square and level when the filler is poured in.

The filling procedure should be performed before any machine work is performed. The block will be filled to the bottom of the freeze plug for this application. The block should be as clean as possible.

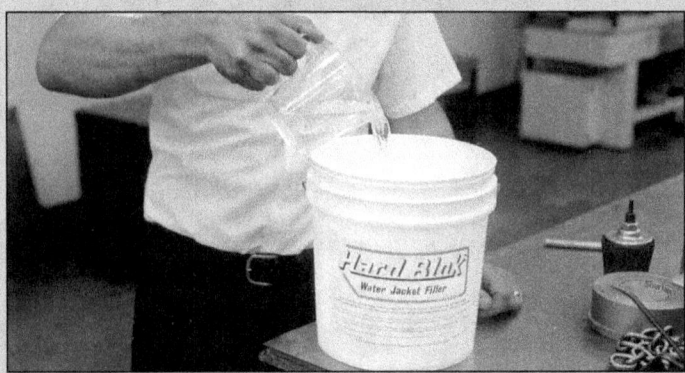

The water is poured into the bucket supplied with the kit. Precisely follow the instructions to avoid adding too much or too little water.

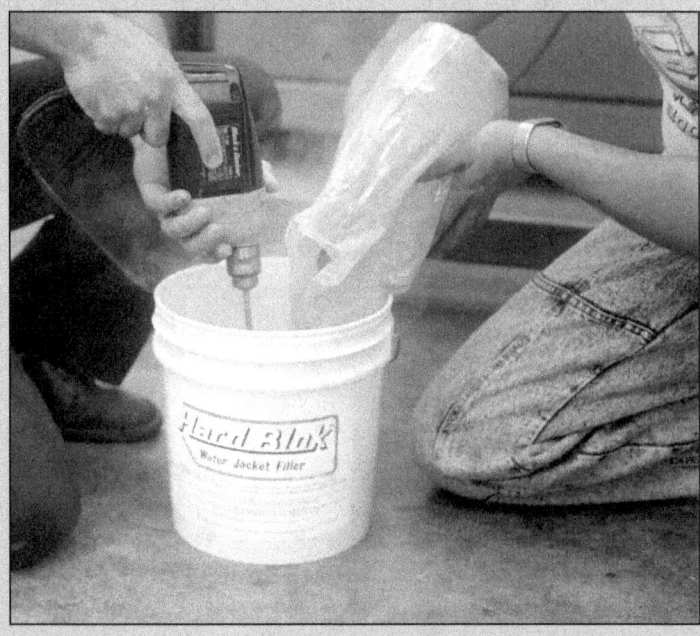

A drill-driven mixer blends the powder and water into filler.

block filler poured up to the bottom of the freeze plugs. This limits the reduction of the water jackets but would certainly add a good deal of strength to the block.

Another tip is to torque down the main caps, so that everything stays aligned. The filler expands slightly as it hardens, so any tweaking would be reduced with the caps in place. It is a good idea to have the caps align-honed after filling the block. The actual installation of the filler

RACE ENGINES

Once mixed, the filler is slowly poured into the block using a funnel to guide it into the water jackets. Pour the filler separately into each water jacket to get a proportionate fill.

Using a drill bit, rod, or other long, thin tool, spread the filler around the cylinder walls to work out the air pockets. Let it cure for 24 hours, and the job is complete.

might take a few applications; only mix up what you can use in 20–30 minutes.

Depending on how much you plan to fill the block, tape up a portion of the water jacket on the front of the engine. Install the timing cover to hold the filler in place while it sets up (this will be removed so everything can be cleaned after the initial setup has occurred). If the temperature is below 65 degrees, the filler will take twice as long to set up, so take that into consideration. The ambient temperature must be at least 50 degrees for proper installation for water jacket fillers. With the engine block mounted to an engine stand and sitting level, the pouring procedure can begin. Using a level, make sure the deck is level.

When using Hard Blok, the amount needed to fill the engine is predetermined with the kit. Fill a large bucket with the appropriate amount of water, then pour in the filler mix. Mix the compound thoroughly; a drill-mounted paint mixer works great for this task. Continue mixing for 5 minutes. The compound should look creamy and be pourable. If it is too thick, add water, 1 ounce at a time, and remix. There should be no water on the top of the mixture, and the heavy particles should be distributed evenly. If there is settling, there is too much water. Once the mixture starts to set, you cannot add any more mix or water, and you have to start over if it's not correct, so be careful, patient, and pay attention to the instructions. Once mixed, the compound will begin to harden in about 30 minutes.

The properly mixed compound should be poured into the water jackets in the deck of the block via a funnel. Using a stiff wire brush or other device, work the compound around the cylinder walls to eliminate air pockets. Using a DA sander or other tool to create mild vibration on the block will help level the surface and further evacuate air bubbles from the compound. Using an impact wrench is not recommended because the vibrations are too strong. Once the filler has been filled to the point you want it, let it sit for at least 12 hours (24 if the temp is below 65 degrees). Once the compound is cured, the block can safely be machined and assembled. Hard Blok and other block fillers are permanent; they cannot be removed once cured, so be careful and take your time when filling a block. If you do, then the results will be a stronger block that resists harmonic vibrations and has excellent thermal expansion.

CHAPTER 9

This heavy-duty electric water pump from TA performance offers exceptional reliability.

Factory Racer Kits

Buick offered a few kits for the racer back in the glory days of the muscle car and factory-sponsored race cars. This continued up to 1972 with the Stage 2 and then spawned once again in the mid-1980s with the GNX. For FAST-class racers, these parts offer the ability to step up the power with a better base platform to build off of. While the factory no longer makes any of these parts, they can sometimes be found on eBay and at swap meets.

Buick offered the factory Export kits for the Nailhead. Buick sold these kits to the racers who asked for them; the kits consisted of higher compression (10.0:1) pistons, a solid lifter cam, lightweight hollow lifters, longer push rods, and adjustable rockers. The 1956 kit could be used in 1954–1955 322s. The second kit was made for 1957–1958 364 engines, but had 11.0:1 pistons and intake gaskets with exhaust heat passages blocked, keeping the intake cooler. This was good for 10 hp more.

For the big-blocks, the Stage 2 kits began production in late 1968 — early 1969 for the 400 powerplant — and consisted of better flowing heads, a too-hot-for-the-street camshaft, and an Edelbrock B4B intake. These Stage 2 heads were produced in limited numbers, estimated at about 75 pair, from 1969 to 1970. Very few of these kits were actually assembled in the Buick plant, and most were used on Buick test cars. The Stage 2 package also included forged 11.0:1 pistons, two 1/8-inch headers, and a Holley 850 or a Rochester Super Stock Quadrajet. In 1972, Buick made the Stage 2 package a public offering, so you could walk into a Buick dealership and purchase the Stage 2 parts as a kit or by themselves. TA Performance has taken the reins on the Stage 2 head design and continues to manufacture the original design and modified versions in aluminum.

Factory racing packages for the average Joe disappeared for a while until Buick resurrected them with the GNX. In 1987, Buick dealers offered the GNX package, which consisted of a basic Grand National, but then the car was shipped off to ASC/McLaren Specialty Products and was seriously modified. The upgrades included a more efficient Garrett air-to-air intercooler and an intercooler pipe that was ceramic coated. This pipe was designed to reject heat. The front fenders received vents that were added to suck heat out of the engine compartment. The GNX also received a Garrett hybrid T-s turbocharger that used a very lightweight ceramic impeller, which is different from the standard metal impeller the regular GN received. This special impeller allowed faster spin-up, reducing turbo lag. The boost was set at 15 psi and an electric wastegate was installed. The modified turbo also featured low-drag turbine shaft seals, and a built-in contamination trap. The end result was a 275-hp, 360-ft-lb V-6. In addition to the engine, the GNX received a heavy-duty transmission with tighter shifts and a ladder bar and panhard bar to help plant the massive torque to the ground. The chassis was modified with steel crossmember braces. The body was tweaked with fender flares for the larger 16-inch wheels and big tires. The total for this package was $11,000, which gave the GNX an MSRP of just under $30,000—quite a bit for any car in 1987, but fewer than 547 GNXs were produced.

CHAPTER 10

V-6 Turbo

The 3.8-liter V-6 turbo Buick engine shares a good deal with its normally aspirated Buick V-8 brethren. But there are quite a few areas in which the turbo engines differ, as well. This chapter will define and break down the various turbo-specific systems and discuss all available performance modifications. While the focus will be the fuel-injected engines because they are the most popular and are the focus of the aftermarket industry for the V-6 turbo, there are some mods that are specific to both the hot-air (non-intercooled) and carbureted engines.

The stock Garrett turbo is suitable for cars running upper 12s in the quarter mile, but getting beyond that usually requires some modification, if not outright replacement. The stock turbo is fairly quick to spool up and has less turbo lag than most other stock turbos of that time. While they work great for a mild street engine, once these units get some miles on them, they simply do not create as much manifold pressure. If you are looking for a little extra out of the stock turbo unit, porting the stock turbo is a cheap way to increase HP.

This 1983 carbureted hot-air turbo motor was the last of its kind. These engines in stock trim can run low to mid-14-second quarter-mile times. There is a lot that can be done to these motors to increase output, even while keeping the carb. An intercooler will drastically increase power output.

The stock turbo is capable of low 12-second ETs. Upgrading to a larger turbo will bring down the time.

CHAPTER 10

The downpipe on the carbureted V-6 turbo mounts to the left side of the exhaust manifold, and the right side mounts to the turbo.

This unique carburetor mount fastens to the driver side of the engine, making room for the rear-mounted turbo.

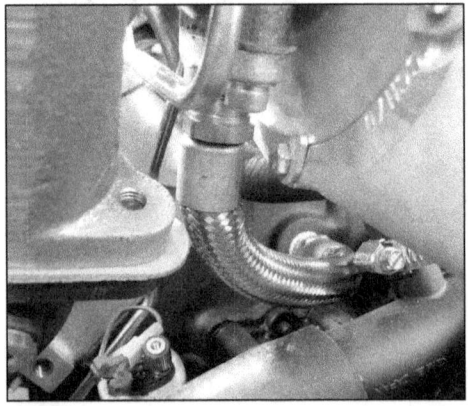

The turbo generates a lot of heat and needs a strong source of oil to dissipate the heat. This braided-steel oiling line runs from the block to the turbo.

Turbo System Porting

Porting the stock turbo requires a die grinder, fine-tooth carbide bits, sanding rolls, and Roloc-style Scotch-Brite pads. Before doing any work, inspect the housing. If you have the stock inlet bell, it should have a 0.10- to 0.15-inch lip all the way around where the bell meets the compressor housing. The opening for the compressor should look smaller than the inlet bell. You can leave the gasket in place and simply grind it off, leaving a correctly sized gasket.

With a cone-shaped carbide bit, begin cutting on the lip from the inlet bell side. Grind this lip until it is flush with the rest of the surface. Do not cut too much, and only remove the lip. Do not touch the polished area near the compressor blades. Complete the initial work with the carbide, then move to a sanding roll, smoothing out the rough spots, and blending the two areas. Once the lip is blended in, you can use a modified Roloc-style Scotch Brite pad to finish off the surface. To modify a standard Roloc pad, remove five pie-shaped pieces from the pad, which will allow the pad to flex inside the housing. You can purchase these pads, but you can also make them.

To port the outlet of the compressor on the intercooler side, you will remove enough material on the intercooler inlet while leaving the wall thickness at about 0.150-inch. Use the same process as the previous segment. Smoothing the interior cast surface on the compressor outlet is another bonus. This increases flow as the turbulence is reduced. Using a sanding roll and modified Roloc pads is the easiest way to accomplish this task. If you have a remote-motor die grinder, you will be able to get to more of the housing. When this is completed, do the same thing to the intercooler inlet. Stuff some rags or an old T-shirt inside the intercooler to keep shavings and debris from getting inside.

With the porting finished, clean the housing with hot, soapy water. Use a degreaser and either compressed air or a blow dryer to dry the inside of all the pieces.

The same thing goes for the turbine housing and elbow. The inside surface is very rough, and this creates a lot of turbulence and friction. *Do not* do anything to the large hole where the blades exit to the elbow.

Start with a clean, dry housing. The inlet to the housing should measure between 0.100 and 0.125 inch smaller than the outlet of the stock headers along the radius, which is about 1/4 inch on the diameter. If you use a copper turbo gasket, this will indicate the size difference. If not using the copper gasket, you can make a paper gasket that is the same size of the outlet of the headers. Use this as a template for the turbine housing, and mark the area that needs to be removed. With a carbide or stone, remove the metal and create a sloping entrance to the turbo. Match the outlet of the headers to the inlet; this should be a gradual slope, not sharp. Again, using the sanding rolls, clean up the cut marks and smooth the casting. Finish up the job with a Roloc pad.

Clean up the wastegate elbow using the same method as for the turbine housing, removing all of the rough surfaces and smoothing it as much as possible. The sanding rolls and Roloc pads make quick work of this task. *Do not* work the mating edge of the elbow-to-turbine surface or the gasket surface to the downpipe.

V-6 TURBO

Be sure to clean and degrease the parts when you are done; the cleaner the better.

Upgrading the turbo certainly pushes up the power output of the engine, but getting the most out of it will require other modifications, such as injectors, intercoolers, downpipes, etc. The idle air control valve (IACV) unit is another area for improvement that should be considered. The IACV relocator from BOP Engineering allows for the use of larger diameter inlet tubes on the turbo compressor. By installing one of these relocators, it also allows the IACV to be removed without having to remove other parts, which is nice for cleaning.

Turbo Replacement

For serious performance engines, replacing the turbo is a must. When the stock turbo is replaced, the stock oil-feed and return lines must be replaced, too. Aftermarket lines, such as the ESP Products Teflon high-pressure lines, ensure the turbo will have adequate oil pressure, and they do not degrade over time, thus keeping the oil clean.

Increasing boost always produces more HP. If you crank up the boost too much, there will be consequences, and the most serious consequence is detonation. As the cylinder pressure increases, the air/fuel mixture is compressed, and the intense heat will pre-ignite the gas, knocking the piston on the upstroke. This is the ping or knock noise you hear under heavy acceleration. Turbo motors are notorious for having knock issues, which is why they come with knock sensors. Left uncontrolled, detonation will destroy an engine in short order. Adding boost just makes it worse.

This ESP Products oil line for the turbo is braided steel and provides more flex than the stock line.

Adding an alcohol injection is a great way to control detonation at high boost levels. This dual-feed nitrous nozzle directs the alcohol mixture into the engine.

Alcohol injection is a solution for high-boost levels and detonation problems. The idea is to cool the cylinder down slightly, reducing the possibility of detonation while not affecting the combustion process. An alcohol-injection kit can be purchased from just about any turbo specialty shop, or you can build your own. Building your own alcohol injector setup is not as difficult as it sounds. You only need a few items that can be purchased from a catalog or local parts house. These parts are an electric fuel pump, Bosch-style relay, MAP switch, nozzle injectors and jets, and fuel tank.

An electric fuel pump will work, but a pump with stainless-steel internals is best because it will resist corrosion from the alcohol. A basic four-

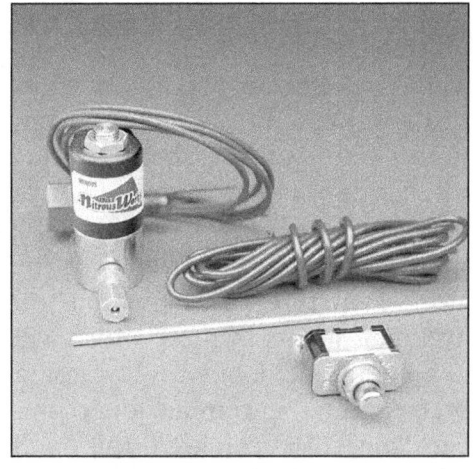
Another option for the alcohol kit is to buy a purge system. The solenoid and hard line can plug directly into the up-pipe, reducing the level of fabrication.

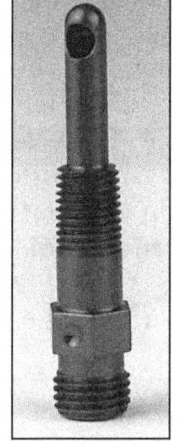
While the dual feed looks good, this single inlet may be the better choice.

A single nitrous solenoid controls the amount of alcohol mix sprayed in the motor.

or five-prong Bosch-style relay is needed to safely switch the current flow to the pump. (See the relay wiring diagram for wiring.) *Do not just wire the pump to a switch* because you will start a fire. An adjustable MAP-boost switch needs to be used to turn on the pump. The boost setting can be set wherever you want it; 10 psi is a good start.

HOW TO BUILD MAX-PERFORMANCE BUICK ENGINES

CHAPTER 10

In addition, you will need nozzle (injector) and jets. Any nozzle will work, but nitrous fogger-style nozzles are the best. Using this type of nozzle gives you the ability to tune the nozzle with the jets. The nozzle needs to be capable of fanning the spray for proper atomization of the alcohol mixture; otherwise you will just get a stream of fluid, which will not be a benefit but could cause a problem in the combustion chamber. You will also need fittings and line to run to the nozzle and the fluid tank. A fluid tank will hold the alcohol mix. A windshield washer tank provides a convenient reservoir.

Wiring the relay is probably the most difficult part. Relays can be confusing. If you get confused, simply refer back to the diagram. The following is a written diagram. Wire the fuel pump's positive terminal to Terminal 87 using an 8- or 10-gauge wire. Run a wire (8 to 10 gauge) with an inline fuse (matching the fuse rating on the pump's instructions) from the battery to Terminal 30. The MAP switch wire goes to Terminal 86. Wire Terminal 85 goes to a good solid ground. Wire the negative terminal on the fuel pump to ground with an 8- or 10-gauge wire. The wire routing depends on where you mount your pump. For a clean installation, use wire ties and flex loom. Be sure to keep all the wires from lying on or near hot surfaces, including the turbo, downpipe, etc.

The mounting location of the injector nozzle is up to you. The best location is in the up-pipe near the bend, which allows the alcohol to atomize properly. The up-pipe should be removed before proceeding. Drill the pipe with a 3/16-inch drill bit (or other, depending on your injector). Since the up pipe is not made of metal thick enough to support the nozzle reliably, a secondary mount must be made. This should be a properly sized nut that matches the nozzle. The nut can either be welded on (if you have a welder, this is the best method), or you can use an epoxy such as JB Weld. If using the epoxy method, make sure the up-pipe is as clean as possible with a die grinder and a Scotch-Brite pad or other device. If the up-pipe is not clean, the epoxy will not stick. Take your time to make it look nice. If you are using a 90-degree nozzle for aiming, mark the spray side.

You can mount the fuel pump in any suitable location. The plastic wheel well is a great place for mounting. The liquid tank needs to be mounted above the pump so that the pump always sees liquid and does not get a lot of air bubbles. The MAP switch can be mounted to the pressure switch on the passenger-side fender. Locate a good place to splice into the boost system for your switch. Mounting the relay next to the MAP switch makes wiring a little easier.

If you are using epoxy, you will need to wait 24 hours before the nozzle can be threaded in. The epoxy needs to be cured so it will take the added weight. Thread the nozzle in the nut until it is snug, then back it off until it points in the desired direction, via the mark you put on it earlier. It should spray into the flow so air/fuel mixing is maximized.

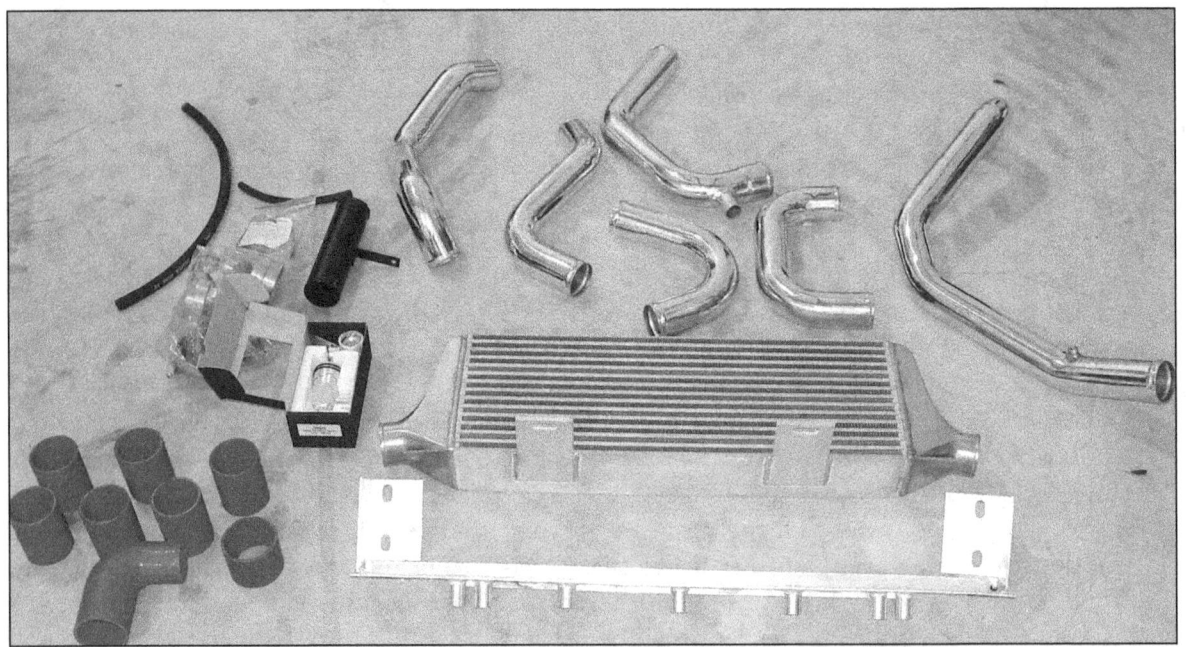

Intercoolers provide cooler, denser air for making more power with a turbo motor. This Turbo XS kit is a front-mounted unit and came with silicone rubber hoses and hard pipe.

The Nitrous Express Intercooler ring sprays a dense charge of liquid nitrous in the intercooler. The air charge quickly cools and performance dramatically increases, so you shave a couple of tenths off your timeslips.

The ring mounts on the intercooler in the center, and the solenoid mounts directly on the ring.

Reinstall the up-pipe. Plumbing the nozzle can be a little tricky if you don't have the right parts. Order all of your plumbing from the same place you get the nozzle. They will help you get the specific parts you need for your nozzle. Install the jet you are running, and then continue with the plumbing job. The placement of the lines is crucial for ease of use. You do not want the feed line too tight or it can bind. You also must make sure the line is not touching anything that generates heat — a melted line does no good. *Do not* use vacuum line because the pressure will pop it off and make a mess. Test the system and make sure fluid is spraying out. Running a 50/50 mix of rubbing alcohol and water is about the best ratio for this type of system. Adding alcohol can allow you to increase the boost 6 psi without detonation.

Intercoolers

For a hot-air car (1978–1985) adding an intercooler will make significant increase in power as the pressurized air runs get cooled, which makes it much more dense, allowing the engine to burn fuel more efficiently. For the later engines (1986–1987), increasing the size of the intercooler is a sure-fire way to add power. There are two main intercooler styles: air-to-air, and air-to-water. Air-to-air are the most common and the least expensive. These intercoolers use large passages to split the intake charge into rows of finned hollow tubes, much like a radiator. Cold-air cars carry this type of stock intercooler. An air-to-water intercooler uses a liquid core to cool the intake charger similar to an engine's coolant system. The water-to-air units use a radiator mounted in front of the engines radiator. There are several vehicles that use water-to-air intercoolers, such as the Ford Lightning and the GM Cyclone/Typhoon.

For performance engines, any intercooler is better than no intercooler. Running much more than 20 psi of boost without an intercooler is often lethal for the engine. Which type of intercooler you chose depends on your intended use of the vehicle. For most turbo Buicks, a drag-strip-ready street car is the goal. For this, an air-to-air intercooler is most likely the best bet. The plumbing lines for an ATA intercooler require some planning and a little skill, but the benefits of an ATA on the highway far outweigh the quick-cool charge from an ATW unit. If the application is strip-only, an ATW will provide a much faster cooling effect, and the cooling box can be packed with ice, giving even more of a boost in temperature drop. The ATW systems cost considerably more, but they can be installed under the hood and the liquid coolant lines are easier to route. A majority of the street-driven factory ATW-cooled vehicles get an ATA cooler installed as a performance upgrade, since the ATA works better in street-driven applications.

There is another option when it comes to cooling the intake charge. Adding a nitrous oxide cooling ring on the intercooler is a great way to drop the temperature of the intake charge for those quick blasts down the dragstrip. As the compressed nitrous oxide is sprayed out, the gas literally freezes the tubes of the intercooler, which makes a drastic change in temp. These systems are great for street-driven vehicles that see any amount of dragstrip action.

Mounting the intercooler is also an important issue. The stock intercooler is mounted behind the radiator, in front of the crank pulley. This means that the air must pass through the hot radiator before it passes through the intercooler. This does not help matters. Placing the intercooler in front of the radiator won't affect the engine's coolant system, but will increase the cooling effect that the intercooler can provide. Increasing the size of the intercooler will allow the unit to have more surface area, which will make for a cooler charge. There are several custom-fit intercoolers available, as well as universal-fit intercoolers. A universal fit will require a lot of cutting and fitting of the piping, so be careful if you decide to go this route.

The wastegate prevents the turbo from generating too much pressure and damaging the engine. The diaphragm on this wastegate is completely gone, so it needs to be repaired.

Downpipes and Wastegates

The downpipe for the turbo system is the exiting portion of the turbo impeller. This is where the exhaust gases flow to the catalytic converter and mufflers. The stock downpipe is fairly restrictive because of several hard bends and a shrunken neck (the input side) that restricts flow. The wastegate is also on this end and is an internal-style unit. That means the actual release port of the wastegate is inside the downpipe.

Upgrading the downpipe is one of the first mods to make a serious performance engine. TA Performance and Southeast Turbo Performance offer a few select downpipes. In addition, the Terry Houston downpipe was once quite popular but is no longer made. Southeast Turbo decided to re-issue the Houston-style downpipe with its own version. There are some issues with the aftermarket downpipes, which relate to the installation and require that some specific details be paid attention to.

John Pearcy, of johnsperformance.com, a turbo Buick specialty shop,

This replacement diaphragm seals the wastegate, so it can do its job.

recommends having an experienced shop install the downpipe. "The main problem with the aftermarket downpipe is the installation," said Pearcy. "The weight of the downpipe hangs on the turbo housing, which, after the engine torques over, puts pressure on the headers, eventually cracking them." The issue at hand is that the Buick V-6 turbo downpipe mounts to the transmission crossmember and leaves the bulk of the weight hanging on the turbo. A correct installation requires custom fabrication of an upper downpipe support that removes the hanging weight from the turbo housing. The

V-6 TURBO

The stock fuel-injection plenum has a few issues. The intake increases air flow to the front two cylinders and is fixed. The intake also reduces backpressure, so power output is increased.

turbo Trans-Am cars use a downpipe that mounts to the passenger side header; this eliminates the problem.

Another turbo Buick specialty shop is ESP Products (espperformance.com). They offer a custom-made 3-inch downpipe with optional wastegate placement options.

The stock wastegate is suitable for mid-level performance use, but it should be checked for deterioration of the rubber flapper and the mechanism. If the wastegate is not in excellent condition, it should be

COURTESY OF TRX PERFORMANCE, LOWELL IN.

PERFORMANCE, HORSEPOWER, INJECTOR, FUEL, & TURBO REFERENCE

1/4 MPH SPEED	TYPICAL E.T.	TURBO REGAL VEHICLE WEIGHT & DRIVER						V-6 INJ. SIZE # PER/HR			GAL./HR
		3300	3400	3500	3600	3700		80% D.C	90% D.C	100% DC	TYPICAL
95	14.39	219	225	232	239	245		26	23	20	20
100	13.67	255	263	271	278	286		30	26	24	23
105	13.02	295	304	313	322	331		34	31	28	27
110	12.43	340	350	360	370	381		40	35	32	31
112	12.21	358	369	380	391	402	H	42	37	33	32
114	11.99	378	389	401	412	424	O	44	39	35	34
116	11.79	398	410	422	434	446	R	47	41	37	36
118	11.59	419	432	445	457	470	S	49	44	39	38
120	11.39	441	454	468	481	494	E	51	46	41	40
122	11.21	463	477	491	505	519	P	54	48	43	42
124	11.03	486	501	516	531	545	O	57	50	45	44
126	10.85	510	526	541	557	572	W	60	53	48	46
128	10.68	535	551	567	584	600	E	62	56	50	48
129	10.60	548	564	581	597	614	R	64	57	51	50
130	10.52	560	577	594	611	628		65	58	52	51
131	10.44	574	591	608	626	643		67	60	54	52
132	10.36	587	605	622	640	658		69	61	55	53
133	10.28	600	618	637	655	673		70	62	56	54
134	10.20	614	632	651	670	688		72	64	57	56
135	10.13	628	647	666	685	704		73	65	59	57
136	10.05	642	661	681	700	720		75	67	60	58
137	9.98	656	676	696	716	736		77	68	61	59
HORSEPOWER REQUIRED AT VEHICLE WEIGHT								INJ.SIZE BASED ON		3700	LB. WT.
NOTE: E.T. & MPH ARE TYPICAL WITHIN +/- .10 AND +/- 1 MPH.								VEHICLE @.5 BSFC & DUTY CYCLE			

INJECTOR DATA

V-6 INJECTOR SIZE/TYPE		TYPICAL HORSEPOWER RANGE		
HIGH IMPEDANCE				
1 – 28#	STOCK- BOSCH	220	360	H.P.
2 – 30#	GRN-STRP-TOMCO	250	380	H.P.
3 – 36#	BLUETOP-BOSCH	330	445	H.P.
4 – 40#	RED-STRP-TOMCO	380	485	H.P.
5 – 43#	GRN-STRP-TOMCO	410	545	H.P.
6 – 50#	M.S.D.	460	600	H.P.
LOW IMPEDANCE				
7 – 52#	BOSCH	500	650	H.P.
8 – 55#	BENDIX-SIEMANS	530	690	H.P
9 – 72#	M.S.D.	685	875	H.P.
10 – 83#	BENDIX-SIEMANS	785	1000+	H.P.

TURBO DATA

TURBO TYPE 3-BOLT	TYPICAL MAX HP	TURBO TYPE 4-BOLT	TYPICAL MAX HP
STOCK	N/A	TE-63	725
TA-49	545	TE-69	780
TA-60	565	TE-70	820
TA-61	580	TE-72	850
TA-62	615	TE-75	1000
TE-32	480	TE-80	1200
TE-34	530	TE-90	1450
TE-44	580	60-1	580
TE-60	600	60-1 4" inlet	640
TE-62	630		
TE-63	670		
TE-70	775		

This 3.8-liter V-6 turbo chart provides performance targets for turbo cars, injector capability, and other valuable turbo data.

CHAPTER 10

The Mototron fuel injectors are the most versatile injectors available. The stock computer and upgraded chips control these units, and these injectors deliver a precise fuel mixture. Before, you had to match the injectors with the turbo, but the Mototron injectors are very versatile.

replaced. The factory wastegate is not adjustable, which makes it difficult to change the boost level. A simple cut and splice of the actuator rod will make the wastegate adjustable; you can also purchase an adjustable wastegate actuator rod. The alternative is to replace the factory unit altogether, which is more appropriate for a high-performance application. The aftermarket wastegates are external, so installing one requires either a new downpipe or a wastegate flange. There are hundreds of wastegate manufacturers, and once you have a flange mounted, you can use just about any wastegate. ESP offers the Evolution wastegate, which is good to 500 hp, and the Racegate unit is capable of supporting 900 hp.

The stock exhaust crossover pipe is another area that could use some modification. The stock pipe is restrictive due to the serious reduction in diameter on the driver-side connection. Adding an aftermarket crossover pipe can yield a 25 percent increase in flow area. This equates to more torque and HP throughout the power band. By decreasing the backpressure, the torque power band will move to a lower RPM, resulting in quicker ETs on the track, and certainly more passing power on the highway. Most aftermarket crossover pipes are ceramic coated, as well, which reduces heat under the hood and promotes exhaust gas scavenging.

Intakes

The stock turbo intake does not distribute the air charge equally throughout the engine. The problem is that the back four cylinders get all the air, and the front two cylinders are starved. This leads to an overly rich condition in the front two cylinders. In high-performance applications, this is a problem. There are several supposed fixes for this problem that involve welding plates and pouring epoxies in the stock plenum, but replacing the plenum is the best fix for the problem. Hemco offers the Buick V-6 turbo plenum in two versions: stock, and race. Each is available in different throttle body sizes: 58 mm (stock style only), 62 mm, 65 mm, and 70 mm. These plenums eliminate the sloping rear plenum, which causes the problem. The Hemco plenum provides as much as 0.2 second in quarter-mile improvement.

TA Performance offers its own version, but as an entire intake assembly for both stock off-center blocks and aftermarket on-center blocks. These intakes come with the upper plenum and fuel rails. For a race engine, the TA intake provides a little extra power.

If the stock look is needed, wanted, or you simply don't want to swap out the plenum, adding a

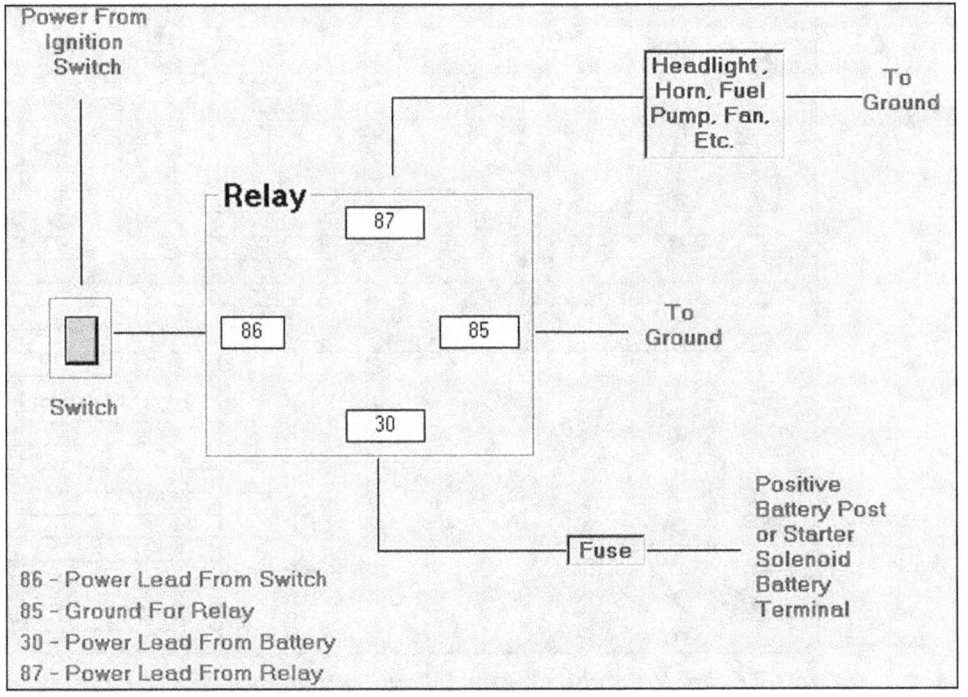

This wiring diagram for Bosch-style relays keeps things nice and easy.

plenum spacer can be worth 10 hp. By using a non-conductive material, the plenum spacer helps keep the upper plenum cool, which provides a more dense air charge. The plenum spacer also helps the distribution of the intake charge due to the extra volume. This can also be added to the Hemco plenum for even more effect.

When the stock turbo is replaced with an aftermarket unit, the throttle body needs to be replaced, as well. The factory 58-mm throttle body is good to the mid 12 seconds in the quarter-mile, but going much faster is going to require more air flow. The throttle body needs to match the turbo. The important thing is to at least run the smallest throttle body capable of supporting the turbo cfm. If you do not add at least the minimum size, you will restrict the turbo and not get the benefit of the upgrade. While you can go too big, it is the small side that makes the biggest difference. But you want to match the capability of the turbo as best you can. Consult the manufacturer of the turbo you purchase on what size throttle body will work best for that turbo.

The fuel injectors also need to match the turbo. The stock injectors are 28 lbs per hour. These injectors can take a V-6 turbo to the upper 12-second range, but beyond that, you will need to upgrade. The stock ECM can control up to 50–55-lb-per-hour injectors; if you want to run bigger injectors than that, you will have to upgrade the ECM.

That said, there is an injector that can be operated with the stock ECM and is capable of delivering 60 lbs of fuel. The Siemens DEKA IV 63PPH injector, more commonly known as the Mototron 60-lb injector, has become very popular for use in the turbo Buick. This injector is very efficient and can be installed in place of the stock injectors in an otherwise stock car and not over-fuel the engine. As the turbo and other components are replaced, this injector will deliver more fuel, as needed. This is probably the most versatile injector currently on the market.

This coil pack replacement from ESP Products for the 1986–1987 Buick turbo engines increases the voltage spark output considerably.

The American-made ESP Products main girdle for the V-6 turbo block was the first girdle available. Stay away from poor-quality, Chinese-made girdles.

CHAPTER 10

The ESP Products twin-turbo package made over 700 hp on the initial dyno testing. Perfect for street and track driving, the twin-turbo kit is designed to lower the boost levels and keep detonation at a minimum.

Fuel Pump

Along with bigger injectors, the fuel pump needs to be replaced. The problem here is that the original design of the fuel system placed the fuel pump inside the gas tank, which is where it stays. The stock fuel pump is really not even capable of supporting the stock fuel-injection system, much less a high-performance engine. Unless you are keeping the car completely stock, the fuel pump must be upgraded. The stock pump is rated at 28 gph, and aftermarket units start at around 41 gph, so you see the difference. There are quite a few in-tank high-performance fuel pumps available. As long as the unit can support the injectors, the choice is yours. EPS Products offers a 41-gph unit as a high-volume unit, while the high-performance units are 50 and 60 gph. The later is capable of supporting over 800 hp.

When the fuel pump is being upgraded, the stock fuel pump wiring needs to be addressed. The stock wiring is barely sufficient to handle the current draw of the stock pump. An aftermarket pump will seriously tax the original wiring and cause a fire. There are kits available that make this a plug-and-play operation, but those who are feeling saucy can build their own.

The main idea behind this is to use the factory fuel pump power wire as the trigger for a relay, which then allows current to flow through a larger 10- or 12-gauge wire. This wire has a higher current flow capability; therefore it won't get as hot and will not lose as much current as the stock 18-gauge wire. To wire the system, simply run 10- or 12-gauge wire from the battery to the fuel tank. Then, wire a Bosch-style relay to supply current to the new wire when current is applied to the relay (see sidebar on relay wiring). With this completed, the electrical burden is removed from the stock wiring, and the new wire will be fully capable of supplying the full current draw of the new fuel pump. Be sure to properly fuse the new wire within 18 inches of the battery with the correct fuse size as stated in the instructions for the fuel pump. When making the connections, use a high-quality crimping tool and use heat-shrink tubing around the wire-side of the terminals on the wire. This will eliminate the possibility of the wires touching the chassis, and then causing a short, which will start a fire. Too many cars catch fire because of faulty wiring—do not let it be yours.

Electronics

While the electronics do not pertain to building the engine, they certainly affect the engine's ability to make power when you are dealing with fuel and spark control. There are several pieces of electronics that must be dealt with when building a Buick V-6 turbo.

On the 1978–1983 engines, the ignition is based on an HEI unit, and engine is equipped with a knock sensor. If the engine begins to knock, the knock sensor retards the timing to protect the engine. These systems are adequate. But if you want to make substantial power with these engines, you need to install an aftermarket ignition system, such as an

MSD 6 or 6al. These units will give you the hotter spark needed to fire a high-performance, carbureted turbo Buick. It is also recommended that you install a knock gauge so you can monitor the detonation inside the engine.

For the 1984–1985 turbo engines, the ignition is controlled by an ECM, and the aftermarket chips are fairly limited in their capability. The later-style ECMs are much better and have quite a few more options in performance chips. Kits are available to convert the 1986–1987 ECM to the earlier cars, such as those from Casper Electronics. Their adapter costs about $60 and adds a lot of options to the older engines.

Upgrading the ignition module to the later 1986–1987 unit is another inexpensive option for the 1984–1985 engines. This requires a little more work than the ECM conversion, which is a plug-and-play operation. Converting the C3I ignition module allows for a more consistent spark and generates a more efficient burn. There are two ways to perform this task; the first requires new pins and removal of the existing pin in the harness plug. This would be the better looking option, but getting the tiny pins to release can be a nightmare. The other option is to cut the wires and solder the wires together in the proper configuration. Do *not* use butt-connectors; this is an important piece, and solder is much more reliable. Which method you choose is up to you. Keep in mind the factory wiring harness leaves only enough room to plug the module in; if you cut off too much, things will become very difficult.

After you have decided which method will be used, the process is fairly simple. The wires need to be repositioned in the correct placement for the newer module. The pin placement is as follows:

Pin A: This pin remains the same. ("ECM B4 EST," white wire, number 423)

Pin B: This pin remains the same. ("ECM D5 BYPASS," tan/black wire, number 424)

Pin C: This pin remains the same. ("ECM B5 REF. LOW," purple/white wire, number 430)

Pin D: Remove "TACH LEAD" (white wire, number 121). Splice in "ECM B-3 REF. LOW" (black/red wire, number 453; previously located at pin F position).

Pin E: Remove "ECM ALL CAM" (yellow wire, number 951). Splice in "TACH LEAD"(white wire, number 121; previously located at pin D position).

Pin F: Splice in "CRANK SENSOR B" (green wire, number 918 previously located at pin G position).

Pin G: Splice in "CRANK SENSOR C GRND" (black wire, number 952 previously located in pin H position).

Pin H: Splice in "CRANK SENSOR A 12V" (white/red wire, number 916 previously located in pin J position).

Pin I not used.

Pin J: Splice in "ECM ALL CAM" (yellow wire, number 951 previously located in pin E position).

Pin K: Splice in "CAM SENSOR B SIGNAL" (light blue wire, number 917 previously located at pin L position).

Pin L: Splice in "CAM SENSOR C GRND" (black wire, number 952 previously located at pin K position).

Pin M: Remove "CAM SENSOR A 12V" (white/red wire, number 916). Splice in "IGNITION POWER" (pink/black wire, number 839 previously installed in pin P position).

Pin N: Remove "IGNITION POWER" (pink/black wire, number 439). Splice in "CAM SENSOR A 12V"" (white/red wire, number 916previously installed in pin M position).

Pin O not used.

Pin P: Splice in "IGNITION POWER" (pink/black wire, number 439 previously located in pin N position).

Once the wiring is completed, the new module can be plugged in, and the car started for a test. If everything fires up and the car runs, the module is correctly hooked up. The later module requires a new mounting plate. This can be built with a simple 4.5 x 6-inch aluminum plate.

The most popular turbo Buicks are the 1986–1987 engines. These engines represent the culmination of 15 years of R&D in its family of engines. As such, these engines are capable of 2,000 hp with relatively simple modifications. The stock ECM is fully capable of serving a stock engine all the way up to even the most extreme race engine. That is not to say that all of the electronics are up to snuff. The stock coil packs are not very hot, and when the boost gets going, it is much more difficult to light the fire. ESP, through years of research and development, came up with the first high-voltage turbo Buick coil pack. This unit is capable of feeding all levels of turbo engines, including the twin-turbocharged 1,500-hp monster ESP built for their shop car. This is one mod that every high-performance Buick needs to have.

The throttle-position sensor (TPS) is a required piece of equipment on every throttle-body-injected engine. The basic function of this sensor is to let the computer know the position of the throttle. The computer then knows how much fuel to send to the cylinders and when to spark the plugs. On the 1984–1987 turbo Regals and Grand Nationals, the mass air flow (MAF) sensor controls the turbo boost. At a specific point, the MAF sensor bypasses the TPS signal and puts the computer into enrichment mode.

Throttle Position Sensor

This is great for a street car, but there are drawbacks. For modified performance vehicles, quicker, firmer shifts are always better. There is an easy mod that allows the stock transmission to give those tighter shifts. By

The ESP Twin Turbo Kit

Engineered for quick throttle response and near-zero turbo lag, the ESP Twin Turbo kit provides a broader power range with both impressive low-end power and top-end speed. Initial Dyno results have shown 700 hp and 720-plus ft-lb of torque at a modest 18 psi of boost.

The lower boost level of the ESP Twin Turbo kit means lower cylinder temperature and pressure. This translates into less detonation, saved head gaskets, and more power. Having the engine operate at these lower boost levels will benefit the engine bearings, fuel system function, and overall engine durability. At only 10 psi of boost, you can still produce 500 hp (380 hp and 425 ft-lb to the tires). That's more power and torque than the Dodge Viper.

The ESP Twin Turbo kit delivers the unique combination of serious turbocharged power and V-8 responsiveness never seen before in the V-6 Turbo Buick. This kit is a clean installation that can bolt onto all stock block and aftermarket engines. Complete from the heads to the cat-back, the ESP Twin Turbo kit is not a patchwork of parts to fit a second turbo into your car; it's a complete kit. Imagine yourself driving to the drag strip, changing tires, and running low 10s at over 130 mph with unleaded fuel* in the tank, and through the exhaust! You can turn the boost down to 10 lbs and still know you have the power for mid to low 11s. Raise the boost to 15 lbs and you're at the high 10-second range at about 120 mph, and it's all designed for the street-performance car.

The ESP Twin Turbo kit will support up to 800 hp; custom applications up to 1,200-plus hp. Stock long blocks and balanced and blueprinted engines will experience huge gains in power and performance without the need to run damaging boost levels. The ESP shop car qualified at the 2007 GS Nationals with a 10.1 at 133 mph.

ESP Twin Turbo Kit:

- T3/T4 turbos**
- TiAL wastegates
- 3-inch Inlet tubes
- S&B Air Filters
- S.S. Headers**
- 3-inch Downpipes**
- 2 S.B. Oil Feed & Return Lines
- 1 Twin F.M. Intercooler
- 1 ARP Header Bolts
- 1 Accessory Bracket
- 1 Serpentine Belt & Tensioner
- 1 Misc. Fitting & hose kit

* Any and all race conditions should have appropriate-octane race gas or alcohol injection.
** All Exhaust components are Jet-Hot Coated, 2,000-degree Black.

The ESP twin turbo kit is a serious piece of engineering. With only 10 psi of boost, an otherwise stock engine can build 500 hp.

V-6 TURBO

The ESP Twin Turbo Kit *continued*

The twin turbo setup even fits in the Buick Regal's or GM G-body's engine compartments without modification. The 3.8-liter V-6 fitted with twin turbos can easily push a Buick to a 10-second quarter-mile time. These kits can be configured in custom application to support over 1,200 hp.

Engine Package:

- Block: Stock
- Support: ESP Engine Girdle
- Compression Ratio: 8.3:1
- Pistons: J.E. Pistons
- Rings: Speed-Pro (File-Fit)
- Cam Shaft: ESP Custom Hydraulic Roller (212-224)
- Cam Bearings: Durabond
- Push Rods: Chrome-moly
- Heads: Stock ESP CNC-Ported Iron Heads
- Rocker Arms: 1.65 T-&-D Roller Rockers
- Intake Manifold: Stock; Port Match by ESP
- Connecting Rods: Stock
- Crankshaft: Stock
- Bearings: King
- Throttle Body: 70-mm AccuFab
- Fuel Injectors: 85# Delphi
- Ignition: ESP High-Output Coilpack
- Engine Management: FAST
- Hardware: ARP Fasteners
- Forced Induction: ESP Twin Turbo Kit (up to 800 hp)

Performance Statistics
- Best E.T. to date: 10.12 seconds
- Best MPH to date: 133 mph
- Best 60-foot to date: 1.47 seconds

John Perri, mgr.
ESP Products
2203 N. Charlotte Street
Pottstown, PA 19464
610-970-8944
www.espperformance.com; www.pre-luber.com

CHAPTER 10

adjusting the throttle valve (TV) cable out one or two positions, the transmission shifts at a higher rpm, yielding tighter, snappier shifts. The big problem with this is that the throttle is held back slightly, not quite hitting the previous wide open throttle (WOT) position. This leaves the WOT performance a little lacking because the computer is not enhancing fuel and spark, and the TPS is not hitting its WOT mark. The computer is looking for 4.5 volts to trigger WOT performance.

By modifying the TPS signal, the computer will produce the WOT performance. This is done with a throttle position sensor/throttle enhancer calibrator (TPS-TEC) module. This module is a plug-and-play unit that mounts under the hood and plugs in line with the TPS. At 60 percent throttle, the TPS-TEC sends the computer a 4.5-volt signal. The computer thinks the engine is running at WOT and alters the fuel and timing maps accordingly. This means you have the WOT performance enhancements at 60 percent throttle, which means more mid-range HP and torque — not bad for a five-minute bolt on. The TPS-TEC has a built-in safety that will not allow the unit to send too much voltage to the computer. In addition to the better performance, the TPS-TEC has a TPS calibrator that allows you to test the operation of your TPS unit.

A Scanmaster unit is also a must-have for every turbo Buick. This tool allows the driver to monitor boost, knock, oxygen voltage, mass air flow (MAF), coolant and air temps, TPS readings — everything you need to know when tuning your turbocharged engine. If you own a turbo-powered Buick, you need a Scanmaster. The Scanmaster is about the size of a radar detector and can be mounted just about anywhere. On a Regal, the ledge just above the radio and A/C controls is perfect, like it was made to go there. If you do not have one, go get one. They are invaluable.

Oxygen Sensor

The oxygen sensor in the 1984–1987 turbo Buicks is flawed. The problem is that after about 20,000 miles, or sooner if you use fuel additives, the oxygen sensors burn up. When the oxygen sensor goes out, the engine runs rough; fuel economy goes down; and Codes 13, 44, and 45 show; there is a whole host of problems that are difficult to diagnose. There is a simple fix, however: installing a heated oxygen sensor. These kits are plug and play; no modifications to the wiring harness and simple Weatherpack connections are made. The heated sensor sends the computer into closed-loop operation much faster, eliminating the up-and-down idle issues, and the sensor is smaller than the original oxygen unit, reducing exhaust restrictions. This modification is race proven and allows the engine to be fed a steady diet of fuel additives or leaded race fuel without fouling the sensor.

Another oxygen change is to run the Tomco platinum oxygen sensor. While not as efficient as the heated oxygen unit, the Tomco sensor resists fouling and lasts 25–30 percent longer than a stock sensor. The platinum tip heats up much faster than a stock unit, which allows the computer to operate more efficiently. These cost less than the heated oxygen kits and are a good option for those on a budget.

MAF Sensor

The MAF sensors are no longer made by GM; they have been discontinued. As these vehicles age, more of these MAF units will be needed. There are rebuilt units available from the local parts stores, but these units barely function well enough for a stock engine. Putting one of these units on a high-performance application is not a suitable fix. There is another option available from Buick specialty dealers, such as Poston Buick. The Translator MAF replacement unit plugs into the stock MAF wiring harness, allowing the use of a new high-flow GM MAF sensor. These high-flow MAF sensors flow 800–1,000 cfm, whereas the stock MAF flows 750 cfm. This increase in flow leads to quicker spool-up and yields better drivability. The newer MAF units are suitable for use with bigger injectors with better economy.

The high-flow MAF sensors also increase the tuning capabilities of the engine. Each MAF sensor has adjustments for fuel delivery, and they work with aftermarket chips, as well. The Pro version of the high-flow MAF plugs into the spark timing wire and allows you to tune the timing curve based on driving conditions.

The Gen 2 MAF flow unit adds even more adjustability. This sensor is based on the Translator Pro and allows the user to adjust the fuel output up to 60 percent (plus or minus) in 1/2-percent steps, across 14 rpm bands. The Gen 2 also features wideband tracking, which allows the unit to tie into any 0–5 volt wideband oxygen sensor and the MAF sensor will adjust the air/fuel ratio to maintain the AFR for optimum performance. These units are not cheap, but adding even the base translator will provide an increase in performance that makes the base unit's $200 price tag worth it.

APPENDIX A

Source Guide

ARP
1863 Eastman Avenue
Ventura, CA 93003
www.arp-bolt.com
info@arpfasteners.com

Auto Meter
413 West Elm Street
Sycamore, IL 60178
(866) 248-6356
www.autometer.com

Barry Grant Incorporated
1450 McDonald Road
Dahlonega, Georgia 30533
Phone: (706) 864-8544
Fax: (706) 864-2206
www.barrygrant.com

BOP Engineering
N3651 Schmidt Road
Jefferson, WI 53549-9768
Phone: (920) 674-6058
Fax: (920) 674-6059
www.bopengineering.com

Buick Performance Group
www.buickperformance.com

CarChemistry
Waxahachie, TX
Phone: (972) 937-7735
Fax: (972) 937-7714
www.carchemistry.com

Centerville Auto Repair
Grass Valley, CA 95945
(530) 272-1564
www.nailheadbuick.com
nailhead_russ@yahoo.com

Champion Racing Heads
13 Hargrove Grade
Palm Coast, FL 32137-5114
Phone: (386) 446-4488
Fax: (386) 446-2090
www.championracingheads.com

Comp Cams
3406 Democrat Road
Memphis, TN 38118
(901) 795-2400
www.compcams.com

Edelbdrock
2700 California Street
Torrance, CA 90503
Phone: 310-781-2222
Fax: 310-320-1187
www.edelbrock.com

Egge
11707 Slauson Avenue
Santa Fe Springs, CA 90670
Phone: (866) 534-3443
Fax: (562) 693-1635
www.egge.com

ESP Products
2203 N. Charlotte Street
Pottstown, PA 19464
(610) 970-8944
contactus@espperformance.com

Flex-a-lite
P.O. Box 580
Milton, WA 98354
(800) 851-1510
www.flex-a-lite.com

GN T-Type Forum
www.gnttype.org

Gessler Head Porting
25 Four Corners Road
Blairstown, NJ 07825-2402
(908) 362-7692
www.gesslerheadporting.com

HardBlok
P.O. Box 1274
Brentwood, TN 37024-1274
(865) 457-0509
www.hardblok.com

Holley
P.O. Box 10360
1801 Russellville Road
Green, KY 42101
(270) 782-2900
www.holley.com

Hooker Headers
P.O. Box 10360
1801 Russellville Road
Bowling Green, KY 42101
(270) 782-2900
www.holley.com

Jack Merkel Performance Engines
25 Walnut Avenue
Clark, NJ 07066
Phone: (732) 388-7088
Fax: (732) 388-1110
www.merkelengines.com

John's Performance
10315 86th Street N.E.
Lake Stevens, WA 98258
(360) 658-9966
www.johnsperformance.com

HOW TO BUILD MAX-PERFORMANCE BUICK ENGINES

APPENDIX A

Kring Buick Parts
www.milrproducts.com

Magnuson Products, Inc.
1990 Knoll Drive
Ventura, CA 93003
Phone: (805) 642-8833
Fax: (805) 677-4897
www.magnusonproducts.com

Mallory
10601 Memphis Avenue #12
Cleveland, OH 44144
(216) 688-8300
www.malloryperfromance.com

March Performance
16160 Performance Way
Naples, FL 34110
Phone: (239) 593-4074
Fax: (239) 593-4564
www.marchperf.com

Meziere
220 S. Hale Avenue
Escondido, CA 92029
(800) 208-1755
www.meziere.com

Moroso
80 Carter Drive
Guilford, CT 06437-2216
Phone: (203) 453-6571
Fax: (203) 453-6906
www.moroso.com

MSD
Autotronic Controls Corporation
1350 Pullman Drive, Dock #14
El Paso, TX 79936
(915) 857-5200
www.msdignition.com

Nitrous Express
5411 Seymour Highway
Wichita Falls, TX 76310
Phone: (940) 767-7694
Fax: (940) 767-7697
www.nitrousexpress.com

Nitrous Works
1450 McDonald Road
Dahlonega, Georgia 30533
Phone: (706) 864-8544
Fax: (706) 864-2206
www.barrygrant.com

PartzFinder Performance
Morris Industrial Park
507 Paul Morris Drive
Englewood, FL 34223
(941) 460-0667
www.partzfinder.com

Performance Automotive Engines
4401 Turf Road, Building E
El Paso, TX 79938
Phone: (915) 855-6009
Fax: (915) 855-2424
www.paenterprises.com

Pertronix
440 East Arrow Highway
San Dimas, CA 91773
Phone: (909) 599-5955
Fax: (909) 599-64242
www.pertronix.com

Poston Buick
200 Ewing Lane
Atmore, AL 36502
(800) 635-9781
www.postonbuick.com

Pypes Performance Exhaust
2880 Bergey Road, Unit O
Hatfield, PA 19440
(800) 421-3890
www.pypesexhaust.com

Racetronix
sales@racetronix.com
www.racetronix.com

Rhoads Lifters
202 E. Main Street
San Manuel, AZ 85631
Phone: (520) 229-9375
Fax: (520) 385-4596
www.rhoadslifters.com

Royal Purple
One Royal Purple Lane
Porter, TX 77365
(888) 382-6300
www.royalpurple.com

TA Performance Products, Inc.
16167 N. 81st Street
Scottsdale, AZ 85260
Phone: (480) 922-6807
Fax: (480) 922-6811
www.taperformance.com

Taylor/Vertex
301 Highgrove Road
Grandview, MO 640301
Phone: (816) 765-5011
Fax: (816) 765-2452
www.taylorvertex.com

Team Buick Forum
www.TeamBuick.com

TurboXS
8041 Queenair Drive, Unit 2
Gaithersburg, MD 20879
Phone: (301) 977-4727
Fax: (301) 977-6507
www.turboxs.com

ZEX Nitrous
3418 Democrat Road
Memphis, TN 38118
(888) 817-1008
www.zex.com

APPENDIX B

1953-1955 NAILHEAD ENGINE SPECIFICATIONS

1953 322-ci Engine Specifications

General Specifications

Model Designation: Super V-8, Series 50; Roadmaster V-8, Series 70

Wheel Base: Super V-8: 121-1/2 in (125-1/2 in for 1952 model); Roadmaster V-8: 121-1/2 in (125-1/2 in on model 72R)

Valve Location: In head

Bore and Stroke: 4 x 3.2 in

Piston Displacement: 322-ci

Compression Ratio: Super V-8: 8.0:1; Roadmaster V-8: 8.5:1

Maximum Brake Horsepower: Super V-8: 164 hp @ 4,000 rpm; Roadmaster V-8: 188 hp @ 4,000 rpm

Maximum Torque: Super V-8: 286 ft-lb @ 2,200 rpm; Roadmaster V-8: 300 ft-lb @ 2,400 rpm

Normal Oil Pressure: 35 psi

Tune Up Specifications

Spark Plug: AC 44-5

Spark Plug Gap: .032 in

Firing Order: 12784563 (Front to rear: left bank: 2-4-6-8; right bank: 1-3-5-7)

Ignition Timing: Adv. Timing mark on Flywheel

Engine Idle Speed: 450 rpm

Cylinder Head Torque: 63-73 ft-lb

Compression Pressure & Cranking Speed: 160 Min.

Voltage & Polarity: 12 volts, negative ground

Piston and Ring Specifications

Fitting Pistons with Scale:
Shim thickness: .003 in
Pounds on Scale: 7 to 13 lbs

Ring End Gap:
Compression: .010 in
Oil: .015 in (no fitting required on Flex-Fit oil rings)

Clearance in Groove: Compression: .002-004 in; Oil: .0002-.0025 in

Wristpin Diameter: .940 in

Valve Specifications

Operating Clearance:
Intake: 0; Exhaust: 0

Valve Seat Angle: 45 degrees

Valve Timing: (BTDC = before top dead center; ATDC = after top dead center)
Intake Opens: 25 degrees BTDC
Exhaust Closes: 42 degrees ATDC

Valve Spring Pressure Pounds at Inches Length:
Inner Spring: 53 lbs @ 1.15 in; Outer Spring: 85 lbs @ 1.12 in

Valve Stem Clearance: Intake: .0025; Exhaust: .003

Engine Bearing Specifications

Connecting Rod Bearings:
Journal Diameter: 2.249-2.250 in
Bearing Clearance: .0002-.0023 in
Rod End Play: .006-.011 in
Rod Bolt Tension: 45-55 ft-lb

Main Bearings:
Journal Diameter: 2.498-2.499 in
Bearing Clearance: .0005-.0025 in
Shaft End Play: .004-.008 in (Thrust on Bearing No. 3)
Main Bolt Tension: 100-110 ft-lb

Capacity Data

Cooling System:
Super V-8:
Without Heater: 16-1/2 qts (18 qts with Dynaflow)
With Heater: 18 qts (19-1/2 qts with Dynaflow)
Roadmaster V-8:
Without Heater: 18 qts
With Heater: 19-1/2 qts

Fuel Tank: 19 gal

Engine Oil: 6 qts

Transmission: 2-1/2 w/auto 10 qts

Rear Axle: 4-1/2 pts

Delco-Remy Distributor Specifications

Distributor Part Number: 1110827 (Distributor rotates clockwise.)

Cam Angle: 26-33 degrees (Do not use dwell meter for setting point opening.)

Breaker Point Opening: .016 in

Condenser Capacity: .18-.23 mfds

Breaker Arm Spring Tension: 19-23 oz

Centrifugal Advance: (Degrees at rpm of distributor)
Advance Starts: 1 degree @ 350 rpm
Full Advance: 15 degrees @ 2,000 rpm

Vacuum Advance Data:
Inches of vacuum to start plunger movement: 5 - 7 in
Inches of vacuum for full plunger travel: 11 - 14 in
Maximum vacuum advance: 11 - 12-1/2 Dist. degrees

Delco-Remy Distributor Specifications

Generator Number: 1102003 (Generator rotates clockwise; negative ground)

Generator Output: 30 amps @ 2,300 rpm

APPENDIX B

Regulator Specifications

Regulator Number: 1118749

Cutout Relay:
Voltage to close points: 12.8 volts
Armature air gap: .020 in

Voltage Regulator Setting: 14.5 volts

Current Regulator Setting: 30 volts

Current and Voltage Armature Air Gap: .075 in

Delco-Remy Starting Motor Specifications

Part Number: 1107601 (Starter rotates clockwise.)

Bush Spring Tension: 24-28 oz

No Load Test: 75 amps, 10.3 volts @ 6,500 rpm

Torque Test: 460 amps, 5.2 volts, torque: 11.5

1954 322-ci Engine Specifications

General Specifications

Model Designation: Super V-8, Series 50; Century V-8, Series 60; Roadmaster V-8, Series 70

Wheel Base: Super V-8: 127; Century V-8: 122; Roadmaster V-8: 127-1/2

Valve Location: In head

Bore and Stroke: 4 x 3.2 in

Piston Displacement: 322-ci

Compression Ratio: Super V-8: 8.0:1 (8.5:1 w/Dynaflow); Century V-8: 8.0:1 (8.5:1 w/Dynaflow) Roadmaster V-8: 8.5:1

Maximum Brake Horsepower: Super V-8: 177 hp @ 4,100 rpm (182 hp w/Dynaflow); Century V-8: 195 hp @ 4,100 rpm (200 hp w/Dynaflow); Roadmaster V-8: 200 hp @ 4,100 rpm

Maximum Torque: Super V-8: 295 ft-lb @ 2,000 rpm (300 ft-lb w/Dynaflow); Century V-8: 302 ft-lb @ 2,400 rpm (309 ft-lb w/Dynaflow); Roadmaster V-8: 309 ft-lb @ 2,400 rpm

Normal Oil Pressure: 35 psi

Tune Up Specifications

Spark Plug: AC 44-5

Spark Plug Gap: .032 in

Firing Order: 12784563 (Front to rear: left bank 2-4-6-8; right bank 1-3-5-7)

Ignition Timing: Yellow timing mark aligns with "5" on timing indicator; Location: vibration damper

Engine Idle Speed: 450 rpm

Cylinder Head Torque: 63-73 ft-lb

Compression Pressure & Cranking Speed: 150 min

Voltage & Polarity: 12 volts, negative ground

Piston and Ring Specifications

Fitting Pistons with Scale:
Shim thickness .003 in
Pounds on Scale: 7 - 13 lbs

Ring End Gap:
Compression: .010 in
Oil: .015 in (no fitting required on Flex-Fit oil rings)

Clearance in Groove: Compression: .002-004 in; Oil: .0035-.0095 in

Wristpin Diameter: .940 in

Valve Specifications

Operating Clearance:
Intake: 0; Exhaust: 0

Valve Seat Angle: 45 degrees

Valve Timing: (BTDC = Before Top Dead Center; ATDC = After Top Dead Center)
Intake Opens: 25 degrees BTDC
Exhaust Closes: 42 degrees ATDC

Valve Spring Pressure Pounds at Inches Length:
Inner Spring: 53 lbs @ 1.15 in; Outer Spring: 85 lbs @ 1.12 in

Valve Stem Clearance: Intake: .0025 in; Exhaust: .003 in

Engine Bearing Specifications

Connecting Rod Bearings:
Journal Diameter: 2.249-2.250 in
Bearing Clearance: .0002-.0023 in
Rod End Play: .006-.011 in
Rod Bolt Tension: 45-55 ft-lb

Main Bearings:
Journal Diameter: 2.498-2.499 in
Bearing Clearance: .0005-.0025 in
Shaft End Play: .004-.008 in (Thrust on Bearing No. 3)
Main Bolt Tension: 100-110 ft-lb

Capacity Data

Cooling System:
Super V-8; Century V-8:
Without Heater: 16-1/2 qts (18 qts with Dynaflow)
With Heater: 18; qts (18 qts with Dynaflow)
Roadmaster V-8:
Without Heater: 18 qts
With Heater: 20 qts

Fuel Tank: 19 gal

Engine Oil: 6 qts

Transmission: 2-1/2 w/auto 10 qts

APPENDIX B

Rear Axle: 4-1/2 pts

Delco-Remy Distributor Specifications

Distributor Part Number: 1110849 (Distributor rotates clockwise.)

Cam Angle: 26-33 (Do not use dwell meter for setting point opening.)

Breaker Point Opening: .016 in

Condenser Capacity: .18-.23 mfds

Breaker Arm Spring Tension: 19-23 oz

Centrifugal Advance: (Degrees at rpm of distributor)
Advance Starts 1-1/2 degrees @ 375 rpm
Full Advance: 12 degrees @ 1750 rpm

Vacuum Advance Data:
Inches of vacuum to start plunger movement: 6.5 - 8.5 in
Inches of vacuum for full plunger travel: 11-1/2 - 15 in
Maximum vacuum advance: 9 - 10-1/2 dist. Degrees

Delco-Remy Distributor Specifications

Generator Number: 1102008 (Generator rotates clockwise; 12 volt, negative ground)

Generator Output: 30 amps @ 2,300 rpm

Brush Spring Tension: 28 oz

Field Current: 1.48-1.62 amps

Regulator Specifications

Regulator Number: 1118825

Cutout Relay:
Voltage to close points: 12.8 volts
Armature air gap: .020 in

Voltage Regulator Setting: 14.5 volts

Current Regulator Setting: 30 volts

Current and Voltage Armature Air Gap: .075 in

Delco-Remy Starting Motor Specifications

Part Number: 1107621 (starter rotates clockwise)

Bush Spring Tension: 30-40 oz

No Load Test: 95 amps; 10.1 volts @ 3,500 rpm

Torque Test: 460 amps, 5.2 volts, torque: 11

1955 322-ci Engine Specifications

General Specifications

Model Designation: Special V-8, Series 40

Wheel base: Special V-8: 122 in

Valve Location: In head

Bore and Stroke: 3.625 x 3.2 in

Piston Displacement: 264-ci

Compression Ratio: 8.4:1

Maximum Brake Horsepower: 188 hp @ 4,800 rpm

Maximum Torque: 256 ft-lb @ 2,400 rpm

Normal Oil Pressure: 35 psi

Tune Up Specifications

Spark Plug: AC 44-5

Spark Plug Gap: .032 in

Firing Order: 12784563 (Front to rear: left bank 2, 4, 6, 8; right bank 1, 3, 5, 7)

Ignition Timing: Adv. timing mark on pulley

Engine Idle Speed: 450 rpm

Cylinder Head Torque: 63-73 ft-lb

Compression Pressure & Cranking Speed: 140 Min.

Voltage & Polarity: 12 volts; negative ground

Piston and Ring Specifications

Fitting Pistons with Scale:
Shim thickness: .003 in
Pounds pull on scale: 7 to 13 lbs

Ring End Gap:
Compression: .015 in
Oil: .025 in

Clearance in Groove: Compression: .002-004 in; Oil: .0035-.0095 in

Wristpin Diameter: .940 in

Valve Specifications

Operating Clearance:
Series 40: Intake: 0; Exhaust: 0

Valve Seat Angle: 45 degrees

Valve Timing: (BTDC = Before Top Dead Center; ATDC = After Top Dead Center)
Intake Opens: 25 degrees BTDC
Exhaust Closes: 42 degrees ATDC

Valve Spring Pressure Pounds at Inches Length:
Inner Spring: 21-1/2 lbs @ 1-1/2 in; Outer Spring: 40-1/2 lbs @ 1-1/2 in

Valve Stem Clearance: Intake: .0025 in; Exhaust: .003 in

Engine Bearing Specifications

Connecting Rod Bearings:
Journal Diameter: 2.249-2.250 in
Bearing Clearance: .0002-.0023 in
Rod End Play: .006-.011 in
Rod Bolt Tension: 45-55 ft-lb

Main Bearings:
Journal Diameter: 2.498-2.499 in

APPENDIX B

Bearing Clearance: .0005-.0025 in
Shaft End Play: .004-.008 in (Thrust on Bearing No. 3)
Main Bolt Tension: 100-110 ft-lb

Capacity Data

Cooling System:
Without Heater: 16-1/2 qts (18-1/2 qts with Dynaflow)
With Heater: 18 qts (20 qts with Dynaflow)

Fuel Tank: 19 gal

Engine Oil: 6 qts

Transmission: 1-3/4 w/auto 10 qts

Rear Axle: 4-1/2 pts

Delco-Remy Distributor Specifications

Distributor Part Number: 1110849 (Distributor rotates counter-clockwise.)

Cam Angle: 26-33 degrees (Do not use dwell meter for setting point opening.)

Breaker Point opening: .016 in

Condenser Capacity: .18-.23 mfds

Breaker Arm Spring Tension: 19-23 oz

Centrifugal Advance: (degrees at RPM of distributor)
Advance starts 1-1/2 degrees @ 375 rpm
Full Advance: 12 degrees @ 1,750 rpm

Vacuum Advance Data:
Inches of vacuum to start plunger movement: 6.5 - 8.5 in
Inches of vacuum for full plunger travel: 11-1/2 - 15 in
Maximum vacuum advance, Dist. degrees: 9 - 10-1/2 in

Delco-Remy Distributor Specifications

Generator Number: 1102008 (Generator rotates clockwise; negative ground)

Generator output: 30 amps @ 2,300 rpm

Brush Spring Tension: 28 oz

Field Current: 1.48-1.62 amps

Regulator Specifications

Regulator Number: 1118825

Cutout Relay:
Voltage to close points: 12.8 volts
Armature air gap: .020 in

Voltage Regulator Setting: 14.5 volts

Current Regulator Setting: 30 volts

Current and Voltage Armature Air Gap: .075 in

Delco-Remy Starting Motor Specifications

Part Number: 1107621 (Starter rotates clockwise.)

Bush Spring Tension: 30-40 oz

No Load Test: 95 amps, 10.1 volts @ 3,500 rpm

Torque Test: 460 amps, 5.2 volts, torque: 11

1956 322-ci Engine Specifications

General Specifications

Model Designation: Special V-8, Series 40; Super V-8, Series 50; Century V-8, Series 60; Roadmaster V-8, Series 70

Wheel base: Special V-8 122-ci; Super V-8 127-ci; Century V-8 122-ci; Roadmaster V-8 127-ci

Valve Location: In head

Bore and Stroke: 4.000 x 3.2 in

Piston Displacement: 322-ci

Compression ratio: Special V-8: 7.6:1 (8.9:1 w/Dynaflow) Super V-8: 9.5:1; Century V-8: 9.5:1; Roadmaster V-8: 9.5:1

Maximum Brake Horsepower: Special V-8: 220 hp @ 4,400 rpm; Super V-8: 255 hp @ 4,400 rpm; Century V-8: 255 hp @ 4,400; Roadmaster V-8: 255 hp @ 4,400 rpm

Maximum Torque: Special V-8: 319 ft-lb @ 2,400; Super V-8: 341 ft-lb @ 3,200 rpm; Century V-8: 341 ft-lb @ 3,200 rpm; Roadmaster V-8: 341 ft-lb @ 3,200 rpm

Normal Oil Pressure: 35 psi

Tune Up Specifications

Spark Plug: AC 44

Spark Plug Gap: .032 in

Firing Order: 12784563 (Front to rear: left bank 2-4-6-8; right bank 1-3-5-7)

Ignition Timing: Yellow timing mark aligns with "5" on timing indicator; Location: vibration damper

Engine Idle Speed: 450 rpm

Cylinder Head Torque: 63-73 ft-lb

Voltage & Polarity: 12 volts, negative ground

Piston and Ring Specifications

Fitting Pistons with Scale:
Shim Thickness .003 in
Pounds on Scale: 7 - 13 lb

Ring End Gap:
Compression: .015 in
Oil: .025 in

Clearance in Groove: Compression: .002-004 in; Oil: .0035-.0095 in

Wristpin Diameter: .940 in

APPENDIX B

Valve Specifications

Operating Clearance:
Intake: 0; Exhaust: 0

Valve Seat Angle: 45 degrees

Valve Timing: (BTDC = Before Top Dead Center; ATDC = After Top Dead Center)
Intake Opens: 30 degrees BTDC
Exhaust Closes: 44 ATDC

Valve Spring Pressure Pounds at Inches Length:
Inner Spring: 24 lbs @ 1-1/2 in; Outer Spring: 43 lbs @ 1-1/2 in

Valve Stem Clearance: Intake: .0025 in; Exhaust: .004 in

Engine Bearing Specifications

Connecting Rod Bearings:
Journal Diameter: 2.249-2.250 in
Bearing Clearance: .0002-.0023 in
Rod End Play: .006-.011 in
Rod Bolt Tension: 45-55 ft-lb

Main Bearings:
Journal Diameter: 2.498-2.499 in
Bearing Clearance: .0005-.0025 in
Shaft End Play: .004-.008 in (Thrust on Bearing No. 3)
Main Bolt Tension: 100-110 ft-lb

Capacity Data

Cooling System:
Without Heater: 17-1/2 qts
With Heater: 19 qts

Fuel Tank: 19 gal

Engine Oil: 6 qts

Transmission: 2-1/2 w/auto 10 qts

Rear Axle: 6 pts

Delco-Remy Distributor Specifications

Distributor Part Number: 1110861 (Distributor rotates clockwise.)

Cam Angle: 26-33 degrees (Do not use dwell meter for setting point opening.)

Breaker Point Opening: .016 in

Condenser Capacity: .18-.23 mfds

Breaker Arm Spring Tension: 19-23 oz

Centrifugal Advance: (degrees at RPM of distributor)
Advance Starts 1-1/2 degrees @ 375 rpm
Full Advance: 12 degrees @ 1,750 rpm

Vacuum Advance Data:
Inches of vacuum to start plunger movement: 6.5 - 8.5 in
Inches of vacuum for full plunger travel: 12 - 14 in
Maximum vacuum advance: 9 - 10-1/2 Dist. Degrees

Delco-Remy Distributor Specifications

Generator Number: 1102008, 1102028 (Generator rotates clockwise; 12 volt; negative ground)

Generator Output: 30 amps @ 2,150 rpm

Brush Spring Tension: 28 oz

Field Current: 1.48-1.62 amps

Regulator Specifications

Regulator Number: 1119003

Cutout Relay:
Voltage to Close Points: 12.8 volts
Armature Air Gap: .020 in

Voltage Regulator Setting: 14.5 volts

Current Regulator Setting: 30 volts

Current and Voltage Armature Air Gap: .075 in

Delco-Remy Starting Motor Specifications

Part number: 1107646 (Starter rotates clockwise.)

Bush Spring Tension: 35 oz

No Load Test: 95 amps, 10.1 volts @ 3,500 rpm

Torque Test: 470 amps, 5.4 volts, torque: 10.5 ft-lb

1954 264-ci Engine Specifications

General Specifications

Model Designation: Special V-8, Series 40

Wheel Base: Special V-8: 122-ci

Valve Location: In head

Bore and Stroke: 3.625 x 3.2 in

Piston Displacement: 264-ci

Compression Ratio: 7.2:1 (8.1:1 w/Dynaflow)

Maximum Brake Horsepower: 143 hp @ 4,200 rpm; (150 hp @ 4,200 rpm w/Dynaflow)

Maximum Torque: 228 ft-lb @ 2,400 rpm (240 ft-lb @ 2,400 rpm w/Dynaflow)

Normal Oil Pressure: 35 psi

Tune Up Specifications

Spark Plug: AC 44-5

Spark Plug Gap: .032 in

APPENDIX B

Firing Order: 12784563 (Front to rear: left bank 2, 4, 6, 8; right bank 1, 3, 5, 7)

Ignition Timing: Adv. timing mark on flywheel

Engine Idle Speed: 450 rpm

Cylinder Head Torque: 63-73 ft-lb

Compression Pressure & Cranking Speed: 130 min

Voltage & Polarity: 12 volts, negative ground

Piston and Ring Specifications

Fitting Pistons with Scale:
Shim thickness: .003 in

Ring End Gap:
Compression: .010 in
Oil: .015 in (no fitting necessary with Flex-Fit oil rings)

Clearance in Groove: Compression .002-004 in; Oil: .0035-.0095 in

Wristpin Diameter: .940 in

Valve Specifications

Operating Clearance:
Series 40: Intake: 0 Exhaust: 0

Valve Seat Angle: 45 degrees

Valve Timing: (BTDC = before top dead center; ATDC = after top dead center)
Intake Opens: 25 degrees BTDC
Exhaust Closes: 42 degrees ATDC

Valve Spring Pressure Pounds at Inches Length:
Inner Spring: 53 lbs @ 1.15 in; Outer Spring: 85 lbs @ 1.12 in

Valve Stem Clearance: Intake: .0025 in; Exhaust: .003 in

Engine Bearing Specifications

Connecting Rod Bearings:
Journal Diameter: 2.249-2.250 in
Bearing Clearance: .0002-.0023 in
Rod End Play: .006-.011 in
Rod Bolt Tension: 45-55 ft-lb

Main Bearings:
Journal Diameter: 2.498-2.499 in
Bearing Clearance: .0005-.0025 in
Shaft End Play: .004-.008 in (Thrust on Bearing No. 3)
Main Bolt Tension: 100-110 ft-lb

Capacity Data

Cooling System:
Without Heater: 16-1/2 qts (18-1/2 qts with Dynaflow)
With Heater: 18 qts (20 qts with Dynaflow)

Fuel Tank: 19 gal

Engine Oil: 6 qts

Transmission: 1-3/4 w/auto 9-1/2 qts

Rear Axle: 4-1/2 pts

Delco-Remy Distributor Specifications

Distributor Part Number: 1110849 (Distributor rotates counter-clockwise.)

Cam Angle: 26-33 degrees (Do not use dwell meter for setting point opening.)

Breaker Point opening: .016 in

Condenser Capacity: .18-.23 mfds

Breaker Arm Spring Tension: 19-23 oz

Centrifugal Advance: (degrees at RPM of distributor)
Advance Starts 1-1/2 degrees @ 375 rpm
Full Advance: 12 degrees @ 1,750 rpm

Vacuum Advance Data:
Inches of vacuum to start plunger movement: 6.5 - 8.5 in
Inches of vacuum for full plunger travel: 11-1/2 - 15 in
Maximum vacuum advance: 9 - 10-1/2 Dist. degrees

Delco-Remy Distributor Specifications

Generator Number: 1102008 (generator rotates clockwise; negative ground)

Generator output: 30 amps @ 2,300 rpm

Brush Spring Tension: 28 oz

Field Current: 1.48-1.62 amps

Regulator Specifications

Regulator Number: 1118825

Cutout Relay:
Voltage to close points: 12.8 volts
Armature air gap: .020 in

Voltage Regulator Setting: 14.5 volts

Current Regulator Setting: 30 volts

Current and Voltage Armature Air Gap: .075 in

Delco-Remy Starting Motor Specifications

Part Number: 1107621 (Starter rotates clockwise.)

Bush Spring Tension: 30-40 oz

No Load Test: 95 amps; 10.1 volts @ 3,500 rpm

Torque Test: 460 amps, 5.2 volts, torque: 11

1955 264-ci Engine Specifications

General Specifications

Model Designation: Special V-8, Series 40

Wheel Base: Special V-8: 122 in

APPENDIX B

Valve Location: In head

Bore and Stroke: 3.625 x 3.2 in

Piston Displacement: 264-ci

Compression ratio: 8.4:1

Maximum Brake Horsepower: 188 hp @ 4,800 rpm

Maximum Torque: 256 ft-lb @ 2,400 rpm

Normal Oil Pressure: 35 psi

Tune Up Specifications

Spark Plug: AC 44-5

Spark Plug Gap: .032 in

Firing Order: 12784563 (Front to rear: left bank 2, 4, 6, 8; right bank 1, 3, 5, 7)

Ignition Timing: Adv. timing mark on pulley

Engine Idle Speed: 450 rpm

Cylinder Head Torque: 63-73 ft-lbs

Compression Pressure & Cranking Speed: 140 min

Voltage & Polarity: 12 volts, negative ground

Piston and Ring Specifications

Fitting Pistons with Scale:
Shim thickness: .003 in
Pounds Pull on Scale: 7-13 lbs

Ring End Gap:
Compression: .015 in
Oil: .025 in

Clearance in Groove: Compression: .002-004 in; Oil: .0035-.0095 in

Wristpin Diameter: .940 in

Valve Specifications

Operating Clearance:
Series 40: Intake: 0; Exhaust: 0

Valve Seat Angle: 45 degrees

Valve Timing: (BTDC = Before Top Dead Center; ATDC = After Top Dead Center)
Intake Opens: 25 degrees BTDC
Exhaust Closes: 42 degrees ATDC

Valve Spring Pressure Pounds at Inches Length:
Inner Spring: 21-1/2 lbs @ 1-1/2 in; Outer Spring: 40-1/2 lbs @ 1-1/2 in

Valve Stem Clearance: Intake: .0025 in; Exhaust: .003 in

Engine Bearing Specifications

Connecting Rod Bearings:
Journal Diameter: 2.249-2.250 in
Bearing Clearance: .0002-.0023 in
Rod End Play: .006-.011 in
Rod Bolt Tension: 45-55 ft-lb

Main Bearings:
Journal Diameter: 2.498-2.499 in
Bearing Clearance: .0005-.0025 in
Shaft End Play: .004-.008 in (Thrust on Bearing No. 3)
Main Bolt Tension: 100-110 ft-lb

Capacity Data

Cooling System:
Without Heater: 16-1/2 qts (18-1/2 qts with Dynaflow)
With Heater: 18 qts (20 qts with Dynaflow)

Fuel Tank: 19 gal

Engine Oil: 6 qts

Transmission: 1-3/4 w/auto 10 qts

Rear Axle: 4-1/2 pts

Delco-Remy Distributor Specifications

Distributor Part Number: 1110849 (Distributor rotates counter-clockwise.)

Cam Angle: 26-33 degrees (Do not use dwell meter for setting point opening.)

Breaker Point Opening: .016 in

Condenser Capacity: .18-.23 mfds

Breaker Arm Spring Tension: 19-23 oz

Centrifugal Advance: (degrees at RPM of distributor)
Advance Starts 1-1/2 degrees @ 375 rpm
Full Advance: 12 degrees @ 1,750 rpm

Vacuum Advance Data:
Inches of vacuum to start plunger movement: 6.5 - 8.5 in
Inches of vacuum for full plunger travel: 11-1/2 - 15 in
Maximum vacuum advance: 9 - 10-1/2 Dist. degrees

Delco-Remy Distributor Specifications

Generator Number: 1102008 (Generator rotates clockwise; negative ground)

Generator Output: 30 amps @ 2,300 rpm

Brush Spring Tension: 28 oz

Field Current: 1.48-1.62 amps

Regulator Specifications

Regulator Number: 1118825

Cutout Relay:
Voltage to close points: 12.8 volts
Armature air hap: .020 in

Voltage Regulator Setting: 14.5 volts

Current Regulator Setting: 30 volts

Current and voltage armature air gap: .075 in

Delco-Remy Starting Motor Specifications

Part number: 1107621 (starter rotates clockwise)

Bush Spring Tension: 30-40 oz

No Load Test: 95 amps, 10.1 volts @ 3,500 rpm

Torque Test: 460 amps, 5.2 volts, torque: 11

APPENDIX C

1953-1969 Engine Specifications

Year	Engine Model	Series	Bore and Stroke	Displacement	Compression Ratio	Max HP	Max Torque	Oil Pressure	Spark Plug Gap	Breaker Point Gap	Armature Spring Tension	Firing Order	Ignition Timing
1953	Special 8	Series 40	3 3/16 x 4 1/8 in	263.3 ci	7.0:1	125 hp @ 3,800 rpm	224 ft-lb @ 2,200 rpm	35 psi	.025 in	.016 in	26-33	16258374	"ADV"
	Super V-8	Series 50	4 x 3.2 in	322.0 ci	8.0:1	164 hp @ 4,000 rpm	286 ft-lb @ 2,200 rpm	35 psi	.032 in	.016 in	26-33	12784563	5°
	Super V-8	Series 52	4 x 3.2 in	322.0 ci	8.0:1	164 hp @ 4,000 rpm	286 ft-lb @ 2,200 rpm	35 psi	.032 in	.016 in	26-33	12784563	5°
	Roadmaster V-8	Series 70	4 x 3.2 in	322.0 ci	8.5:1	188 hp @ 4,000 rpm	300 ft-lb @ 2,400 rpm	35 psi	.032 in	.016 in	26-33	12784563	5°
	Roadmaster V-8	Series 72	4 x 3.2 in	322.0 ci	8.5:1	188 hp @ 4,000 rpm	300 ft-lb @ 2,400 rpm	35 psi	.032 in	.016 in	26-33	12784563	5°
1954	Special V-8 Man	Series 40	3.625 x 3.2 in	264 ci	7.2:1	143 hp @ 4,200 rpm	228 ft-lb @ 2,400 rpm	35 psi	.032 in	.016 in	26-33	12784563	5°
	Special V-8 Auto	Series 40	3.625 x 3.2 in	264 ci	8.1:1	150 hp @ 4,200 rpm	240 ft-lb @ 2,400 rpm	35 psi	.032 in	.016 in	26-33	12784563	5°
	Super V-8 Man	Series 50	4 x 3.2 in	322 ci	8.0:1	177 hp @ 4,100 rpm	295 ft-lb @ 2,000 rpm	35 psi	.032 in	.016 in	26-33	12784563	5°
	Super V-8 Auto	Series 50	4 x 3.2 in	322 ci	8.5:1	182 hp @ 4,100 rpm	300 ft-lb @ 2,000 rpm	35 psi	.032 in	.016 in	26-33	12784563	5°
	Century V-8 Man	Series 60	4 x 3.2 in	322 ci	8.0:1	195 hp @ 4,100 rpm	302 ft-lb @ 2,400 rpm	35 psi	.032 in	.016 in	26-33	12784563	5°
	Century V-8 Auto	Series 60	4 x 3.2 in	322 ci	8.5:1	200 hp @ 4,100 rpm	309 ft-lb @ 2,400 rpm	35 psi	.032 in	.016 in	26-33	12784563	5°
	Roadmaster V-8	Series 70	4 x 3.2 in	322 ci	8.5:1	200 hp @ 4,100 rpm	309 ft-lb @ 2,400 rpm	35 psi	.032 in	.016 in	26-33	12784563	5°
1955	Special V-8	Series 40	3.625 x 3.2 in	264 ci	8.4:1	188 hp @ 4,800 rpm	256 ft-lb @ 2,400 rpm	35 psi	.032 in	.016 in	26-33	12784563	5°
	Super V-8	Series 50	4.000 x 3.2 in	322 ci	8.4:1	188 hp @ 4,800 rpm	256 ft-lb @ 2,400 rpm	35 psi	.032 in	.016 in	26-33	12784563	5°
	Super V-8 Auto	Series 50	4.000 x 3.2 in	322 ci	9.0:1	236 hp @ 4,600 rpm	330 ft-lb @ 3,000 rpm	35 psi	.032 in	.016 in	26-33	12784563	5°
	Century V-8 Man	Series 60	4.000 x 3.2 in	322 ci	8.4:1	188 hp @ 4,800 rpm	250 ft-lb @ 2,400 rpm	35 psi	.032 in	.016 in	26-33	12784563	5°
	Century V-8 Auto	Series 60	4.000 x 3.2 in	322 ci	9.0:1	236 hp @ 4,600 rpm	330 ft-lb @ 3,000 rpm	35 psi	.032 in	.016 in	26-33	12784563	5°
	Roadmaster V-8	Series 70	4.000 x 3.2 in	322 ci	9.0:1	236 hp @ 4,600 rpm	330 ft-lb @ 3,000 rpm	35 psi	.032 in	.016 in	26-33	12784563	5°
1956	Special V-8	Series 40	4.000 x 3.2 in	322 ci	8.9:1	220 hp @ 4,400 rpm	319 ft-lb @ 2400 rpm	35 psi	.032 in	.016 in	26-33	12784563	5°
	Super V-8	Series 50	4.000 x 3.2 in	322 ci	9.5:1	255 hp @ 4,400 rpm	341 ft-lb @ 3,200 rpm	35 psi	.032 in	.016 in	26-33	12784563	5°
	Century V-8	Series 60	4.000 x 3.2 in	322 ci	9.5:1	255 hp @ 4,400 rpm	341 ft-lb @ 3,200 rpm	35 psi	.032 in	.016 in	26-33	12784563	5°
	Roadmaster V-8	Series 70	4.000 x 3.2 in	322 ci	9.5:1	255 hp @ 4,400 rpm	341 ft-lb @ 3,200 rpm	35 psi	.032 in	.016 in	26-33	12784563	5°
1957	Special V-8 Auto	Series 40	4.125 x 3.4 in	364 ci	9.5:1	250 hp @ 4400 rpm	380 ft-lb @ 2,400 rpm	40 psi	.032 in	.016 in	30	12784563	5°
	Super V-8	Series 50	4.125 x 3.4 in	364 ci	10.0:1	300 hp @ 4,600 rpm	400 ft-lb @ 3,200 rpm	40 psi	.032 in	.016 in	30	12784563	5°
	Century V-8	Series 60	4.125 x 3.4 in	364 ci	10.0:1	300 hp @ 4,600 rpm	400 ft-lb @ 3,200 rpm	40 psi	.032 in	.016 in	30	12784563	5°
	Roadmaster V-8	Series 70	4.125 x 3.4 in	364 ci	10.0:1	300 hp @ 4,600 rpm	400 ft-lb @ 3,200 rpm	40 psi	.032 in	.016 in	30	12784563	5°
1958	Special V-8	Series 40	4.125 x 3.4 in	364 ci	9.5:1	250 hp @ 4,400 rpm	380 ft-lb @ 2,400 rpm	40 psi	.032 in	.019 in	30	12784563	5°
	Super V-8	Series 50	4.125 x 3.4 in	364 ci	10.0:1	300 hp @ 4,600 rpm	400 ft-lb @ 3,200 rpm	40 psi	.032 in	.019 in	30	12784563	5°
	Century V-8	Series 60	4.125 x 3.4 in	364 ci	10.0:1	300 hp @ 4,600 rpm	400 ft-lb @ 3,200 rpm	40 psi	.032 in	.019 in	30	12784563	5°
	Roadmaster V-8	Series 70	4.125 x 3.4 in	364 ci	10.0:1	300 hp @ 4,600 rpm	400 ft-lb @ 3,200 rpm	40 psi	.032 in	.019 in	30	12784563	5°
	Limited V-8	Series 700	4.125 x 3.4 in	364 ci	10.0:1	300 hp @ 4,600 rpm	400 ft-lb @ 3,200 rpm	40 psi	.032 in	.019 in	30	12784563	5°
1959	Le Sabre V-8 Man	4400	4.125 x 3.4 in	364 ci	8.5:1	250 hp @ 4,400 rpm	380 ft-lb @ 2,400 rpm	40 psi	.032 in	.019 in	30	12784563	5° Std 12° Auto
	Le Sabre V-8 Auto	4400	4.125 x 3.4 in	364 ci	10.5:1	250 hp @ 4,400 rpm	384 ft-lb @ 2,400 rpm	40 psi	.032 in	.019 in	30	12784563	5° Std 12° Auto
	Invicta V-8	4600	4.1875 x 3.64 in	401 ci	10.5:1	324 hp @ 4,400 rpm	445 ft-lb @ 2,800 rpm	40 psi	.032 in	.019 in	30	12784563	5° Std 12° Auto
	Electra V-8	4700	4.1875 x 3.64 in	401 ci	10.5:1	324 hp @ 4,400 rpm	445 ft-lb @ 2,800 rpm	40 psi	.032 in	.019 in	30	12784563	5° Std 12° Auto
	Electra V-8	4800	4.1875 x 3.64 in	401 ci	10.5:1	324 hp @ 4,400 rpm	445 ft-lb @ 2,800 rpm	40 psi	.032 in	.019 in	30	12784563	5° Std 12° Auto
1960	Le Sabre 364 V-8 2-bbl		4.125 x 3.40 in	364 ci	8.5:1	210 hp @ 4,000 rpm	340 ft-lb @ 2,400 rpm	40 psi	.032 in	.016 in	30	12784563	5° std 12° auto
	Le Sabre 364 V-8 2-bbl		4.125 x 3.40 in	364 ci	10.25:1	250 hp @ 4,400 rpm	384 ft-lb @ 2,400 rpm	40 psi	.032 in	.016 in	30	12784563	5° std 12° auto
	Le Sabre 364 V-8 2-bbl		4.125 x 3.40 in	364 ci	9.0:1	235 hp @ 4,400 rpm	362 ft-lb @ 2,400 rpm	40 psi	.032 in	.016 in	30	12784563	5° std 12° auto
	Le Sabre 364 V-8 4-bbl		4.125 x 3.40 in	364 ci	10.25:1	300 hp @ 4,400 rpm	405 ft-lb @ 2,800 rpm	40 psi	.032 in	.016 in	30	12784563	5° std 12° auto
	Invicta 401 V-8 4-bbl		4.1875 x 3.64 in	401 ci	10.25:1	325 hp @ 4,400 rpm	445 ft-lb @ 2,800 rpm	40 psi	.032 in	.016 in	30	12784563	5° std 12° auto
	Electra 401 V-8 4-bbl		4.1875 x 3.64 in	401 ci	10.25:1	325 hp @ 4,400 rpm	445 ft-lb @ 2,800 rpm	40 psi	.032 in	.016 in	30	12784563	5° std 12° auto
1961	Special 215 V-8 2-bbl		3.50 x 2.80	215 ci	8.80:1	155 hp @ 4,600 rpm	220 ft-lb @ 2,400 rpm	33 psi	.035 in	.016 in	30	18436572	5°
	Special 215 V-8 4-bbl		3.50 x 2.80 in	215 ci	10.25:1	185 hp @ 4,800 rpm	230 ft-lb @ 2,800 rpm	33 psi	.035 in	.016 in	30	18436572	5°
	Le Sabre 364 V-8 2-bbl		4.125 x 3.40 in	364 ci	10.25:1	250 hp @ 4,400 rpm	384 ft-lb @ 2,400 rpm	40 psi	.032 in	.016 in	30	12784563	12°
	Le Sabre 364 V-8 2-bbl		4.125 x 3.40 in	364 ci	9.0:1	235 hp @ 4,400 rpm	375 ft-lb @ 2,400 rpm	40 psi	.032 in	.016 in	30	12784563	12°
	Invicta 401 V-8 4-bbl		4.1875 x 3.64 in	401 ci	10.25:1	325 hp @ 4,400 rpm	445 ft-lb @ 2,800 rpm	40 psi	.032 in	.016 in	30	12784563	12°
	Electra 401 V-8 4-bbl		4.1875 x 3.64 in	401 ci	10.25:1	325 hp @ 4,400 rpm	445 ft-lb @ 2,800 rpm	40 psi	.032 in	.016 in	30	12784563	12°
1962	198 V-6 2-bbl		3.625 x 3.20 in	198 ci	8.80:1	135 hp @ 4,600 rpm	205 ft-lb @ 2,400 rpm	33 psi	.035 in	.016 in	30	165432	5°
	215 V-8 2-bbl		3.50 x 2.80 in	215 ci	9.00:1	155 hp @ 4,600 rpm	220 ft-lb @ 2,400 rpm	33 psi	.035 in	.016 in	30	18436572	5°
	215 V-8 2-bbl		3.50 x 2.80 in	215 ci	10.25:1	185 hp @ 4,800 rpm	230 ft-lb @ 2,800 rpm	33 psi	.035 in	.016 in	30	18436572	5°
	401 V-8 2-bbl		4.1875 x 3.64 in	401 ci	9.0:1	265 hp @ 4,400 rpm	412 ft-lb @ 2,400 rpm	40 psi	.032 in	.016 in	30	12784563	12°
	401 V-8 2-bbl		4.1875 x 3.64 in	401 ci	10.25:1	280 hp @ 4,400 rpm	424 ft-lb @ 2,400 rpm	40 psi	.032 in	.016 in	30	12784563	12°
	401 V-8 4-bbl		4.1875 x 3.64 in	401 ci	10.25:1	325 hp @ 4,400 rpm	445 ft-lb @ 2,800 rpm	40 psi	.032 in	.016 in	30	12784563	12°
1963	198 V-6 2-bbl		3.625 x 3.20 in	198 ci	8.80:1	135 hp @ 4,600 rpm	205 ft-lb @ 2,400 rpm	33 psi	.035 in	.016 in	30	165432	5°
	215 V-8 2-bbl		3.50 x 2.80 in	215 ci	9.00:1	155 hp @ 4,600 rpm	220 ft-lb @ 2,400	33 psi	.035 in	.016 in	30	18436572	5°
	215 V-8 2-bbl		3.50 x 2.80 in	215 ci	11.00:1	200 hp @ 5,000 rpm	240 ft-lb @ 3,200 rpm	33 psi	.035 in	.016 in	30	18436572	5°
	401 V-8 2-bbl		4.1875 x 3.64 in	401 ci	9.0:1	265 hp @ 4,400 rpm	412 ft-lb @ 2,400 rpm	40 psi	.035 in	.016 in	30	12784563	12°
	401 V-8 2-bbl		4.1875 x 3.64 in	401 ci	10.25:1	280 hp @ 4,400 rpm	424 ft-lb @ 2,400 rpm	40 psi	.035 in	.016 in	30	12784563	12°
	401 V-8 4-bbl		4.1875 x 3.64 in	401 ci	10.25:1	325 hp @ 4,400 rpm	445 ft-lb @ 2,800 rpm	40 psi	.035 in	.016 in	30	12784563	12°
	425 V-8 4-bbl		4.3125 x 3.64 in	425 ci	10.25:1	340 hp @ 4,400 rpm	465 ft-lb @ 2,800 rpm	40 psi	.035 in	.016 in	30	12784563	12°

APPENDIX C

Year	Engine Model	Series	Bore and Stroke	Displacement	Compression Ratio	Max HP	Max Torque	Oil Pressure	Spark Plug Gap	Breaker Point Gap	Armature Spring Tension	Firing Order	Ignition Timing
1964	225	V-6 1-bbl	3.75 x 3.40 in	225 ci	9.00:1	155 hp @ 4,400 rpm	225 ft-lb @ 2,400 rpm	33 psi	.035 in	.016 in	30	165432	5°
	300	V-8 2-bbl	3.75 x 3.40 in	300 ci	9.00:1	210 hp @ 4,600 rpm	310 ft-lb @ 2,400 rpm	33 psi	.035 in	.016 in	30	18436572	2 1/2°
	300	V-8 4-bbl	3.75 x 3.40 in	300 ci	11.00:1	250 hp @ 4,800 rpm	335 ft-lb @ 3,000 rpm	33 psi	.035 in	.016 in	30	18436572	2 1/2°
	401	V-8 2-bbl	4.1875 x 3.64 in	401 ci	9.0:1	265 hp @ 4,400 rpm	412 ft-lb @ 2,400 rpm	40 psi	.035 in	.016 in	30	12784563	2 1/2°
	300	V-8 2-bbl	3.75 x 3.40 in	300 ci	9.0:1	210 hp @ 4,600 rpm	310 ft-lb @ 2,400 rpm	33 psi	.035 in	.016 in	30	18436572	2 1/2°
	300	V-8 4-bbl	3.75 x 3.40 in	300 ci	11.0:1	250 hp @ 4,800 rpm	335 ft-lb @ 3,000 rpm	33 psi	.035 in	.016 in	30	18436572	2 1/2°
	401	V-8 4-bbl	4.1875 x 3.64 in	401 ci	10.25:1	325 hp @ 4,400 rpm	445 ft-lb @ 2,800 rpm	40 psi	.035 in	.016 in	30	12784563	2 1/2°
	425	V-8 4-bbl	4.3125 x 3.64 in	425 ci	10.25:1	340 hp @ 4,400 rpm	465 ft-lb @ 2,800 rpm	40 psi	.035 in	.016 in	30	12784563	2 1/2°
	425	V-8 Two 4-bbl	4.3125 x 3.64 in	425 ci	10.25:1	360 hp @ 4,400 rpm	465 ft-lb @ 2,800 rpm	40 psi	.035 in	.016 in	30	12784563	2 1/2°
1965	225	V-6 1-bbl	3.75 x 3.40 in	225 ci	9.0:1	155 hp @ 4,400 rpm	225 ft-lb @ 2,400 rpm	33 psi	.035 in	.016 in	30	165432	5°
	300	V-8 2-bbl	3.75 x 3.40 in	300 ci	9.0:1	210 hp @ 4,600 rpm	310 ft-lb @ 2,400 rpm	33 psi	.035 in	.016 in	30	18436572	2 1/2°
	300	V-8 4-bbl	3.75 x 3.40 in	300 ci	11.0:1	250 hp @ 4,800 rpm	335 ft-lb @ 3,000 rpm	33 psi	.035 in	.016 in	30	18436572	2 1/2°
	401	V-8 4-bbl	4.1875 x 3.64 in	401 ci	10.25:1	325 hp @ 4,400 rpm	445 ft-lb @ 2,800 rpm	40 psi	.035 in	.016 in	30	12784563	2 1/2°
	425	V-8 4-bbl	4.3125 x 3.64 in	425 ci	10.25:1	340 hp @ 4,400 rpm	465 ft-lb @ 2,800 rpm	40 psi	.035 in	.016 in	30	12784563	2 1/2°
	425	V-8 Two 4-bbl	4.3125 x 3.64 in	425 ci	10.25:1	360 hp @ 4,400 rpm	465 ft-lb @ 2,800 rpm	40 psi	.035 in	.016 in	30	12784563	2 1/2°
1966	225	V-6 2-bbl	3.75 x 3.40 in	225 ci	9.0:1	160 hp @ 4,200 rpm	235 ft-lb @ 2,400 rpm	33 psi	.035 in	.016 in	30	165432	5°
	300	V-8 2-bbl	3.75 x 3.40 in	300 ci	9.0:1	210 hp @ 4,600 rpm	310 ft-lb @ 2400 rpm	33 psi	.035 in	.016 in	30	18436572	2 1/2°
	340	V-8 2-bbl	3.75 x 3.85 in	340 ci	9.0:1	220 hp @ 4,000 rpm	340 ft-lb @ 2,400 rpm	33 psi	.035 in	.016 in	30	18436572	2 1/2°
	340	V-8 4-bbl	3.75 x 3.85 in	340 ci	10.25:1	260 hp @ 4,000 rpm	365 ft-lb @ 2,800 rpm	33 psi	.035 in	.016 in	30	18436572	2 1/2°
	401	V-8 4-bbl	4.1875 x 3.64 in	401 ci	10.25:1	325 hp @ 4,400 rpm	445 ft-lb @ 2,800 rpm	40 psi	.035 in	.016 in	30	12784563	2 1/2°
	425	V-8 4-bbl	4.3125 x 3.64 in	425 ci	10.25:1	340 hp @ 4,400 rpm	465 ft-lb @ 2,800 rpm	40 psi	.035 in	.016 in	30	12784563	2 1/2°
	425	V-8 Two 4-bbl	4.3125 x 3.64 in	425 ci	10.25:1	360 hp @ 4,400 rpm	465 ft-lb @ 2,800 rpm	40 psi	.035 in	.016 in	30	12784563	2 1/2°
1967	225	V-6 2-bbl	3.75 x 3.40 in	225 ci	9.0:1	160 hp @ 4,200 rpm	235 ft-lb @ 2,400 rpm	33 psi	.035 in	.016 in	30	165432	5°
	300	V-8 2-bbl	3.75 x 3.40 in	300 ci	9.0:1	210 hp @ 4,600 rpm	310 ft-lb @ 2,400 rpm	33 psi	.035 in	.016 in	30	18436572	2 1/2°
	340	V-8 2-bbl	3.75 x 3.85 in	340 ci	9.0:1	220 hp @ 4,000 rpm	340 ft-lb @ 2,400 rpm	33 psi	.035 in	.016 in	30	18436572	2 1/2°
	340	V-8 4-bbl	3.75 x 3.85 in	340 ci	10.25:1	260 hp @ 4,000 rpm	365 ft-lb @ 2,800 rpm	33 psi	.035 in	.016 in	30	18436572	2 1/2°
	400	V-8 4-bbl	4.04 x 3.90 in	400 ci	10.25:1	340 hp @ 5,000 rpm	440 ft-lb @ 3,200 rpm	30 psi	.035 in	.016 in	30	18436572	2 1/2°
	430	V-8 4-bbl	4.1875 x 3.90 in	430 ci	10.25:1	360 hp @ 5,000 rpm	475 ft-lb @ 3,200 rpm	30 psi	.035 in	.016 in	30	18436572	2 1/2°
1968	250	I-6 1-bbl	3.875 x 3.53 in	250 ci	8.5:1	155 hp @ 4,200 rpm	235 ft-lb @ 1,600 rpm	30 - 45 psi	.030 in	.019 in	32	153624	TDC std 4° auto
	350	V-8 2-bbl	3.80 x 3.85 in	350 ci	9.0:1	230 hp @ 4,400 rpm	350 ft-lb @ 2,400 rpm	37 psi	.030 in	.016 in	30	18436572	TDC
	350	V-8 4-bbl	3.80 x 3.85 in	350 ci	10.25:1	280 hp @ 4,800 rpm	375 ft-lb @ 3,200 rpm	37 psi	.030 in	.016 in	30	18436572	TDC
	400	V-8 4-bbl	4.04 x 3.90 in	400 ci	10.25:1	340 hp @ 5,000 rpm	440 ft-lb @ 3,200 rpm	30 psi	.030 in	.016 in	30	18436572	TDC
	430	V-8 4-bbl	4.1875 x 3.90 in	430 ci	10.25:1	360 hp @ 5,000 rpm	475 ft-lb @ 3,200 rpm	30 psi	.030 in	.016 in	30	18436572	TDC
1969	250	I-6 1-bbl	3.875 x 3.53 in	250 ci	8.5:1	155 hp @ 4,200 rpm	235 ft-lb @ 1,600 rpm	30 - 45 psi	.035 in	.019 in	32	153624	TDC std 4° auto
	350	V-8 2-bbl	3.80 x 3.85 in	350 ci	9.0:1	230 hp @ 4,400 rpm	350 ft-lb @ 2,400 rpm	37 psi	.030 in	.016 in	30	18436572	TDC
	350	V-8 4-bbl	3.80 x 3.85 in	350 ci	10.25:1	280 hp @ 4,800 rpm	375 ft-lb @ 3,200 rpm	37 psi	.030 in	.016 in	30	18436572	TDC
	400	V-8 4-bbl	4.04 x 3.90 in	400 ci	10.25:1	340 hp @ 5,000 rpm	440 ft-lb @ 3,200 rpm	30 psi	.030 in	.016 in	30	18436572	TDC std 2 1/2° ATDC auto
	430	V-8 4-bbl	4.1875 x 3.90 in	430 ci	10.25:1	360 hp @ 5,000 rpm	475 ft-lb @ 3,200 rpm	30 psi	.030 in	.016 in	30	18436572	TDC

1970-1971 Engine Specifications

Year	Engine	Series	Bore and Stroke	Displacement	Compression Ratio	Max HP	Max Torque	Spark Plug Gap	Point Dwell	Point Gap	Ignition Timing
1970	350	V-8 4-bbl	3.80 x 3.85 in	350 ci	9:1	285 hp @ 4,600 rpm	375 ft-lb @ 2,800 rpm	.030	.30	.016	6° BTDC
1970	350	V-8 4-bbl	3.80 x 3.85 in	350 ci	10.25:1	315 hp @ 4,800 rpm	410 ft-lb @ 3,200 rpm	.030	.30	.016	6° BTDC
1970	455	V-8 4-bbl	4.31 x 3.90 in	455 ci	10:1	350 hp @ 4,600 rpm	510 ft-lb @ 2,800 rpm	.030	.30	.016	6° BTDC
1970	455	V-8 4-bbl	4.31 x 3.90 in	455 ci	10:1	360 hp @ 5,000 rpm	510 ft-lb @ 2,800 rpm	.030	.30	.016	6° BTDC
1970	455	V-8 4-bbl	4.31 x 3.90 in	455 ci	10:1	370 hp @ 5,000 rpm	510 ft-lb @ 2,800 rpm	.030	.30	.016	10° BTDC
1971	350	V-8 2-bbl	3.80 x 3.85 in	350 ci	9:1	230 hp @ 4,400 rpm	350 ft-lb @ 2,800 rpm	.030	.30	.016	6° BTDC
1971	350	V-8 4-bbl	3.80 x 3.85 in	350 ci	9:1	260 hp @ 4,600 rpm	360 ft-lb @ 3,200 rpm	.030	.30	.016	6° BTDC
1971	455	V-8 4-bbl	4.31 x 3.90 in	455 ci	8.5:1	315 hp @ 4,400 rpm	450 ft-lb @ 2,800 rpm	.030	.30	.016	6° BTDC
1971	455	V-8 4-bbl	4.31 x 3.90 in	455 ci	8.5:1	345 hp @ 5,000 rpm	460 ft-lb @ 3,000 rpm	.030	.30	.016	10° BTDC
1971	455	V-8 4-bbl	4.31 x 3.90 in	455 ci	8.5:1	330 hp @ 4,600 rpm	455 ft-lb @ 2,800 rpm	.030	.30	.016	10° BTDC

APPENDIX D

1987 3.8L V-6 Turbo Engine Specifications

Engine Dimensions and Fitment Specifications

General

Piston Clearance Limits

Top Land	.046 in. - .056 in
Skirt Top	.0008 in. - .0020 in
Skirt Bottom	.0013 in. - .0035 in

Ring Groove Depth

#1 - Compression Ring	.185 in. - .194 in
#2 - Compression Ring	.186 in. - .194 in
#3 - Oil Ring	.188 in. - .196 in

Ring Width

#1 - Compression Ring	.077 in. - .078 in
#2 - Compression Ring	.077 in. - .078 in
#3 - Oil Ring	183 in. - .189 in

Ring Gap

#1 - Compression Ring	.010 in. - .020 in
#2 - Compression Ring	.010 in. - .020 in
#3 - Oil Ring	.015 in. - .055 in

Piston Pin Length	2.900 in
Diameter of Pin	.9391 in. - .9394 in
Pin Clearance in Piston	.0004 in. - .0007 in
Pin Press Fit in Rod	.0007 in. - .0017 in
Pin Direction and Amount Offset in Piston	.040 in Major Thrust Side

Connecting Rod Specifications

Bearing Length	.654 in
Bearing Clearance (Limits)	.0005 in. - .0026 in
End Play	.003 in. - .015 in

Crankshaft Specifications

End Play at Thrust Bearing	.003 in. - .011 in
Main Bearing Journal Diameter	2.4995 in
Crankpin Journal Diameter	2.2487 in - 2.2495 in
Main Bearing Overall Length	
#1	.864 in
#2	1.057 in
#3	.864 in
#4	.864 in
Main Bearing to Journal Clearance	.0003 in. - .0018 in

Camshaft Specifications

Bearing Journal Diameter	1.785 in. - 1.786 in
Journal Clearance in Bearings	
#1	.0005 in. - .0025 in
#2,3,4	.0005 in. - .0035 in

Valve System Specifications

Rocker Arm Ratio	1.55:1
Valve Lifter Diameter	.8420 in. - .8427 in
Valve Lifter Clearance in Crankcase	.0008 in. - .0025 in
Minimum Valve Margin	.025

Intake Valve

Head Diameter	1.715 in. - 1.705 in
Seat Angle	45 degrees
Stem Diameter	.3412 in. - .3401 in
Clearance in Guide	.0015 in. - .0035 in

Exhaust Valve

Head Diameter	1.505 in. - 1.495 in
Seat Angle	45 degrees
Stem Diameter	.3412 in. - .3405 in
Clearance in Guide	.0015 in. - .0032 in

Valve Spring

Valve Closed	90 lbs +or- 4 @ 1.727 in
Valve Open	245 lbs +or- 10 @ 1.340 in

More great titles available from CarTech®...

S-A DESIGN

Super Tuning & Modifying Holley Carburetors — Perf, street and off-road applications. *(SA08)*

Custom Painting — The book, in full color, gives you an overview of the broad spectrum of custom painting types and techniques available today. *(SA10)*

Street Supercharging, A Complete Guide to — Bolt-on buying, installing and tuning blowers. *(SA17)*

Engine Blueprinting — Using tools, block selection & prep, crank mods, pistons, heads, cams & more! *(SA21)*

David Vizard's How to Build Horsepower — Building horsepower in any engine. *(SA24)*

How To Build Max Performance Chevy Rat Motors — Hot rodding big-block Chevys. *(SA48)*

How To Build Horsepower, Vol. 2 — Carbs & intake manifolds. *(SA52)*

Chevrolet Small-Block Parts Interchange Manual — Selecting & swapping high-perf. small-block parts. *(SA55)*

High-Performance Ford Engine Parts Interchange — Selecting & swapping big- and small-block Ford parts. *(SA56)*

How To Build Max Perf Chevy Small-Blocks on a Budget — Would you believe 600 hp for $3000? *(SA57)*

How To Build Max Performance Ford V-8s on a Budget — Dyno-tested engine builds for big- & small-block Fords. *(SA69)*

How To Build Max-Perf Pontiac V8s — Mild perf apps to all-out performance build-ups. *(SA78)*

How To Build High-Performance Ignition Systems — Complete guide to understanding auto ignition systems. *(SA79)*

How To Build Max Perf 4.6 Liter Ford Engines — Building & modifying Ford's 2- and 4-valve 4.6/5.4 liter engines. *(SA82)*

How To Build Big-Inch Ford Small-Blocks — Add cubic inches without the hassle of switching to a big-block. *(SA85)*

How To Build High-Perf Chevy LS1/LS6 Engines — Modifying and tuning Gen-III engines for GM cars and trucks. *(SA86)*

How To Build Big-Inch Chevy Small-Blocks — Get the additional torque & horsepower of a big-block. *(SA87)*

Honda Engine Swaps — Step-by-step instructions for all major tasks involved in engine swapping. *(SA93)*

How to Build Big-Inch Mopar Small Blocks — How to get big-block power out of your Mopar small-block. *(SA104)*

How to Build High-Performance Chevy Small — Block Cams/Valvetrains — Camshaft & valvetrain function, selection, performance, and design. *(SA105)*

High-Performance Jeep Cherokee XJ Builder's Guide 1984-2001 — Build a useful, Cherokee for mountains, the mud, the desert, the street, and more. *(SA109)*

How to Build and Modify Rochester Quadrajet Carburetors — Selecting, rebuilding, and modifying the Quadrajet Carburetors. *(SA113)*

Rebuilding the Small-Block Chevy: Step-by-Step Videobook — 160-pg book plus 2-hour DVD show you how to build a street or racing small-block Chevy. *(SA116)*

How to Paint Your Car on a Budget — Everything you need to know to get a great-looking coat of paint and save money. *(SA117)*

How to Drift: The Art of Oversteer — This comprehensive guide to drifting covers both driving techniques and car setup. *(SA118)*

High-Performance Jeep Wrangler TJ Builder's Guide 1997-2006 — How to upgrade your Wrangler's suspension, axles, differentials, engine, transfer case, wheels and tires, skid plates, and more. *(SA120)*

How to Build Chevy Small-Block Circle-Track Racing Engines — Learn all the insider tricks and secrets to keep your car in front of the pack. *(SA121)*

Turbo: Real World High-Performance Turbocharger Systems —*Turbo* is the most practical book for enthusiasts who want to make more horsepower. Foreword by Gale Banks. *(SA123)*

High-Performance Chevy Small-Block Cylinder Heads — Learn how to make the most power with this popular modification on your small-block Chevy. *(SA125)*

High Performance Brake Systems — Design, selection, and installation of brake systems for Musclecars, Hot Rods, Imports, Modern Era cars and more. *(SA126)*

High Performance C5 Corvette Builder's Guide — Improve the looks, handling and performance of your Corvette C5. *(SA127)*

High Performance Diesel Builder's Guide — The definitive guide to getting maximum performance out of your diesel engine. *(SA129)*

How to Rebuild & Modify Carter/Edelbrock Carbs — The only source for information on rebuilding and tuning these popular carburetors. *(SA130)*

Building Honda K-Series Engine Performance — The first book on the market dedicated exclusively to the Honda K series engine. *(SA134)*

Engine Management-Advanced Tuning — Take your fuel injection and tuning knowledge to the next level. *(SA135)*

How to Drag Race — Car setup, beginning and advanced techniques for bracket racing and pro classes, and racing science and math, and more. *(SA136)*

4x4 Suspension Handbook — Includes suspension basics & theory, advanced/high-performance suspension and lift systems, axles, how-to installations, and more. *(SA137)*

GM Automatic Overdrive Transmission Builder's and Swapper's Guide — Learn to build a bulletproof tranny and how to swap it into an older chassis as well. *(SA140)*

High-Performance Subaru Builder's Guide — Subarus are the hottest compacts on the street. Make yours even hotter. *(SA141)*

Car Care for Car Guys: Tips & Techniques Beyond Auto Maintenance 101 — Uses more than 300 color photos with direct instruction to provide more project detail and greater depth. *(SA144)*

How to Build Max-Performance Buick Engines — Covers all performance Buick engines, from the big-inch cars of the '50s and '60s, through the turbo models of the '80s. *(SA146)*

How to Build Max-Performance Mitsubishi 4G63t Engines — Covers every system and component of the engine, including a complete history. *(SA148)*

Dyno-Proven Small-Block Ford Performance — Includes valuable dyno test information to help readers choose the right performance parts for their vehicles. *(SA153)*

How to Swap GM LS-Series Engines Into Almost Anything — Includes a historical review and detailed information so you can select and fit the best LS engine. *(SA156)*

How to Autocross — Covers basic to more advanced modifications that go beyond the stock classes. *(SA158)*

Designing & Tuning High-Performance Fuel Injection Systems — Complete guide to tuning aftermarket stand-alone systems. *(SA161)*

Design & Install In Car Entertainment Systems — The latest and greatest electronic systems, both audio and video. *(SA163)*

How to Build Max-Performance Hemi Engines — Build the biggest baddest vintage Hemi. *(SA164)*

How to Digitally Photograph Cars — Learn all the modern techniques and post processing too. *(SA168)*

High-Performance Differentials, Axles, & Drivelines — Must have book for anyone thinking about setting up a performance differential. *(SA170)*

How To Build Max-Performance Mopar Big Blocks — Build the baddest wedge Mopar on the block. *(SA171)*

How to Build Max-Performance Oldsmobile V-8s — Make your Oldsmobile keep up with the pack. *(SA172)*

How to Make Your Muscle Car Handle — Upgrade your musclecar suspension to modern standards. *(SA175)*

Full-Size Fords 1955-1970 — A complete color history of full sized fords. *(SA176)*

Rebuilding Any Automotive Engine: Step-by-Step Videobook — Rebuild any engine with this book DVD combo. DVD is over 3 hours long! *(SA179)*

The New MINI Performance Handbook — All the performance tricks for your new MINI. *(SA182)*

How to Build Max-Performance Ford FE Engines — Finally, performance tricks for the FE junkie. *(SA183)*

How to Build Altered Wheelbase Cars — Build a wild altered car. Complete history too! *(SA189)*

S-A DESIGN RESTORATION SERIES

How to Restore Your Mustang 1964 1/2-1973 — Step by step restoration for your classic Mustang. *(SA165)*

Muscle Car Interior Restoration Guide — Make your interior look and smell new again. Includes dash restoration. *(SA167)*

How to Restore Your Camaro 1967-1969 — Step by step restoration of your 1st gen Camaro. *(SA178)*

S-A DESIGN WORKBENCH® SERIES

Workbench® Series books feature step by step instruction with hundreds of color photos for stock rebuilds and automotive repair.

How To Rebuild the Small-Block Chevrolet — *(SA26)*
How to Rebuild the Small-Block Ford — *(SA102)*
How to Rebuild & Modify High-Performance Manual Transmissions — *(SA103)*
How to Rebuild the Big-Block Chevrolet — *(SA142)*
How to Rebuild the Small-Block Mopar — *(SA143)*
How to Rebuild GM LS-Series Engines — *(SA147)*
How to Rebuild Any Automotive Engine — *(SA151)*
How to Rebuild Honda B-Series Engines — *(SA154)*
How to Rebuild the 4.6/5.4 Liter Ford — *(SA155)*
Automotive Welding: A Practical Guide — *(SA159)*
Automotive Wiring and Electrical Systems — *(SA160)*
How to Rebuild Big Block Ford Engines — *(SA162)*
Automotive Bodywork & Rust Repair — *(SA166)*

HISTORIES AND PERSONALITIES

Duece — 75 Years of the 32 Ford. This beautiful book is a tribute to all things 32 Ford. *(CT413)*

Quarter-Mile Chaos — Rare & stunning photos of terrifying fires, explosions, and crashes in drag racing's golden age. *(CT425)*

Factory Lightweights: Detroit's Drag Racing Specials of the '60s — Relive the thrilling past of factory produced cars designed to win on Sunday and sell on Monday. *(CT444)*

Fuelies: Fuel Injected Corvettes 1957-1965 — The first Corvette book to focus specifically on the fuel injected cars, which are among the most collectible. *(CT452)*

Slingshot Spectacular: Front-Engine Dragster Era — Relive the golden age of front engine dragsters in this photo packed trip down memory lane. *(CT464)*

The Electroline Diaries: A Journey with the Burbank Choppers Car Club — Take a unique look at this popular car club, their cars, and their lifestyle. *(CT465)*

Chrysler Concept Cars 1940-1970 — Fascinating look at the concept cars created by Chrysler during this golden age of the automotive industry. *(CT470)*

Fuel Altereds Forever — Includes more than 250 photos of the most popular drivers and racecars from the Fuel Altered class. *(CT475)*

Yenko — Complete and thorough of the man, his business and his legendary cars. *(CT485)*

Von Dutch: The Art, The Myth, The Legend — Chronicles the life & art of pinstriper Von Dutch. *(CT998)*

CarTech®, Inc. 39966 Grand Ave., North Branch, MN 55056. Ph: 800-551-4754 or 651-277-1200 • Fax: 651-277-1203
Brooklands Books Ltd., PO Box 146 Cobham, Surrey KT11 1LG, England. Ph: 01932 865051 • Fax 01932 868803
Brooklands Books Aus., 3/37-39 Green Street, Banksmeadow, NSW 2019, Australia. Ph: 2 9695 7055 • Fax 2 9695 7355

Visit us online at www.cartechbooks.com for more info!

More Information for Your Project ...

HOW TO BUILD AND MODIFY ROCHESTER QUADRAJET CARBURETORS *by Cliff Ruggles* This book lifts the veil of mystery surrounding the Q-Jet and show owners how to tune and modify their carbs for maximum performance. The book is a complete guide to selecting, rebuilding, and modifying the Q-Jet, aimed at both muscle car restorers and racers. It includes a history of the Q-Jet, an explanation of how the carb works, a guide to selecting and finding the right carb, instructions on how to rebuild the carb, and extensive descriptions of high-performance modifications that will help anyone with a Q-Jet car crush the competition. Softbound, 8-1/2 x 11 inches, 128 pages, approx. 300 color photos. *Item # SA113*

HOW TO BUILD HIGH-PERFORMANCE IGNITION SYSTEMS (New Edition) *by Todd Ryden* How to Build High-Performance Ignition Systems is the complete guide to understanding automotive ignition systems, from old-school points and condensers to modern computer-controlled distributorless systems, from bone-stock to totally aftermarket. In this all-color updated edition, author Todd Ryden leads you through the various components, systems, and subsystems, including coils, wires, spark plugs, distributors, magnetos, inductive systems, CD ignitions, multiple-spark systems, computer ignition controls, and rev limiters. Softbound, 8-1/2 x 11 inches, 144 pages, approx. 375 color photos. *Item # SA79*

SUPER TUNING AND MODIFYING HOLLEY CARBURETORS *by David Emanuel* Super tuning and modifying of Holley carburetors for performance, street, and off-road applications. Shows how to select, install, tune, and modify all popular Holley performance 4-barrel models 4150/4160, 4165/4175, 4500, 4360, and the 2300 two barrel. 8-3/8 x 10-7/8 inches, 144 pages, and over 300 b/w photos. *Item #SA08*

AUTOMOTIVE BODYWORK & RUST REPAIR *by Matt Joseph* Matt Joseph shows you the ins and outs of tackling both simple and difficult rust and metalwork projects. This book teaches you how to select the proper tools for the job, common sense approaches to the task ahead of you, preparing and cleaning sheetmetal, section fabrications and repair patches, welding options such as gas and electric, forming fitting and smoothing, cutting metal, final metal finishing including filling and sanding, the secrets of lead filling, making panels fit properly, and more. Softbound, 8-1/2 x 11 inches, 160 pages, 400 color photos. *Item #SA166*

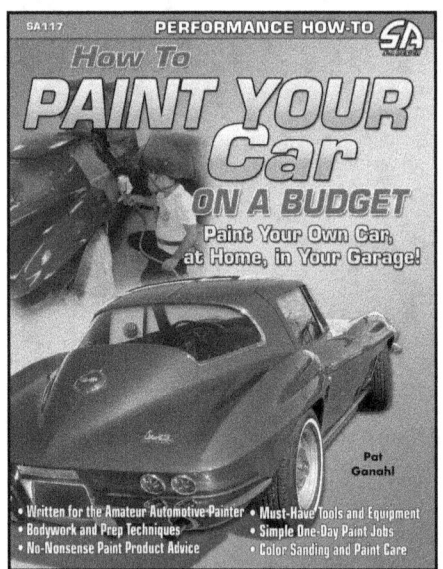

HOW TO PAINT YOUR CAR ON A BUDGET *by Pat Ganahl* If your car needs new paint, or even just a touch-up, the cost involved in getting a professional job can be more than you bargained for. In this book, author Pat Ganahl unveils dozens of secrets that will help anyone paint their own car. From simple scuff-and-squirt jobs to full-on, door-jambs-and-everything paint jobs, Ganahl covers everything you need to know to get a great-looking coat of paint on your car and save lots of money in the process. Covers painting equipment, the ins and outs of prep, masking, painting and sanding products and techniques, and real-world advice on how to budget wisely when painting your own car. Softbound, 8-1/2 x 11 inches, 128 pages, approx. 400 color photos. *Item #SA117*

HOW TO DESIGN AND INSTALL IN-CAR ENTERTAINMENT SYSTEMS *by Jefferson Bryant* The author presents the entire spectrum of audio/video, navigation, communication, and entertainment technology, and how the enthusiast can create a complete custom system or an integrated stock/aftermarket system. Featuring how-to installations, thorough explanations of professional-only builds, descriptions of hook-ups, mechanical upgrades, such as charging systems, and a comprehensive resource guide. Softbound, 8-1/2 x 11 inches, 144 pages, 375 color photos. *Item #SA163*

www.cartechbooks.com or 1-800-551-4754

www.ingramcontent.com/pod-product-compliance
Lightning Source LLC
Chambersburg PA
CBHW051412070526
44584CB00023B/3399